WILLS, PROBATE AND ADMINISTRATION

To the memory of Richard and Thomas
For Rosie, Alice, Edward and Jennie
For Hannah, Alex and Rod

WILLS, PROBATE AND ADMINISTRATION

George Miles LLB (Exon), Solicitor
Associate Dean, Head of Professional Studies
Faculty of Law, University of the West of England, Bristol

and

Paulene Denyer LLB (Hull), LLM (Lond), Solicitor
Senior Lecturer, Faculty of Law,
University of the West of England, Bristol

First published in Great Britain 1993 by Blackstone Press Limited,
9-15 Aldine Street, London W12 8AW. Telephone 081-740 1173

© G. Miles and P. Denyer, 1993

ISBN: 1 85431 295 2

British Library Cataloguing in Publication Data
A CIP catalogue record for this book is available from the British Library

Typeset by Style Photosetting Limited, Mayfield, East Sussex
Printed by Loader Jackson Printers, Arlesey, Bedfordshire

All rights reserved. No part of this book may be reproduced or transmitted in any form or by any means, electronic or mechanical, including photocopying, recording, or any information storage or retrieval system without prior permission from the publisher.

CONTENTS

Preface vii

1 Wills 1

1.1 Validity — 1.2 Revocation and alterations — 1.3 Republication, revival and incorporation — 1.4 Construction

2 Intestacy 21

2.1 The basic position — 2.2 Entitlement where there is a surviving spouse — 2.3 Issue — 2.4 Other relatives — 2.5 The Crown — 2.6 Hotchpot

3 Provision for Family and Dependants 31

3.1 The basis of the claim — 3.2 The application — 3.3 Categories of applicant — 3.4 Reasonable financial provision — 3.5 The guidelines (s. 3(1)) — 3.6 Types of family provision order (s. 2) — 3.7 Property available for financial provision orders — 3.8 The anti-avoidance provisions (ss. 10 and 11)

4 Income Tax 43

4.1 The personal representatives and the deceased's income — 4.2 Personal representatives and the estate's income — 4.3 The beneficiaries

5 Capital Gains Tax 49

5.1 The personal representatives and the gains of the deceased — 5.2 Personal representatives and gains of the estate — 5.3 The beneficiaries

6 Inheritance Tax 53

6.1 Lifetime dispositions — 6.2 Transfers on death — 6.3 Exemptions and reliefs — 6.4 Calculation of tax on death — 6.5 Valuation — 6.6 Liability — 6.7 Burden — 6.8 Accounts and payment of tax

7 Taxation of Trusts and Settlements 69

7.1 Income tax — 7.2 Capital gains tax — 7.3 Inheritance tax

8 Grants of Representation 81

8.1 Background — 8.2 Responsibilities of solicitors instructed by personal representatives — 8.3 The effect of the issue of a grant — 8.4 Grant not necessary — 8.5 Types of grant — 8.6 Amendment and revocation of grants — 8.7 Personal representatives – capacity — 8.8 Personal representatives – several claimants — 8.9 Personal representatives – number — 8.10 Personal representatives – renunciation

CONTENTS

9 Oaths 97

9.1 Generally — 9.2 Oaths for executors — 9.3 Oaths for administrators with will annexed — 9.4 Oaths for administrators — 9.5 Oaths for administrators *de bonis non*

10 Inland Revenue Accounts 111

10.1 Generally — 10.2 Excepted estates — 10.3 Form IHT 202 — 10.4 Form IHT 200 — 10.5 Funding the payment of inheritance tax — 10.6 Corrective account — 10.7 Form CAP A-5C

11 Affidavit Evidence 127

11.1 Generally — 11.2 Due execution – r. 12, NCPR — 11.3 Knowledge and approval – r. 13, NCPR — 11.4 Terms, condition and date of will – r. 14, NCPR — 11.5 Attempted revocation – r. 15, NCPR — 11.6 Other cases

12 Court Proceedings 133

12.1 Introduction — 12.2 Standing searches – r. 43, NCPR — 12.3 Caveats – r. 44, NCPR — 12.4 Citations – rr. 46 to 48, NCPR — 12.5 Solemn form procedure

13 Powers and Duties of Personal Representatives 139

13.1 Duties of personal representatives — 13.2 Administrative powers of personal representatives — 13.3 Beneficiaries' rights during administration — 13.4 Remedies available to beneficiaries

14 Administering the Estate – Some Practical Considerations 153

14.1 General matters — 14.2 The early stages — 14.3 On receipt of the grant — 14.4 Financial services

15 Post Mortem Changes 171

15.1 Disclaimers — 15.2 Variations — 15.3 Orders under the Inheritance (Provision for Family and Dependants) Act 1975 — 15.4 'Flexible' wills — 15.5 Capitalisation of a life interest on intestacy

16 Distributing the Estate 181

16.1 Payment of legacies — 16.2 Ascertainment of residue — 16.3 Estate accounts — 16.4 Assents — 16.5 Financial services — 16.6 Personal representatives as trustees

17 Tax and Estate Planning 193

17.1 Inheritance tax: the nil rate band, exemptions, reliefs and excluded property — 17.2 Taking account of capital gains tax — 17.3 Lifetime tax planning — 17.4 Will planning

18 Will Drafting 209

18.1 Why make a will? — 18.2 Duties of solicitor instructed to prepare a will — 18.3 Taking instructions — 18.4 Structure and content of the will — 18.5 Codicils

Index 231

PREFACE

This book is offered as a Guide for those studying this subject on the Legal Practice Course – or rather *Courses*, since under the new regime for the training of would-be solicitors, each approved institution's LPC is its own (subject to meeting The Law Society's written standards). The national yardstick of The Law Society's Final and its accompanying Core Material have gone, to be replaced by as many different variations upon a theme as there are providers of the new courses.

Whilst such diversity may be healthy and welcome, it does present problems to those rash enough to undertake the task of trying to write a 'Course Guide'. Whilst there is probably not much argument about what should be included in a course on Wills, Probate and Administration, there can certainly be a variety of views as to how to present the various elements and as to the order in which to do so. This 'problem' is compounded by the fact that this is an area of practice which does not readily lend itself to compartmentalisation into neat and self-contained chapters. We have tried to present the material in (what seems to us) a logical sequence, with extensive cross-referencing to other parts of the book where the issues under discussion are also considered.

In writing this book, we have been conscious that our brief was to prepare a Guide for the course(s) and not to provide (in effect) the course itself! Thus, for example, in the chapters concerned with the completion of the forms of Oath and Inland Revenue Account we have concentrated upon an explanation of what is required, leaving it to each course to provide exemplars of the practice through its own exercises. Similarly, in the context of will drafting, we have focused upon explaining what a precedent for a particular clause needs to achieve (and why), since such an appreciation is fundamental to successful drafting. We have not sought to provide detailed precedents for all the standard clauses which would, we admit, make this work more self-contained. It is our conviction that students should expect in their courses to be driven to use the sorts of source materials which they will encounter in practice. We have, therefore, quite deliberately not included our own additional offerings which might enable a student to 'get by' without learning something about the use of practitioner texts and collections of precedents.

We would like to place on record our gratitude for all the assistance afforded to us by the staff at Blackstone Press — with a special word of thanks to Mandy Preece for her efficiency and patience (qualities which do not always go hand in hand!).

Above all, however, we acknowledge the understanding of our respective nearest and dearest, who have suffered with us over the last months as we have struggled to meet deadlines. It is but scant recompense for our enforced neglect of them that this book should be dedicated to them.

George Miles
Paulene Denyer
Bristol, July 1993

ONE

WILLS

This book is essentially about what happens to a person's property on their death. The answer will very largely depend upon whether there is a valid will. What happens if there is not, or if the deceased's will is for some reason only partially effective, will be considered in **Chapter 2**. This chapter is concerned with the legal background to the making and construction of valid wills.

A will has no effect until the testator dies — until then it is said to be 'ambulatory'. No benefits are conferred whilst the testator is still alive, nor are the testator's rights of ownership in any way restricted by the terms of the will. Further, the will itself generally remains revocable by the testator.

Although testators can determine the distribution of their estates by making wills, it is important to appreciate that often substantial assets will pass on death quite independently of the terms of any will (or, indeed, the operation of the intestacy rules discussed in **Chapter 2**). We will consider such assets in more detail later (in **8.4.2** and **8.4.3**) but they include property held as beneficial joint tenants, which accrues by right of survivorship; life policies written under s. 11, Married Women's Property Act 1882 and other trust policies; certain pension-scheme benefits; property the subject of a statutory nomination; and *donationes mortis causa*.

This chapter will cover a lot of ground, and for convenience will be broken down into four parts.

The first part (**1.1**) will consider issues relating to the validity of wills. The second part (**1.2**) looks at how a will may be revoked and the rules relating to alterations. The third part (**1.3**) deals with some technical matters — republication, revival and incorporation. And, finally, the fourth part (**1.4**) is concerned with the construction of wills and the effect of the various types of gift which they may contain, and discusses the various ways in which a gift under a will may fail.

1.1 Validity

1.1.1 GENERALLY

English law will generally recognise a will as valid (Wills Act 1963) if it accords with the internal law of either

(a) the country in which it was executed, or
(b) the country in which the deceased was domiciled or of which he was a national — either at the time of its execution or of the deceased's death.

So far as English domestic law is concerned, a valid will requires that the testator should have the *capacity* and *intention* to make the will, and compliance with the prescribed *formalities*.

1.1.2 CAPACITY

At the date of making the will, the testator must not (normally) have been under the age of 18. (Being of age is, however, not a requirement if the testator was in a position to make a 'privileged' will as a soldier on actual military service or a seaman at sea.) Additionally, the testator must have had the necessary mental capacity.

1.1.2.1 The basic test

The test for mental capacity was laid down in *Banks* v *Goodfellow* (1870) LR 5 QB 549. Testators must have understood three things:

(a) the nature of the act (i.e. the making of a will) and its effects;
(b) the extent of their property;
(c) the claims to which they ought to give effect.

Generally, it must be shown that the requisite understanding existed at the date of execution of the will. However, the rule in *Parker* v *Felgate* (1883) 8 PD 171 lays down an acceptable alternative where this cannot be done. Under this rule, it will be sufficient to show that:

(a) the requisite capacity existed at the date of giving instructions for the preparation of the will;
(b) the will was prepared in accordance with those instructions;
(c) at the time of execution the testators understood that they were signing a will for which instructions had previously been given (though it is not necessary for the testators at that time to be able either to remember what those instructions were, or to understand the will if read over to them).

1.1.2.2 Proof

The onus of proving the existence of the necessary mental capacity lies with the propounder of the will (i.e. the person seeking to prove it — to have it accepted as valid). In this context, there are two rebuttable presumptions.

(a) Rational will. Capacity is presumed where a duly executed will (i.e. one complying with the formality requirements) appears to be rational. If it does not so appear, the propounder will then have to prove capacity.
(b) Mental illness continues. Where the testator generally lacked capacity, there is a presumption that this state of affairs continues. This may be rebutted by evidence showing that the testator had recovered, or that the will was made in a lucid interval.

1.1.2.3 Lack of capacity

Where capacity is not presumed or proven, the will cannot be admitted to probate (i.e. it will not be accepted by the court as a valid will).

Where a person lacks the necessary mental capacity to make a valid will for himself, the Court of Protection is empowered (under the provisions of s. 96, Mental Health Act 1983) to make a 'statutory will' on behalf of that person.

There are a number of precautions which the prudent solicitor should take when drafting a will where there is any doubt as to the testator's capacity. These are considered later (in **Chapter 18**).

1.1.3 INTENTION

1.1.3.1 The requirement

The testator must have had a general intention to make a will, and a specific intention to make the particular will. Put another way, the testator must know and approve the contents of the will. To the extent that such knowledge and approval are lacking, the will cannot be admitted to probate. The necessary knowledge and approval must normally have existed at the date of the execution of the will: however, the rule in *Parker* v *Felgate* (**1.1.2.1** above) also applies in this context.

1.1.3.2 Proof

Again, the onus of proof lies on the propounder of the will. There is generally a rebuttable presumption that a testator with the necessary mental capacity executed the will with the requisite knowledge and approval of its contents. Those who seek to challenge the will would have to prove that the testator made the will (or perhaps a particular provision in it) as a result of force, fear, fraud or undue influence; or that the necessary knowledge and approval were lacking because of a mistake.

There is no such presumption of knowledge and approval in two situations:

(a) the testator is blind or illiterate, or someone has signed the will on the testator's behalf. We will consider later (**1.1.4.7**) the steps which should be taken in these cases when drafting the will to deal most satisfactorily with the issue of intention.

(b) there are suspicious circumstances — in particular where the will substantially benefits the person who prepared it (or a close relative of that person). In such cases, evidence will be required of the testator's knowledge and approval of the contents of the will, otherwise the gift will fail.

1.1.3.3 Professional conduct

In addition to the legal problem identified above, solicitors drafting wills where the testator proposes a gift to them (or to members of their firms or the families of any of them) must have regard to a ruling by the Council of The Law Society, the breach of which can result in disciplinary proceedings and perhaps striking off the Roll. The ruling is as follows:

> Where a client intends to make a gift *inter vivos* or by will to his solicitor, or to the solicitor's partner, or a member of staff or to the families of any of them and the gift is of a significant amount, either in itself or having regard to the size of the client's estate and the reasonable expectations of prospective beneficiaries, the solicitor must advise the client to be independently advised as to that gift and if the client declines must refuse to act.

1.1.4 FORMALITIES

1.1.4.1 Section 9, Wills Act 1837 (as substituted by s. 17, Administration of Justice Act 1982)

This provides that:

> No will shall be valid unless—
>
> (a) it is in writing, and signed by the testator, or by some other person in his presence and by his direction; and
>
> (b) it appears that the testator intended by his signature to give effect to the will; and

(c) the signature is made or acknowledged by the testator in the presence of two or more witnesses present at the same time; and

(d) each witness either—

(i) attests and signs the will; or
(ii) acknowledges his signature,

in the presence of the testator (but not necessarily in the presence of any other witness),

but no form of attestation shall be necessary.

The section does not apply to privileged wills, which can be made informally — even orally. Nor does it apply to statutory wills under the Mental Health Act 1983, for which that Act lays down special rules.

1.1.4.2 In writing

A will may be typed or handwritten (in ink or pencil — though the use of both will raise a rebuttable presumption that the parts written in pencil are 'deliberative only' and they will only be admitted to probate if there is evidence that the testator intended them to be final). There is no restriction as to the material upon which a will may be written, nor as to the language used: it may even be written in code — provided there is evidence available enabling it to be deciphered.

1.1.4.3 Signature

The testator's usual signature is ideal — but any mark (e.g. a thumbprint or rubber stamp) made by the testator and intended to be a signature will suffice. One of the leading cases on this point is *In the Goods of Chalcraft* [1948] P 222, where a dying testatrix managed to sign 'E. Chal' but was unable to complete her full signature. It was held that this was sufficient; the testatrix intended what she had written (as much as she could manage in the circumstances) to be her signature. In another case, *In the Estate of Cook* [1960] 1 WLR 353, the will began with the name of the testatrix and ended with the words 'Your loving mother'. The court accepted that the testatrix intended this to be her signature.

However, testators do not need to sign their own wills; the Act allows signature by another — at the testator's direction and in the testator's presence. The person so signing (who may be one of the witnesses) may sign their own name or that of the testator.

1.1.4.4 With intent to give effect to the will

It is usual (and logical) for the signature to appear at the end of the will. Indeed, the original version of s. 9, Wills Act required that the signature should be 'at the foot or end' of the will. A strict interpretation of this provision led to the passing of the Wills Amendment Act 1852, and a more lenient approach. The precise scope of the current requirement will have to be decided by the courts. In *Wood v Smith* [1993] Ch 90, the testator had made his signature at the beginning of the will, intending this to give effect to his will, but written before he had made any provisions disposing of his estate. At first instance, the judge refused to accept this because, in his view, the natural construction of the words 'with intent to give effect to the will' was that the testator should sign after the dispositive provisions and that this had not happened here. The Court of Appeal, however, held that this could constitute a valid execution of the will provided the signing and the subsequently written dispositions all formed part of one transaction.

1.1.4.5 Signature made/acknowledged in the presence of two or more witnesses present at the same time

Where the testator is (as is usually the case) signing the will, the signature must be completed in the presence of at least two witnesses, present at the same time. The witnesses do not need to be able to see the contents of the will, or even to know that the testator is signing a will. They must, however, be able to see the testator writing the signature (for this reason a blind person cannot act as a witness), though it is not necessary for them to see the signature itself.

Alternatively, the testator may sign the will and then acknowledge that signature (by words or conduct) in the presence of the (two or more) witnesses, who must be present at the same time and be able to see the signature.

There are no special rules as to the capacity of the witnesses, but they must be bodily and mentally present (not, e.g., drunk or asleep). Although, by s. 15, Wills Act 1837 a beneficiary will normally lose a gift under a will where that beneficiary or their spouse has witnessed the will (see further in **1.4** of this chapter), this does not affect the formal validity of the will.

1.1.4.6 Witnesses attest and sign (or acknowledge their signatures) in the presence of the testator

Attestation is, in effect, the validation of the testator's signature. The witnesses need not sign (or acknowledge) in each other's presence — though in practice this is what usually happens. However, the presence of the testator (bodily and mentally) is required when the signature/acknowledgement is made.

1.1.4.7 Attestation clause

The inclusion of such a clause is specifically not a requirement for formal validity. However, a suitable attestation clause should (as a matter of good practice) be routinely included — since this will raise a presumption of due execution. If there is no such clause (or only an inadequate one) compliance with the requirements of s. 9 will have to be proved (see further **Chapter 11**).

An attestation clause should show (as a minimum) compliance with the statutory requirements. It need not be lengthy: a clause in common use reads simply

> SIGNED by [the Testator] as his
> last will in our joint presence
> and then by us in his

Where the testator is blind or illiterate, or someone else signs on behalf of the testator, we saw, in **1.1.3.2** above, that there is no presumption of knowledge and approval and that this will have to be established if the will is to be admitted to probate. The best way of dealing with this is to have the will read over to the testator in the presence of the witnesses and to include an attestation clause showing that this was done and explaining the circumstances of the execution of the will. For example

> THIS WILL having been read over to [the Testator] in our joint presence when [the Testator] appeared thoroughly to understand it and approve its contents was SIGNED by [the Signatory] in his presence and at his direction as his last will in our joint presence and we then in the presence of [the Testator] and at his request subscribed our names as witnesses

1.1.5 CODICILS

A codicil is used to add to, amend, or partially revoke the terms of an existing will. The requirements for a valid codicil are the same as those required for a valid will.

1.2 Revocation and Alterations

1.2.1 REVOCATION

1.2.1.1 The general position

Provided a testator retains testamentary capacity, a will is revocable at any time during the testator's lifetime. This is so even if the testator has entered into a contract not to revoke the will (though if the will is revoked the estate may be liable for the breach of contract).

Revocation may occur:

(a) automatically by operation of law

    (i) Marriage (see **1.2.1.3**)
    (ii) Divorce or nullity (see **1.2.1.4**);

(b) by deliberate act of the testator

    (i) Later will or codicil (see **1.2.1.5**)
    (ii) Destruction (see **1.2.1.6**).

Sometimes, revocation is regarded as conditional only. This is considered in **1.2.2**.

The law relating to alterations is discussed in **1.2.3**.

1.2.1.2 Mutual wills

A qualification to the principle of revocability is the equitable doctrine of mutual wills. This may be invoked to impose a constructive trust upon the property of the testator where

(a) there is an agreement between (say) husband and wife to confer benefits upon each other by their respective wills and an intention then to benefit the same ultimate person(s) — e.g. their children;
(b) there is an agreement that the survivor shall be bound by the arrangement;
(c) an event has occurred to cause the arrangement to become binding. This will happen when the first of the parties dies not having revoked their will believing that (b) still applies — or perhaps when the survivor accepts the benefit under will of the first to die.

Where these conditions are all met, although the survivor's will must remain revocable, any purported disposition of the property bound by the trust will be ineffectual. This is because the beneficial interests of those claiming under the trust have priority over those of the beneficiaries claiming under the new will or the intestacy rules on the death of the survivor.

1.2.1.3 Marriage

Where the testator has an existing will, the effect of the testator's subsequent marriage is generally to revoke that will — s. 18, Wills Act 1837 (both in its original form and as substituted by Administration of Justice Act 1982).

The scope of the exceptions to this general rule depend upon whether the will was made before 1983 or after 1982. In determining when a will is 'made' for this purpose, the general rule that a codicil has the effect of 're-dating' the will (see further **1.3.1**) does not necessarily apply. Something more than the mere existence of (say) a 1987 codicil to a 1980 will is necessary for the new rules to apply.

(a) *Will made before 1983*. The original s. 18, Wills Act 1837 was subject to the exception in s. 177, Law of Property Act 1925. This provided that, in effect, a will expressed to be made in contemplation of a particular marriage should not be revoked by that marriage. In *Re Coleman* [1976] Ch 1, the judge construed s. 177 as requiring the will as a whole (and not merely particular gifts in it) to be expressed to be made in contemplation of the particular marriage.

(b) *Will made after 1982*. The principal exceptions to the general rule are now found in the new s. 18(3) and (4), Wills Act 1837.

Section 18(3) provides that where '. . . it appears from the will that at the time it was made the testator was expecting to be married to a particular person and that he intended that the will should not be revoked by the marriage, the will shall not be revoked by his marriage to that person'.

Section 18(4) provides that where '. . . it appears from a will that at the time it was made the testator was expecting to be married to a particular person and that he intended that a disposition in the will should not be revoked by his marriage to that person . . .' then that particular disposition will not be revoked by the marriage, and the rest of the dispositions will also be 'saved' unless the contrary appears from the will. This provision is clearly intended to overcome the problem encountered in *Re Coleman* (above).

Only intrinsic evidence is admissible to establish the testator's expectation and intention, so that it is clearly best if an express declaration is included to cover the points — for example:

> I DECLARE that I make this will in the expectation of my marriage to [intended spouse] and that I intend that this will shall not be revoked by that marriage.

It is possible for a testator to make a will conditional upon marriage — i.e. the will does not take effect unless and until the marriage takes place. Clearly, in such cases the question of revocation by subsequent marriage does not arise.

1.2.1.4 Divorce/nullity

In the case of deaths after 1982, s. 18A, Wills Act 1837 (inserted by Administration of Justice Act 1982) provides (subject to any contrary intention in the will) for a sort of 'limited revocation' on a decree absolute of divorce or nullity. Basically, two things will happen (s. 18A(1)):

(a) the will takes effect as if any appointment of the former spouse as executor or trustee were omitted; and

(b) any gift in the will to the former spouse lapses. In *Re Sinclair* [1985] Ch 446, the Court of Appeal held that the word 'lapse' in s. 18A means simply 'fail': it does not mean that the former spouse is deemed to have predeceased the testator. (As to the doctrine of lapse, see further **1.4.3.3** below).

If the gift to the former spouse is of a life interest, the gift to the remainderman is accelerated, even though that interest is expressed to be contingent upon surviving the life tenant (s. 18A(3)). The provisions of s. 18A do not apply on separation, nor do they affect any other provisions of the will.

1.2.1.5 Later will/codicil

By s. 20, Wills Act 1837 a will is revoked (wholly or partially) by a later will or codicil; or 'by some writing declaring an intention to revoke the same and executed in the manner' of a will — as in *Re*

Spracklan's Estate [1938] 2 All ER 345, where the Court of Appeal held that a letter (signed by the testatrix and duly attested) to her bank manager asking him to destroy the will which the bank was keeping for her satisfied this requirement.

A later will or codicil impliedly revokes an earlier testamentary disposition to the extent that it is inconsistent with or merely repeats the terms of the earlier document. However, it is common — and certainly good practice for the avoidance of doubt — for a will to contain an express revocation clause, such as: 'I hereby revoke all previous wills and codicils made by me'. The doctrine of conditional revocation may apply (see **1.2.2** below).

1.2.1.6 Destruction

By s. 20, Wills Act 1837 a will is also revoked by 'burning tearing or otherwise destroying the same by the testator or by some person in his presence and by his direction with the intention of revoking the same'

There are thus two essential elements for an effective revocation:

(a) *An act of destruction*. An act of destruction is necessary; merely writing 'cancelled' or 'revoked' across the will is not enough. Nor is putting a line through parts of the will, or even the signature of the testator — though it will be otherwise if there has been an effective obliteration. In *Re Adams (Dec'd)* [1990] Ch 601, the testator's signature had been heavily scored through with a ball-point pen so as to render it illegible. The court held that a material part of the will had been destroyed with the intention to effect a revocation of the whole.

Where part only of the will is destroyed, this may amount to a revocation of that part of the will only, or of the whole will if of a sufficiently substantial or vital part (e.g. the testator's or witnesses' signatures — *Hobbs* v *Knight* (1838) 1 Curt 769). It is essential, however, that the testator completes the intended act of destruction: *Doe d. Perkes* v *Perkes* (1820) 3 B & Ald 489, where the testator was restrained from further destruction of his will which, in anger, he had torn into four pieces. Later he was heard to observe that it was a good job that it was not worse. The court concluded from this that the testator's intended destruction was incomplete, so that the will had not been revoked.

The court will admit extrinsic evidence of the testator's intention in determining the extent of any revocation, and may infer this from the state of the will at the date of death.

A destruction by someone other than the testator must, to be effective, be done in the testator's presence and at the testator's direction; if not, it is not possible for the testator subsequently to 'ratify' the act.

(b) *An intention to revoke*. The testator must have the intention to revoke at the time of the will's destruction. The necessary mental capacity is the same as that required for the making of a will (see **1.1.2** above).

Accidental revocation is, therefore, an impossibility; so is one based upon a mistaken belief that the will is invalid or has already been revoked.

If a will is found mutilated at the date of death, this will be rebuttably presumed to have been done by the testator with the intention of revoking it (wholly or partially, depending upon the extent of the mutilation). There is a further rebuttable presumption that a will last known to have been in the testator's possession, but which cannot be found at the date of death, has been destroyed by the testator with the intention of revoking it.

The doctrine of conditional revocation may again apply (see **1.2.2** below).

1.2.2 CONDITIONAL REVOCATION

Where an intention to revoke is required, the testator's intention may be absolute — in which event the revocation is effective immediately (assuming the other essential elements are present). However, if that intention is conditional only, the revocation will not be effective unless and until the condition is met. The condition might be, for example, the validity of a new will or codicil, or a particular devolution of the estate under the intestacy rules.

In the case of revocation by later will/codicil (**1.2.1.5** above), the question as to whether the testator's intention is absolute or conditional is a matter of construction.

In *Re Crannis* (1978) 122 SJ 489, a testatrix made a will in 1948 leaving her estate to her sister. In 1958, she executed a codicil providing that if her sister should predecease her, the estate should go to the testatrix's niece. The sister died in 1960 and the testatrix made a new will in 1962: this contained a revocation clause, appointed the niece executrix and left the whole estate to her. The will was witnessed by the niece's husband (so that by virtue of s. 15, Wills Act 1837 the gift to the niece failed). *Held*: the testatrix's intention was that the revocation clause was conditional upon the 1962 will disposing of the estate. As it did not do so, the court admitted all three testamentary documents to probate (omitting the revocation clause from the 1962 will). Thus, the niece took the gift under the codicil and was appointed executrix under the 1962 will.

In *Re Finnemore (Dec'd)* [1991] 1 WLR 793, the deceased made three wills, each of which contained a revocation clause. Each will contained a bequest of certain property to C. The last two wills were witnessed by C's husband. The court held that the revocation clauses in the two later wills were conditional upon the effectiveness of the gifts contained in them. To the extent that these failed (i.e. in the case of the gifts to C) the revocation clauses in the later wills were ineffective (though they did have the effect of revoking the rest of the earlier wills).

In these cases, extrinsic evidence of the testator's intention is only admissible to assist in the interpretation of the document. Where the revocation is by destruction (**1.2.1.6** above), the question as to whether the testator's intention was absolute or conditional is a question of fact. The testator's declarations as to intention are admissible. However, there must be some evidence that the intention was conditional. In *Re Jones* [1976] Ch 200, a testatrix destroyed her existing will and made an appointment to give instructions for a new one. The Court of Appeal held that a mere intention to make a new will at the time of the destruction of the existing one was not sufficient *per se* to render the testatrix's intention to revoke conditional only (i.e. upon the execution of a new will). The doctrine of conditional revocation may also apply in the context of alterations (see **1.2.3.4** below).

1.2.3 ALTERATIONS

1.2.3.1 Section 21, Wills Act 1837

This lays down the basic rule, which is that

> ...no obliteration, interlineation, or other alteration made in any will after the execution thereof shall be valid or have any effect, except so far as the words or effect of the will before such alteration shall not be apparent, unless such alteration shall be executed in like manner as hereinbefore is required for the execution of a will...

1.2.3.2 Effective alterations

An alteration made before execution is clearly acceptable (provided, of course, this is done with the knowledge and approval of the testator). However, an unattested alteration is rebuttably presumed to have been made after execution (except where the 'alteration' is the filling in of a blank space, when the rebuttable presumption is that this was done prior to execution). Either presumption is rebuttable by intrinsic or extrinsic evidence to the contrary.

An alteration made after the will but duly executed is also valid. In practice, it is sufficient if the testator and the witnesses initial the alteration. An alteration may also be validated by the republication of the will (see **1.3.1** below).

Where the original wording or effect of the will is, as a result of the 'alteration', not apparent (i.e. is not decipherable by natural means), the alteration — whenever made — may also be effective if the obliteration was made by the testator with an intention to revoke (see further **1.2.3.4** and **1.2.3.5** below).

1.2.3.3 Ineffective alterations

An unattested alteration by the testator made after (or which cannot be established to have been made before) execution and which does not amount to an obliteration is ineffective. So is an alteration made by someone other than the testator or by the testator without an intention to revoke.

1.2.3.4 Consequences of invalid alteration

This will depend upon whether the original wording is 'apparent' or not. The wording is apparent if it can be deciphered by 'natural means' (such as holding up to the light or using a magnifying glass) without resort to 'forbidden' methods (such as the use of chemicals, infra-red photography or extrinsic evidence).

If the original wording is so apparent, it will be admitted to probate. If it is not so apparent, the will is prima facie admitted to probate with a blank space where the obliteration has occurred. However, where there has been an attempted substitution in place of what has been obliterated, the doctrine of conditional revocation may apply; this will allow the courts to employ any of the forbidden methods mentioned above in an attempt to ascertain the original wording. For a discussion of the procedure in these cases, see further **11.4.1**.

1.2.3.5 Precautions

It is clearly sensible to have all alterations (even those made before execution of the will) initialled by the testator and the witnesses. Further, testators should be discouraged from attempting to make their own 'adjustments' to their wills.

1.3 Republication, Revival and Incorporation

1.3.1 REPUBLICATION

This is really the confirmation of an unrevoked will or codicil. It can be achieved by the formal re-execution of the document. In practice, however, republication usually occurs as a result of a codicil making some reference to the earlier document(s). This may be simply a description of the new document as 'codicil to my will'; however, more commonly the codicil contains an express confirmation, by ending (for example): 'In all other respects I confirm my will'.

The effect of republication is generally that the will takes effect as if executed (with the changes made by the codicil) at the date of the codicil. So, for example, if there is an unattested alteration of the will made before the codicil is executed, the alteration is in principle validated by the republication. However, we have already noted the presumption that an unattested alteration to a will is made after execution (**1.2.3.2** above); where there is a codicil, the presumption is that the alteration was made after both the will and the codicil. The presumption is rebutted by evidence to the contrary (e.g. an express reference in the codicil to the alteration).

For the effect of republication upon the construction of the will, see further **1.4** below.

1.3.2 REVIVAL

By s. 22, Wills Act 1837 a will or codicil which has been wholly or partially revoked may be revived by formal re-execution, or by a duly executed codicil showing an intention to revive. If so revived, the will or codicil takes effect as if made at the date of the revival. The consequences are essentially similar to those described above in relation to republication.

The necessary intention to revive is not shown by a mere reference to the earlier will, or by physical attachment to it. It must be clear from the codicil that the effect of the earlier will was being revived: extrinsic evidence may be admissible to enable the court to ascertain the testator's intention as expressed in the codicil under the 'armchair principle' (see further, **1.1.2** below).

A will can only be revived if it still exists, and the revocation of a will can only be 'reversed' by a formal act of revival. Thus, suppose a testator makes a will in 1985, then makes a will in 1990 which revokes the 1985 will, and then makes a codicil which revokes the 1990 will. This does not have the effect of reviving the 1985 will.

1.3.3 INCORPORATION BY REFERENCE

As we have seen (**1.1.4** above), for a document to be admitted to probate it must be executed in accordance with the requirements of s. 9, Wills Act. However, a document not so executed may, in effect, become part of the will under the doctrine of incorporation by reference. For this to happen, three conditions must be met:

(a) The document must be clearly identified in the will.
(b) The document must already exist at the date of the will (or of a later codicil republishing it). The onus of proving this fact lies with the person seeking incorporation of the document.
(c) The document must be referred to in the will as already in existence at the time of execution. If this is not the case (e.g. because the statement is equivocal or the reference is to a document to be prepared in the future) the document in question cannot be incorporated. Where the will is republished by a codicil, it is sufficient if either the will or the codicil refers to the document's existence.

If it is desired to incorporate a document, care is needed in drafting the will to ensure that the conditions are met. Equally, where incorporation is not wanted, care is needed to avoid an accidental incorporation, with its attendant publicity: once a will (including any incorporated document) is admitted to probate, it becomes available for public inspection.

1.4 Construction

The intention here is to look at some of the basic principles of construction of wills and the various gifts which they may contain. We will also examine the circumstances in which gifts contained in valid wills may fail.

1.4.1 GENERAL PRINCIPLES OF CONSTRUCTION

The object of the court in construing a will is to ascertain the intention of the testator as expressed in the will read as a whole. The language used in the will is central to its construction (though extrinsic evidence may be admissible in certain circumstances — see **1.4.1.2**). In *Perrin* v *Morgan* [1943] AC 399, Lord Simon LC said:

The fundamental rule in construing the language of a will is to put on the words used the meaning which, having regard to the terms of the will, the testator intended. The question is not ... what the testator meant to do when he made his will, but what the written words he uses mean in the particular case — what are the 'expressed intentions' of the testator'.

The court will not speculate as to what the testator might have intended, nor will it rewrite the testator's will (though see **1.4.1.4** below).

1.4.1.1 Presumptions

The court applies two basic presumptions:

(a) Technical words and expressions should be given their technical meaning. In *Re Cook* [1948] Ch 212, the testatrix had given 'all my personal estate whatsoever' to her nephews and nieces. The bulk of her estate comprised realty, which it was held did not pass under the gift of her will.

(b) Non-technical words and expressions should be given their ordinary meaning. Sometimes a word has several 'ordinary' meanings. In *Perrin* v *Morgan* (above) the House of Lords had to determine what was meant by the use of the word 'money'. This can have several 'ordinary' meanings, ranging from 'cash' to all of a person's property (as in 'it's her money he's after'). In such cases, the court construes the word in context, attributing to it the meaning which the testator intended.

These presumptions are rebuttable:

(i) under the 'dictionary principle', where (from the will itself and any admissible extrinsic evidence) it is apparent that the testator has used a word in a different sense from its technical or ordinary meaning.

(ii) where a 'secondary meaning' makes sense in the context. In *Re Smalley* [1929] 2 Ch 112, a testator gave all his property to 'my wife Eliza Ann Smalley'. He was survived by his lawful wife Mary Ann Smalley, and also by his reputed wife Eliza Ann Mercer. The Court of Appeal held that Eliza Ann Mercer was entitled, since the surrounding circumstances indicated that the testator had used the words 'my wife' in their secondary meaning of 'my reputed wife'.

There is an important distinction to be drawn between these two rules. Under (i) it would be possible for the testator to make 'black' mean 'white' or 'personalty' include 'realty' where the sense in which the word is being used is made clear in the will. This could not happen under (ii), since it is necessary that the word or phrase concerned be capable of the secondary meaning.

1.4.1.2 Extrinsic evidence

The general rule is that the court construes the words used in the will and does not admit extrinsic evidence as to the testator's intention.

However, under s. 21, Administration of Justice Act 1982 — which applies on deaths after 1982 — extrinsic evidence of the testator's intention is admissible to assist in the interpretation of the will in three situations. Such evidence may be 'circumstantial' (e.g. where the gift in the will is to 'Mrs G', evidence of the fact that the testator was acquainted with a Mrs Gregg whom he always referred to as 'Mrs G' — *Abbot* v *Massie* (1796) 3 Ves 148); or 'direct' (e.g. that the testator had told a friend that he intended to make the gift).

The cases in which such evidence may be admissible are:

(a) where any part of the will is meaningless. In *Kell* v *Charmer* (1856) 23 Beav 195, a jeweller in his will left 'to my son William the sum of i.x.x. To my son Robert Charles the sum of o.x.x.'

Evidence was admitted to show that in his business the testator used a 'code' to denote his prices, under which the symbols used in the will meant £100 and £200 respectively.

(b) where the language used in any part of the will is ambiguous on the face of it. Such a 'patent ambiguity' arises, for example, in the case of gifts such as 'my money' or 'my effects'.

(c) where evidence (other than evidence of the testator's intention) shows that the language used in any part of the will is ambiguous in the light of the surrounding circumstances. In these cases there is a 'latent ambiguity' — one which does not become apparent until you try to give effect to the will. *Re Smalley* (above) is an example of such a situation. The problem also arises where there is an 'equivocation' — where the description of the subject or object of the gift is applicable to two or more persons or things. For example, in *Re Jackson* [1933] Ch 237, where the gift was to 'my nephew Arthur Murphy' and the testator had three nephews of that name (two legitimate and one illegitimate). Extrinsic evidence (including evidence of the testator's intention) was admitted, which showed that the illegitimate nephew was intended to take. (Ironically, it was only the fact that there were two legitimate nephews fitting the 'description' in the will that enabled this evidence to be admitted. At the time, illegitimate relationships were ignored (unless the will otherwise provided) so that had there been only one legitimate nephew called Arthur Murphy he would have taken — even if there had been evidence of the testator's intention to benefit the illegitimate nephew — because there would not have been an ambiguity!)

Note that in (c) evidence of the testator's intention cannot be introduced to raise the ambiguity — only circumstantial evidence is admissible to do this. However, once the ambiguity has been thus 'established', evidence of the testator's intention is admissible to assist in resolving it.

It is important to appreciate that the section only allows extrinsic evidence to be admitted to assist in interpretation of the testator's will — and not (in effect) to make a new will for the testator. In *Re Williams* [1988] 1 WLR 905, Nicholls J said:

> The evidence may assist by showing which of two or more possible meanings the testator was attaching to a particular word or phrase . . . That meaning may be one which, without recourse to the extrinsic evidence, would not really have been apparent at all. So long as that meaning is one which the word or phrase read in its context is capable of bearing, then the court may conclude that, assisted by the extrinsic evidence, that is its correct construction. But if, however liberal may be the approach of the court, the meaning is one which the word or phrase cannot bear, I do not see how in carrying out a process of . . . interpretation . . . the court can declare that meaning to be the meaning of the word or phrase. Such a conclusion, varying or contradicting the language used, would amount to rewriting part of the will . . .

1.4.1.3 Date from which the will speaks

Unless there is a contrary intention in the will, then:

(a) as to property, the will speaks and takes effect 'as if it had been executed immediately before the death of the testator' — s. 24, Wills Act 1837. Thus a gift of the contents of the testator's house will prima facie be construed as a gift of the contents as at the date of death (rather than at the date of the will).

If a testator intends otherwise, this is best expressly stated; in the absence of such an express statement, the use of words such as 'my', 'now', or 'at present' could be sufficient (but do not of necessity oust s. 24). For example, a gift of 'my 500 shares in ABC plc' would be construed as a gift of the shares owned at the date of the will. On the other hand, a gift of 'all my shares in ABC plc' would prima facie pass the shares owned at the date of death; the subject matter of the gift here is generic and so described as to be capable of increase or decrease between the date of the will and the date of death.

(b) as to the objects of the gift (i.e. the beneficiaries) the will speaks from the date of execution. In other words, s. 24 does not apply (unless a contrary intention appears from the will). As a result, a gift to 'the eldest child of Adam' is prima facie a gift to the person fulfilling that description at the date of the will. If that child should predecease the testator, the gift will not 'pass' to the eldest surviving child of Adam. (If Adam had no children at the date of the will, the gift would be construed as a gift to Adam's first child, rather than (again) the eldest surviving child.)

This rule does not apply to 'class gifts' or to identified gifts to each member of a class (see further **1.4.1.5** below).

In **1.3.1** above, we noted that generally the effect of a codicil is to 're-date' the will. Thus, where under the above rules a will is construed as speaking from the date of execution, the operative date becomes the date of the codicil.

1.4.1.4 Omitting, changing and supplying words

The court, in construing a will, may sometimes be prepared to omit or change words used in the will. It will only do so where it is clear from the will

(a) that something has been omitted, and what that was; or
(b) that there has been an error in the wording, and the substance of the testator's intention is clear. In *Re Whitrick* [1957] 1 WLR 884, the testatrix left all her estate to her husband with a substitutional gift in the event of her husband and herself 'both dying at the same time'. Her husband predeceased her, so that on a strict interpretation of the words used the substitutional gift failed to take effect (they did not die 'at the same time'). The Court of Appeal held that it was clear from the will as a whole that the intention of the testatrix was to provide for what should happen if her husband failed to survive her. The will would be construed as if the substitutional gift was to take effect in this event as well as if they died at the same time.

In the case of deaths after 1982, s. 20, Administration of Justice Act 1982 gives the court a limited power to rectify a will so as to carry out the testator's intentions. The court must be satisfied that as a result of a clerical error, or of a failure to understand the testator's instructions, the will is so expressed that it fails to carry out the testator's intentions. This provision allows the court to supply, omit or change words where the testator's intention may not be clear from the will itself — not previously possible even if it was obvious that they had been accidentally omitted. Application for rectification must normally be made to the court within six months of the date of the grant of representation; a later application is only possible with the leave of the court.

1.4.1.5 Class gifts

A class gift is a gift of property to be divided amongst beneficiaries who fulfil a general description — for example, '£50,000 to the children of Zoe', '£50,000 to the children of Zoe who attain the age of 18'. In such cases, the total value of the gift is clear; the problem is to know how to share it amongst those entitled. This will obviously depend upon how many people fit the description. In the examples given, it would not be possible to answer this question with certainty at least until the death of Zoe; in the meantime, no distribution would be possible.

A similar problem arises where the gift in the will takes the form of an individual gift to the members of a class — for example, '£5,000 to each of the children of Zebedee'. Here, what the prospective beneficiaries are to take is identified, but until the death of Zebedee it cannot be known how many children will qualify.

The courts have invented 'class closing rules' to overcome these problems and allow distribution at an earlier date. The various rules (which one applies to a given case depends upon the type of gift involved) determine when the class will close; in principle, this will generally happen when there is one person fitting the description who has a vested interest. At whatever point the class closes, it does so to the exclusion of any potential beneficiary not then 'living' — a term which includes a child *en ventre sa mère* (i.e. conceived) and subsequently born alive. This is obviously 'unfair' to those thus excluded from benefit; but this disadvantage is considered to be outweighed by the advantage of earlier distribution.

The class closing rules may be excluded by a clear provision in the testator's will — such as 'to the children of Zoe living at my death', 'to the children of Zebedee whenever born'. Further, the rules only apply to gifts of capital: if there is a gift of, for example, '£500,000 upon trust to pay the income therefrom to the children of Alice for twenty-one years', the class remains open so that each income payment is made to the children of Alice then living.

As indicated above, the rules (if not so excluded) differ in detail according to the type of gift involved.

(a) Immediate vested gift — e.g. '£500,000 to the children of Arthur'. The class closes at the date of the testator's death if there is any child of Arthur then living. If there are none, the class remains open until the death of Arthur.

(b) Deferred vested gift — e.g. '£500,000 to Laura for life remainder to the children of Arthur'. In this case, the class will close on the death of Laura provided at that time at least one of the potential class has attained a vested interest. Thus, any children of Arthur born before (or *en ventre sa mère* at) Laura's death will qualify (it is immaterial whether or not they were alive at the death of the testator). The estates of any children of Arthur who had predeceased Laura will also be entitled. If, at the date of Laura's death, no one has attained a vested interest, the class remains open until the death of Arthur.

(c) Immediate contingent gift — e.g. '£500,000 to the children of Arthur who attain the age of 18'. Here, the class closes at the testator's death if any member of the class has then fulfilled the contingency, and will comprise any child of Arthur who is already 18 plus any others then living who subsequently attain that age. The prospective share of any child who dies before attaining a vested interest accrues to those members of the class who do. If at the date of the testator's death no child of Arthur has fulfilled the contingency, the class remains open until one does; the class will then close around that child and any others then living who subsequently attain the age of 18.

(d) Deferred contingent gift — e.g. '£500,000 to Laura for life remainder to the children of Arthur who attain the age of 18'. The class will close here on the death of Laura if at that point any child of Arthur has fulfilled the contingency, and will comprise any such children and any others then living who subsequently attain 18. Again, the prospective share of any child who dies under the age of 18 will accrue to those who attain vested interest. If on the death of Laura there is no class member with a vested interest, the class again remains open until such time as the first child of Arthur attains 18.

(e) 'Early closing'. Where there is a deferred class gift and the prior interest fails (e.g. because in (b) or (d) above, Laura predeceases the testator), the gift to the class (in effect) becomes an immediate class gift and thus subject to the class closing rules appropriate to such gifts. There will probably be no such 'acceleration' of the class gift, however, where the life interest is terminated by the life tenant's disclaimer or surrender of the prior interest — *Re Harker's Will Trusts* [1969] 1 WLR 1124, in which the judge refused to follow a contrary view in *Re Davies* [1957] 1 WLR 922.

(f) Individual gift to members of a class — e.g. '£1,000 to each of the children of Adelaide', '£1,000 to each of the children of Adelaide who attain the age of 18'. In these cases, unless there is a contrary intention in the will, the class will close at the testator's death. If there are no children of Adelaide then living, the gift fails. If the gifts to the class members follow a life interest, the class remains open until the death of the life tenant.

1.4.1.6 Gifts to children

Gifts to 'children' (whether of the testator or anyone else) will be construed as including

(a) legitimate children, unless there is a clear intention to the contrary.
(b) legitimated children, unless there is a clear intention to the contrary (Legitimacy Act 1976). Such children are treated as if born legitimate, whether the legitimation (by their parents' marriage) occurred before or after the testator's death. Where the gift depends upon the child's

date of birth, the rules of construction are similar to those described below in relation to adopted children.

(c) illegitimate children. At common law, such children were not prima facie included. However, in the case of a will/codicil made after 3 April 1988, ss. 1(1) and 19, Family Law Reform Act 1987 have for most succession purposes effectively abolished the concept of illegitimacy. In the absence of contrary intention shown by the testator, references in a will/codicil to any relationship between two persons are to be construed without regard to whether the parents of either of them, or the parents of any person through whom the relationship is traced, were at any time married to each other.

For the purposes of this provision, a will/codicil is not treated as made after 3 April 1988 simply because there is a codicil dated after that date.

Where the will was made after 1969 (but before 4 April 1988) the position is governed by s. 15, Family Law Reform Act 1969.

(d) adopted children (Adoption Act 1976 — governs the construction of wills/codicils on deaths after 1975). In essence, an adopted child is treated as the legitimate child of the adopting parent(s) and no longer the child of its natural parents. This is so whether the adoption order (of a court in the UK, the Isle of Man, the Channel Islands, or certain foreign jurisdictions) is made before or after the death of the testator.

The effect, therefore, is that any reference to 'children' in a will, in the absence of any contrary indication, includes such adopted children — though not in the case of the wills of the natural parents.

If the gift in the will depends upon the date of birth of a child, the Act further provides (in the absence of contrary intention) that the will is to be construed as if the adopted child had been born on the date of the adoption (and if two or more children are adopted on the same day, they are treated as born on that date in the order of their actual births). For example, suppose the gift in the will is to 'the children of Anthony living at the date of my death', and the testator died in 1992. In 1993, Anthony adopts a child who was born in 1990; that child is treated as born in 1993 and so cannot take under the gift in the will.

This rule does not, however, affect any reference to the age of a child. Thus, if the gift is to 'the first child of Anthony to attain the age of 18' and Anthony has a natural child born in 1990 and in 1993 adopts a child (then aged 10), the adopted child will reach the age of 18 first and so take the gift. It is not clear in the case of a gift to 'Anthony's eldest child' whether this would be construed as a 'reference to the age of a child'.

1.4.1.7 Life interest or absolute gift?

There can sometimes be difficulties (hopefully not in any professionally drawn will) in deciding whether the testator intends to give a limited or absolute interest. So, for example, the gift in a homemade will might be 'to Ada and on Ada's death what is left over to Basil'. There are several possible constructions of such a provision, including:

(a) an absolute gift to Ada (the gift over to Basil failing either for uncertainty or because it is repugnant to Ada's absolute interest — it is not possible to give absolute interests in succession).
(b) a life interest to Ada with remainder to Basil absolutely. There are a number of presumptions, applying in the absence of contrary intention in the will, which may assist in the construction of the will in such cases:

(i) that a bequest of personalty is absolute.
(ii) that a devise of realty without words of limitation passes the fee simple or such other interest as the testator has power to dispose — s. 28, Wills Act 1837.

(iii) under s. 22, Administration of Justice Act 1982, which applies where a testator gives property to a spouse in terms which would confer an absolute interest, and in the same instrument purports to give issue an interest in the same property. The presumption in such cases is that the spouse takes an absolute interest.

The rule in *Hancock* v *Watson* [1902] AC 14 (usually referred to as the rule in *Lassence* v *Tierney* (1849) 1 Mac & G 551) is an attempt to reconcile two inconsistent provisions in a will. In effect, it applies where there is initially an absolute gift (of realty or personalty) and trusts are then engrafted upon that gift which fail for any reason. To the extent that such trusts fail, the absolute gift takes effect. So, for example, if there is a gift of property to Alistair absolutely and subsequently the will directs the same property to be held on Alistair's death for Belinda, if Belinda predeceases the testator the purported gift to her fails (under the doctrine of lapse — **1.4.3.3** below). Alistair (or his estate) will take the property absolutely.

1.4.2 LEGACIES AND DEVISES

Technically, a legacy is a gift in a will of personalty, which may be classified as specific, general, demonstrative, pecuniary or residuary. A devise is a gift of realty, and may be either specific or residuary.

1.4.2.1 Specific legacy/devise

This is a gift of particular property owned by the deceased distinguished from any other property of the same kind which may be owned by the deceased — e.g. 'my 500 shares in XYZ plc', 'my freehold property Greenacre'. Such gifts are subject to the doctrine of ademption if the testator does not own the property concerned at the date of death (see **1.4.3.2** below) but abate (i.e. will be used for the payment of debts) after other property in the estate (see **14.3.4**).

1.4.2.2 General legacy

This is a gift of property not distinguished by the testator from other similar property — e.g. '500 shares in XYZ plc'. This is a gift of any 500 shares in the company (even if that was the number which the testator owned at the date of the will). Such gifts are not subject to the doctrine of ademption, so that if in the example the testator did not own any XYZ plc shares at the date of death, the beneficiary is entitled to require estate funds (provided these are sufficient) to be used to buy 500 shares. But such legacies will be used for the payment of debts before specific legacies (see **14.3.4**).

1.4.2.3 Demonstrative legacy

Such legacies are essentially general in character, but a specific source is identified from which it is to be paid — e.g. '£1,000 to Ambrose to be paid from my Newtown Building Society Account'. Such legacies are not adeemed if the account has been closed during the testator's lifetime, or there is insufficient in the account at the date of death to pay the legacy in full. In such circumstances, the beneficiary is entitled to any balance at that time, and to have the deficiency paid as a general legacy. However, for the purposes of abatement, a demonstrative legacy ranks as a specific legacy and is thus used last for the payment of debts (see **14.3.4**).

1.4.2.4 Pecuniary legacy

This is a gift of money, and usually is general in character — e.g. a gift of '£5000'. However, it may be specific (e.g. a gift of 'the £5,000 which I keep in my safe' or 'the £5,000 which Xavier owes me'); or demonstrative (e.g. '£5,000 payable from my current account at Newtown Bank'). Where such a legacy is payable by instalments (e.g. '£5,000 per annum') it is usually called an annuity.

1.4.2.5 Residuary legacy/devise

Residuary gifts embrace all the rest of the deceased's property (i.e. not disposed of by any specific, general or demonstrative gifts).

1.4.3 FAILURE

A gift in a will may fail for a variety of reasons. The will may provide what then is to happen to the gifted property. In the absence of any effective substitutional gift, a failed non-residuary gift forms part of the residuary estate; if it is (part of) the residuary gift which fails, there is property undisposed of by the will which passes in accordance with the intestacy rules — described in **Chapter 2**.

The reasons for the failure of a gift include:

(a) Uncertainty (**1.4.3.1**)
(b) Ademption (**1.4.3.2**)
(c) Lapse (**1.4.3.3**) [& divorce]
(d) Section 15, Wills Act 1837 (**1.4.3.4**)
(e) Gift contrary to public policy (**1.4.3.5**).

In addition, we have already noted the effect of the testator's divorce on any gift to the former spouse (**1.2.1.4** above). Further possible causes of failure include disclaimer (this is discussed more fully in **15.1**), and failure to observe the rules against perpetuity and accumulation. These latter you should have encountered in the course of your studies of land law and trusts, and are not further discussed in this book.

1.4.3.1 Uncertainty

Gifts may fail for uncertainty of either subject matter or objects.

Where it is not possible to identify the property which is the subject of the gift (e.g. a gift of 'some of my jewellery') it will fail. However, this is not so where the gift — although of an uncertain amount — is capable of ascertainment. Thus a gift to a beneficiary of 'such of my jewellery as she may select' is effective. Where the testator has not sufficiently identified the beneficiaries the gift normally fails — e.g. a gift to 'one of my nieces'. However, a gift for charitable purposes which does not clearly identify the particular charity intended to be benefited will not fail, provided it is clear that the gift is for exclusively charitable purposes.

1.4.3.2 Ademption

To the extent that a testator no longer owns the property which is the subject of a specific legacy or devise at the date of death, the gift is adeemed, i.e. it fails, and the disappointed beneficiary is not entitled to any compensation. Ademption may occur because the testator has sold the property, or given it away *inter vivos*; or because there has been a change in substance (as opposed to a mere change of name or form). In *Re Slater* [1907] 1 Ch 665, the testator made a specific bequest of shares in the Lambeth Waterworks Company. This company was subsequently taken over and amalgamated with other companies to form the Metropolitan Water Board, and stock in the new undertaking was issued to replace the original shares. The Court of Appeal held that this was a change of substance so that the gift failed. On the other hand, in *Re Clifford* [1912] 1 Ch 29, the testator's will contained a gift of 'twenty-three of the shares belonging to me' in a particular company. Subsequently, the company changed its name and each of the original shares was subdivided into four new ones. It was held that the original subject matter of the gift remained, though changed in name and form. It was not, therefore, adeemed and took effect as a gift of 92 of the new shares.

The doctrine of conversion may cause ademption to occur by changing the 'substance' of the gift. Thus, a specific gift of Greenacre house is adeemed if the testator has since the date of the will entered into a binding contract for its sale. Again, if the will leaves Greenacre to Arnold and the residuary estate to Brian, and the testator subsequently grants Oliver an option to purchase Greenacre, the gift to Arnold is adeemed by the exercise of the option during the testator's lifetime. If the option is exercised by Oliver after the testator's death, its exercise retrospectively causes the gift to Arnold to be adeemed — *Lawes* v *Bennett* (1785) 1 Cox 167. The result is that the purchase monies will pass to Brian as part of the residuary estate — though Arnold will be entitled to any income produced by the property from the date of death. In *Re Carrington* [1932] 1 Ch 1, the rule in *Lawes* v *Bennett* was applied to a specific gift of shares, which was adeemed by the exercise after the testator's death of an option to purchase granted after the date of the will. However, if the will is made (or republished) after the grant of the option, no ademption occurs when the option is exercised. In such a case, the testator is assumed to have intended the specific beneficiary to take either the property or the proceeds of its sale — *Drant* v *Vause* (1842) 1 Y & CCC 580.

Normally, a codicil to a will (effectively re-dating it, as we have seen) has no effect upon a gift in that will which has been adeemed. However, sometimes a codicil might save a gift which would otherwise have been adeemed. For example, suppose that the will contains a gift to Amber 'of the property in which I now reside', which happens to be Greenacre. Subsequently, Greenacre is sold and is replaced by Brownacre. A later codicil will have the effect (because of the way in which the will is drafted) of passing Brownacre to Amber.

If the subject matter of the gift is to be ascertained at the date of death (e.g. 'the shares in XYZ plc which I own at the date of my death'), the doctrine of ademption is not applicable. However, if the testator owns no such shares at death, the gift will clearly fail completely.

1.4.3.3 Lapse

As a general rule, a beneficiary must survive the testator in order to take a gift under that testator's will, otherwise the gift lapses — in which event prima facie the subject matter of the intended gift will fall into residue, or (if itself a share of residue) pass under the intestacy rules (discussed in **Chapter 2**). However, although the testator cannot preclude the operation of the doctrine by provision in the will that it is not to apply, the inclusion of an effective substitutional gift prevents the consequences just described.

A class gift only lapses if all members of the class predecease the testator; the rule is similar in the case of gifts to beneficial joint tenants.

The order of death, as between testator and beneficiary, will usually be easily determined so that whether or not the gift has lapsed will be clear. Where the order of death is uncertain, the *commorientes* rule (s. 184, Law of Property Act 1925) applies unless excluded by the inclusion in the will of a survivorship clause — see further **18.4.6.3**. Under this rule, where there is no evidence as to the order in which deaths have occurred then, for succession purposes, the younger is deemed to have survived the elder. Thus a gift in the younger's will to the elder would lapse, but not vice versa. The *commorientes* rule generally applies both where there is a will, and where there is no will so that the estate will be distributed under the intestacy rules (see **Chapter 2**). However, the rule is modified in the case of the elder of two spouses who dies without a will, or partially intestate (because the will does not wholly dispose of that spouse's estate). The property of the elder spouse which is not disposed of by any will has to be dealt with in accordance with the intestacy rules. In applying these, the younger spouse is presumed to have predeceased (s. 46, Administration of Estates Act 1925 as amended by s. 1, Intestates' Estates Act 1952). The normal *commorientes* rule applies, however, when considering entitlement to the estate of the younger, whether that spouse left a will or not: and to the property of the elder in so far as disposed of by the elder's will.

The most important exception to the doctrine of lapse is contained in s. 33, Wills Act 1837 (as substituted by s. 19, Administration of Justice Act 1982). This section applies where:

(a) a will contains a gift to the child or issue (i.e. remoter descendant) of the testator; and
(b) the intended beneficiary dies before the testator, leaving issue; and
(c) issue of the intended beneficiary are living (including *en ventre sa mère*) at the testator's death.

If these conditions are met then, in the absence of a contrary intention shown by the will, the gift takes effect as a gift to such issue, who take (in equal shares if more than one) the gift which their parent would have taken. It is not clear whether if the original gift is contingent the gift 'substituted' by s. 33 is subject to the same contingency.

No issue can take whose parent is alive at the date of the testator's death and is thus capable of taking.

The section also applies (in the absence of a contrary intention in the will) to a class gift to the testator's children or remoter issue.

It is important to appreciate that s. 33 cannot prevent the failure of gifts in favour of beneficiaries who predecease but who are not issue of the testator.

1.4.3.4 Section 15, Wills Act 1837 (as amended by s. 1, Wills Act 1968)

A gift in a will fails if the beneficiary or the beneficiary's spouse witnesses the will, though the validity of the will as such is not affected. However, the gift will not fail if, ignoring the attestation by the beneficiary or spouse, the will is duly executed — i.e. because there are at least two other witnesses who are not beneficiaries or their spouses. Further, a gift within the terms of s. 15 may be 'saved' if the will is subsequently confirmed by a codicil which is independently witnessed.

The rule preventing witnesses or their spouses benefiting only applies to beneficial gifts (including the benefit of charging clauses commonly included in wills where solicitors and other professionals are to act as executors and/or trustees — see further **18.4.4.2**). It does not affect a gift to the witness or their spouse as trustee; nor will it matter if the beneficiary (or their spouse) under a fully or half secret trust witnesses the will, since such beneficiary takes under the trust rather than the will — *Re Young* [1951] Ch 344.

Where the beneficiary's spouse has witnessed the will, s. 15 only applies if the beneficiary and the witness were married at the date of the execution of the will; there will be no problem where they only married after that date.

1.4.3.5 Gift contrary to public policy

Gifts for an illegal or immoral purpose, or otherwise contrary to public policy will fail. Thus, as a matter of public policy, a sane person who commits murder or manslaughter (or anyone claiming through that person, such as their issue) is debarred from taking any benefit under the will or intestacy of the victim.

However, under Forfeiture Act 1982 (which does not apply in the case of murder) the court may modify the effect of the general rule if it is satisfied that the justice of the case so requires. Application under the Act must be made within three months of the conviction. Further, except again in the case of murder, the offender may make application for an order under Inheritance (Provision for Family and Dependants) Act 1975 — see **Chapter 3**.

TWO

INTESTACY

In **Chapter 1** we considered the legal background to the making and construction of wills by which testators may achieve distribution of their estates in accordance with their wishes. In this chapter, we will consider the position:

(a) Where someone dies without having effectively disposed of any of their property by will — giving rise to a total intestacy.

(b) Where there is a valid will but this does not dispose of the whole of the estate — causing a partial intestacy. This situation may arise where the will contains no residuary gift, or where there is a gift of residue but this has wholly or partly failed (e.g., because a residuary beneficiary has predeceased the testator, and there is no effective substitutional gift (either in the will or by the operation of s. 33, Wills Act 1837 — see **1.4.3**).

However, certain types of property will pass on death quite independently of the intestacy rules (just as they are unaffected (as we saw in **Chapter 1**) by the terms of any will). Any such property in an estate will not, therefore, be affected by the rules discussed in this chapter. The types of property which pass on death outside the will or the intestacy rules will be examined more closely later (in **8.4.2** and **8.4.3**), but include property held as beneficial joint tenants, which accrues by right of survivorship; life policies written under s. 11, Married Women's Property Act 1882 and other trust policies; certain pension scheme benefits; property the subject of a statutory nomination; and *donationes mortis causa*.

2.1 The Basic Position

Where the deceased left a will, its effective provisions will be implemented. To the extent that the estate is not disposed of by a valid will, its distribution is governed by the rules in Part IV of the Administration of Estates Act 1925 (as amended).

2.1.1 THE STATUTORY TRUST FOR SALE

Section 33(1), Administration of Estates Act 1925 provides that the personal representatives hold the intestate's estate not disposed of by will on trust for sale and conversion into money (with power to postpone such sale and conversion as they think fit).

The subsection specifically provides that (unless there is 'special reason' for doing so) the personal representatives should not sell any reversionary (i.e. future) interest until it falls into possession. Thus, if the deceased's assets include a remainder interest under a trust where the life tenant is still alive, the remainder interest should not normally be sold. It is further provided that personal chattels (see below) must not be sold except for 'special reason', unless there are not sufficient other assets available to enable the personal representatives to discharge the debts and other liabilities of the estate.

INTESTACY

From the proceeds of such sale and conversion (and the intestate's ready money) the personal representatives must pay the funeral, testamentary and administration expenses, debts and other liabilities of the deceased.

The residuary estate (what is left after all the liabilities and expenses have been discharged) is then to be shared amongst those entitled according to the statutory rules.

2.1.2 ENTITLEMENT

The position of any surviving spouse must always be considered first.

(a) A surviving spouse takes everything unless either:

(i) there are issue — i.e. children, grandchildren etc. — in which event (if the estate is large enough) the issue may also be entitled (see **2.2.2** below); or

(ii) there are no issue but certain close relatives — in which event these relatives may also share the estate (see **2.2.3** below).

(b) If there is no surviving spouse, the order of entitlement is set out in **2.3, 2.4** and **2.5** below. The classes of beneficiary entitled must be considered in order, and only if there is no one in a particular category is it necessary to consider the next one.

2.1.3 THE STATUTORY TRUSTS

In the case of issue, brothers and sisters, and uncles and aunts, it will be seen that the class takes 'on the statutory trusts'. Section 47, Administration of Estates Act 1925 defines this expression as meaning:

(a) Equally for all members of the class of relatives concerned living or *en ventre sa mère* (i.e conceived) at the date of the intestate's death who attain the age of 18 or marry under that age.

(b) The issue of any class members who predecease take *per stirpes* their parent's share provided they (i.e. the issue) attain 18 or marry earlier.

This substitution only applies where a potential beneficiary dies before the intestate, leaving issue. If a potential beneficiary is living at the date of the intestate's death but subsequently dies before attaining a vested interest (i.e. before attaining 18 or earlier marriage), the estate will be dealt with as if that person had never existed (even if survived by their issue).

2.1.3.1 Example

Ian has recently died intestate, leaving the following issue:

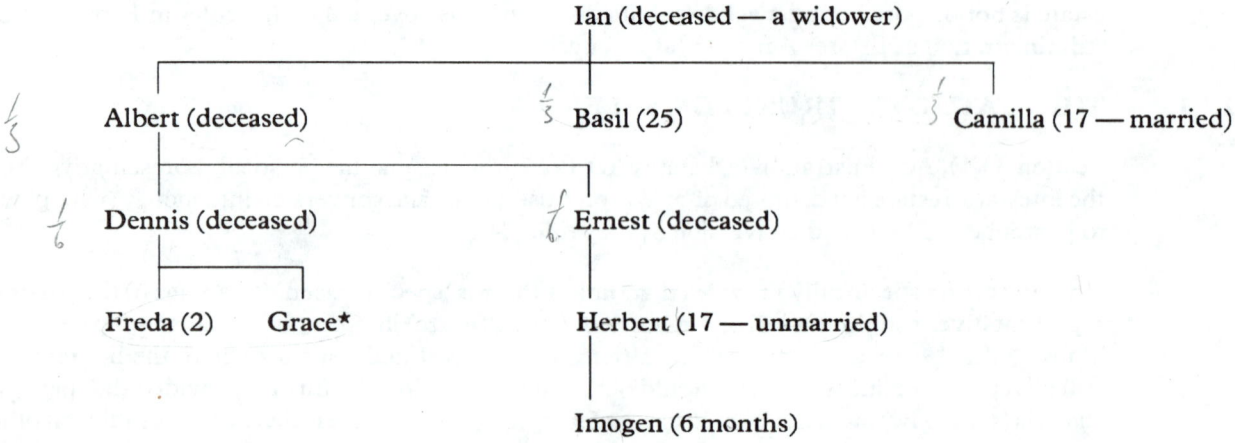

*Grace was *en ventre sa mère* at the date of Ian's death.

Ian's estate will pass to his issue on the statutory trusts. Basil will take a vested one-third share. Camilla has fulfilled the contingency, so that her one-third share also vests. As she is under 18 she will not be able to give an effective discharge to the personal representatives, so that the capital of her share will have to be held for her until she attains her majority. She will, however, be entitled to receive the income in the meantime. Were she to die before attaining 18, her one-third share would pass as part of her estate to those entitled on her intestacy.

Albert's share will pass under the statutory trusts to his issue, i.e., his one-third share will be sub-divided into two equal shares. The (one-sixth) share which Dennis would have inherited had he survived will be held on the statutory trusts for Freda and Grace; Ernest's one-sixth share will similarly be held for Herbert (he does not obtain a vested interest because he is not married). If neither Freda or Grace were to attain vested interests, their one-sixth share would accrue to Herbert, provided he in turn survives to attain a vested interest. If he also fails to do so, the whole of Albert's share will accrue to Basil and Camilla, since these will be the only interests under the statutory trusts which vest. Imogen will not be entitled (she could only take under the statutory trusts if her father had predeceased Ian).

2.2 Entitlement where there is a Surviving Spouse

To be entitled to share in the intestate's estate the spouse (i.e. a person to whom the intestate was lawfully married at the date of death) must survive (however briefly) the intestate. There is no entitlement under the intestacy rules for a divorced spouse (i.e. after decree absolute) or one who is judicially separated.

We noted in **1.4.3.3** the 'commorientes' rule where the order of death is uncertain, and that the rule in such circumstances — that (for succession purposes) the younger is deemed to survive the elder — does not in effect apply as between husbands and wives to the extent that the elder dies intestate.

2.2.1 SPOUSE ALONE

Where there are no issue, parents, or brothers or sisters of the whole blood (or their issue), the personal representatives hold the whole of the residuary estate for the surviving spouse absolutely.

2.2.2 SPOUSE AND ISSUE

2.2.2.1 The spouse

The spouse is entitled to:

(a) the personal chattels absolutely;
(b) a statutory legacy of £75,000, free of tax and costs, with interest (currently at 6%) from the date of death until payment;
(c) a life interest in one half of the residuary estate.

Thus, if anything remains after the personal chattels and the statutory legacy have been paid, the spouse is entitled to the income for life from one half of the balance of the estate.

2.2.2.2 The issue

The issue are entitled (on the statutory trusts) to the other half of the residuary estate and to the remainder interest in that half in which the spouse has a life interest.

INTESTACY

2.2.2.3 Personal chattels

The term 'personal chattels' is defined by s. 55(1)(x), Administration of Estates Act 1925 as including:

> ... carriages, horses, stable furniture and effects (not used for business purposes), motor cars and accessories (not used for business purposes), garden effects, domestic animals, plate, plated articles, linen, china, glass, books, pictures, prints, furniture, jewellery, articles of household or personal use or ornament, musical and scientific instruments and apparatus, wines, liquors and consumable stores, but do not include any chattels used at the death of the intestate for business purposes nor money or securities for money.

In spite of this definition showing signs of its age, it is clear that it is intended to cover items of personal and domestic use and ornament. In most cases there is unlikely to be much difficulty in determining whether a particular item, by its nature, falls within the definition. However, user is sometimes relevant: assets used for business purposes are excluded, so that it would appear that a car used for both business and private purposes falls outside the definition.

The phrase 'articles of household or personal use' has been held to include, for example:

(a) A 60-foot yacht used by the deceased for pleasure — *Re Chaplin* [1950] Ch 507.
(b) A stamp collection made by the deceased as a hobby — *Re Reynold's Will Trusts* [1966] 1 WLR 19.
(c) A collection of watches worth some £50,000 out of an estate of approximately £80,000 — *Re Crispin's Will Trusts* [1975] Ch 245.

2.2.3 SPOUSE, NO ISSUE BUT PARENT(S) OR BROTHERS/SISTERS OF THE WHOLE BLOOD (OR THEIR ISSUE)

In this case, the spouse takes:

(a) the personal chattels absolutely;
(b) a statutory legacy of £125,000, free of tax and costs and with interest (as before);
(c) one half of the residuary estate (i.e. the capital) absolutely.

The other half of the residuary estate passes to the intestate's parent(s) or, if neither survives, to the brothers and sisters of the whole blood or their issue on the statutory trusts.

2.2.4 SPECIAL RULES APPLYING TO SPOUSES

There are two possible elections which may be open to the surviving spouse and, if exercised, will affect the distribution described above. These relate to the surviving spouse's life interest and to the matrimonial home.

2.2.4.1 Redemption of life interest (s. 47A, Administration of Estates Act 1925)

Where the surviving spouse has a life interest in the residuary estate an election may be made, in writing, to the personal representatives to capitalise that life interest. If the spouse is the sole personal representative, the election is made to the Senior District Judge of the Family Division. The time limit for making the election is 12 months from the date of the grant, but the court can, in its discretion, extend the time limit.

The effect of making the election is that, instead of receiving the income only from one half of the residuary estate for life, the spouse takes a capital sum (inevitably less than half of the residuary estate) absolutely. The balance of the residuary estate (after the deduction of the costs of the capitalisation) will then be held for the issue on the statutory trusts.

There is a complex statutory formula for arriving at the capitalised value. However, if the issue are all *sui juris* the figure may be arrived at instead by agreement between the spouse and the issue.

As to the tax consequences of such an election, see **15.5**.

2.2.4.2 Appropriation of the matrimonial home (sch. 2, Intestates' Estates Act 1952)

This provision enables the surviving spouse, in effect, to purchase the matrimonial home (or the deceased's interest in it where they were beneficial tenants in common). The election is not necessary where the deceased and the surviving spouse were beneficial joint tenants because the deceased's interest accrues automatically to the survivor, independently of the intestacy rules.

The 'matrimonial home' is defined as that in which the surviving spouse was resident at the date of death of the intestate; it does not matter whether the deceased was also so resident.

The 1952 Act gives the spouse the right to require the personal representatives to appropriate the matrimonial home (at its value at the date of appropriation — *Re Collins* [1975] 1 WLR 309) — in partial or total satisfaction of the spouse's statutory legacy and/or absolute or capitalised life interest in the residuary estate. If these are not adequate to 'purchase' the deceased's interest, the deficiency may be made up out of the spouse's own resources.

This election too must be made in writing to the personal representatives within 12 months of the grant (the court having again a discretion to extend the time limit). Normally, during this period the personal representatives cannot sell the matrimonial home without the spouse's consent. If the spouse is one of two or more personal representatives, the notice should be given to the others. Schedule 2 does not say what is to happen if the spouse is the sole personal representative.

In four cases, the consent of the court is required before the election can be made. In these cases the court will need to be satisfied that the exercise of the election will not prejudice the rights of others interested in the residuary estate (e.g. by diminishing the value of other assets, or making them harder to sell). Such consent is required where the dwelling:

(a) Forms part of a building, the whole of which is comprised in the residuary estate, e.g. is a flat within a building owned by the intestate.
(b) Is held with agricultural land similarly comprised, e.g. is the farmhouse on a farm owned by the intestate.
(c) Was at the death of the intestate used in whole or in part as a hotel or lodging house.
(d) Was at the death of the intestate used in part for non-domestic purposes (e.g. where part of the house was used as an office or shop).

It may be possible to avoid an application to the court in these cases by the use of the general power of appropriation conferred on personal representatives by s. 41, Administration of Estates Act 1925. This power might also be useful where the election described above is not available, e.g. because the 12 month time limit has expired.

Section 41 allows personal representatives to appropriate assets in or towards satisfaction of any interest in the deceased's estate (whether under the terms of the will or the operation of the intestacy rules), subject to the beneficiary consenting and to any specific legatee not being prejudiced.

The power in s. 41 cannot normally be exercised where the value of the asset to be appropriated exceeds the value of the beneficiary's interest in the estate. However, in the specific case of an appropriation of the matrimonial home on intestacy, the spouse may pay 'equality money', i.e. if necessary make up any deficiency (sch. 2, Intestates' Estates Act 1952).

INTESTACY

2.3 Issue

Subject to the entitlement of any surviving spouse, the residuary estate is held for the issue of the intestate on the statutory trusts.

Effectively, children take to the exclusion of remoter issue, except where a child predeceases the intestate leaving issue, when, as we have seen, the issue take their parent's share on the statutory trusts.

An adopted child is treated as a legitimate child of its adoptive parent(s) and not as the child of its natural parents (s. 39, Adoption Act 1976). A legitimated child is treated as if born legitimate (ss. 5 and 10, Legitimacy Act 1976).

Section 18, Family Law Reform Act 1987 provides that (on a death on/after 4 April 1988) the distribution of assets on intestacy is to be determined without regard to whether the parents of a particular person were (or were not) married to each other. In other words, illegitimacy is ignored, and this applies not only to the intestate's issue but to all other relatives who may be entitled under the intestacy rules. (On a death before 4 April 1988 different rules applied.)

The Family Law Reform Act 1987 provides no special protection for personal representatives who distribute in ignorance of illegitimate claimants. However, under s. 18(2) there is a presumption that an illegitimate child is not survived by its father, or any person related to that child only through its father, unless the contrary is shown.

2.4 Other Relatives

If there are no surviving spouse or issue, the order of entitlement to share in the estate is as follows:

(a) parents (equally if both alive); but if none then
(b) brothers and sisters of the whole blood (i.e. who share the same parents as the deceased) on the statutory trusts; but if none then
(c) brothers and sisters of the half blood (i.e. who share only one parent with the deceased) on the statutory trusts; but if none then
(d) grandparents (equally if more than one); but if none then
(e) uncles and aunts of the whole blood (i.e. brothers and sisters of the whole blood of one of the intestate's parents) on the statutory trusts; but if none then
(f) uncles and aunts of the half blood (i.e. brothers and sisters of the half blood of one of the intestate's parents) on the statutory trusts.

It is blood relatives of the intestate who are entitled, not those related only by marriage.

2.5 The Crown

If the intestate is not survived by any relatives qualifying to share in the estate in any of the above categories then the Crown takes the residuary estate as *bona vacantia*. If the intestate died resident within the Duchy of Lancaster or in Cornwall, the Duchy or Duke of Cornwall respectively, take as *bona vacantia*.

Section 46, Administration of Estates Act 1925 gives the Crown etc. a discretion in such cases to make provision for the intestate's dependants (who need not be related to the deceased) and for 'any other person for whom the intestate might reasonably have been expected to make provision'.

2.6 Hotchpot

2.6.1 THE RULES

The hotchpot rules require that surviving spouses, children and issue should bring into account certain other benefits received from the deceased in calculating their respective entitlements under the intestacy rules. The rules, which do not apply to any other relatives, are found in ss. 47(1) and 49(1), Administration of Estates Act 1925; the former applies on both total and partial intestacy, the latter only on a partial intestacy.

2.6.2 SURVIVING SPOUSE (s. 49(1))

On a partial intestacy the surviving spouse is required to bring into account any benefit received under the will against the appropriate statutory legacy. The spouse's other entitlements under the intestacy rules (to receive the personal chattels and to a share in the residuary estate) are not affected.

2.6.2.1 Example

Henry's will leaves Wendy a legacy of £100,000 and his personal chattels, but makes no other dispositions. On Henry's death there is £100,000 not disposed of by his will. There are no issue, but Henry's mother, Gloria, is still alive.

Wendy takes:

(a) £100,000 and the personal chattels (under the will);
(b) £25,000 being the balance of the (£125,000) statutory legacy;
(c) £37,500 (being one half the residuary estate) absolutely.

Gloria takes the other half of the residuary estate (£37,500) absolutely.

If the benefit received under the will exceeds the amount of the appropriate statutory legacy, the effect is that the spouse will not receive any statutory legacy, but is under no obligation to account for the excess. If the spouse receives a life interest under the will, this has to be brought into account at its <u>actuarial</u> value.

2.6.3 CHILDREN AND ISSUE

The two hotchpot rules here apply in the absence of contrary intention on the part of the deceased 'expressed or appearing from the circumstances of the case'. Underlying them is an assumption that parents would wish to treat their children equally.

It is important to appreciate that the rules discussed below only have any impact upon the entitlement of the intestate's children or issue: they do not affect in any way the rights of the surviving spouse.

2.6.3.1 Section 47(1)

On a total or partial intestacy, in order to determine a child's entitlement under the intestacy rules, any *inter vivos* 'advancements' by the intestate to that child must be brought into account. (If the child concerned is dead, the advancement must be brought into account by those claiming through that child.) Valuation of the advancement is to be made as at the date of death, except in the case of a gift of cash — when the sum given will be the amount to be brought into account.

INTESTACY

An 'advancement' is a substantial provision to set a child up in life, and may take the form of an outright gift to, or a settlement for the benefit of, the child. It is specifically provided by s. 47(1) that a provision on the occasion of the child's marriage is to be brought into account. There is a presumption of advancement where the payment etc. is of such a substantial amount as to represent permanent provision for the child (*Re Hayward* [1957] Ch 528). In *Re Grover's Will Trusts* [1971] Ch 168, it was held that the onus of proving advancement lies on the person alleging it.

The steps required to calculate the child's share where this rule operates are:

(a) Calculate the 'notional estate', i.e. the estate available (after satisfying the entitlement of any surviving spouse) for distribution to the children etc. together with the value of any advancements.
(b) Divide the notional estate between the children to establish their 'total' entitlement.
(c) Distribute what is actually available for distribution, taking into account what is deemed already to have been received 'on account'.

For example, Isabel dies intestate, leaving an estate for distribution amounting to £90,000. She was a widow, who had three children — Anna, Basil and Claire. Anna predeceased and is survived by her daughter, Daisy. Isabel had made *inter vivos* advancements: to Anna (£20,000); to Claire (£10,000); and to Daisy (£20,000).

The calculation is thus:

(a) The notional estate is £120,000, i.e. the amount actually available for distribution on death plus the advancements to Anna and Claire. The payment to Daisy is not brought into account because Daisy is not a child of Isabel. (However, Daisy (who claims Anna's share) has to bring in the advancement to Anna.)
(b) Divide the notional estate by the number of shares (here 3) so that each overall entitlement is £40,000.
(c) Distribute the sum actually available for distribution (here £90,000): to Daisy (Anna's share) £20,000 (i.e. taking into account £20,000 already received); to Basil £40,000 (no advancements); to Claire £30,000 (taking into account £10,000 already received).

If the value of the advancements is greater than the share to which a child is entitled, there is no obligation to refund the excess, i.e. in such circumstances the rule operates so to get as close to 'equality' as possible.

For example, Ivan dies intestate, a widower, leaving two children, Xavier and Yvette. His estate available for distribution is £60,000: he had transferred Greenacre (at the date of death worth £80,000) to Xavier on the occasion of his marriage. Yvette will in the circumstances receive the whole of the estate on death.

2.6.3.2 Section 49(1)

On a partial intestacy, gifts by the will to the deceased's issue must also be brought into account, i.e. in addition to anything caught by s. 47(1).

There are difficulties over the interpretation of this provision, but the generally accepted view favours the 'stirpital construction', i.e. that 'issue must mean children or remoter issue and any member of the family belonging to a certain branch must bring in everything that has been taken or acquired under the will by that branch' (per Harman J in *Re Young* [1951] Ch 185).

For example, suppose in the case of Isabel's estate (**2.6.3.1** above), Isabel had left a will in which the only effective gift was one of £12,000 to her grandchild, Daisy. The notional estate (sum available for distribution + advancements + legacy) would now be £132,000, so that each overall share would be £44,000. On distribution, Daisy (claiming Anna's share) would receive £12,000 (i.e. taking into account the advancement to Anna and Daisy's own legacy); Basil would receive £44,000 (having received nothing on account); and Claire would receive £34,000 (i.e. taking into account her advancement).

THREE

PROVISION FOR FAMILY AND DEPENDANTS

Under English law testators are free to leave their estates to whomever they choose. For instance, a spouse or child has no right to receive any property under a will, though in **Chapter 2** we have seen that an intestate's close relatives are entitled if the deceased dies wholly or partially intestate.

In this chapter we will consider how the Inheritance (Provision for Family and Dependants) Act 1975 encroaches on this general principle of freedom of testamentary disposition. We will see that the statute enables certain classes of persons to apply to the court for provision from the deceased's estate on the basis that the will or intestacy fails to make adequate financial provision for them. The Act only applies if the deceased dies domiciled in England and Wales.

All statutory references in this chapter are to the Inheritance (Provision for Family and Dependants) Act 1975 unless otherwise stated.

3.1 The Basis of the Claim

In order to succeed an applicant must:

(a) apply within the time limit (**3.2**);
(b) fall within one of the five categories of applicant set out in s. 1(1) (**3.3**); and
(c) satisfy the court that the will or intestacy fails to make reasonable financial provision for the applicant (**3.4**).

The court may then order financial provision to be made out of the deceased's net estate (**3.6** and **3.7**). The deceased may have anticipated that a claim might be made under the Act and may have disposed of property prior to death in an attempt to defeat such a claim. The Act contains anti-avoidance provisions enabling an order to be made relating to such property in limited circumstances (**3.8**).

The Act also sets out certain guidelines which the court must take into account both when deciding whether or not reasonable financial provision has been made for the applicant, and if not, whether any order should be made (**3.5**).

3.2 The Application

3.2.1 THE TIME LIMIT FOR MAKING APPLICATIONS

3.2.1.1 The normal time limit

Applications should be made within six months from the first effective grant of representation to the deceased's estate (s. 4).

PROVISION FOR FAMILY AND DEPENDANTS

3.2.1.2 Can a late application be made?

This is only possible if the court gives leave (s. 4). The court will assess the adequacy of the reasons given by the applicant as to why it should exercise its discretion. In *Re Salmon* [1981] Ch 167, Megarry VC stated that there were guidelines to assist the court, and these included the circumstances associated with the delay; how promptly leave was being sought; whether negotiations had been commenced within the time limit; whether the estate had already been distributed; and if leave was refused this would mean that the applicant would be without redress against anybody.

3.2.2 TO WHICH COURT IS THE APPLICATION MADE?

Application may be made in the High Court or in the county court. There is now no financial limit on the jurisdiction of the county court.

Application may be made in the High Court or in the county court, which now have concurrent jurisdiction. This is discussed in greater detail at **15.3.1** together with the factors to be considered in choosing between proceeding in the Family or Chancery Division of the High Court. For an outline of the relevant procedure in the High Court see **15.3.1.2**, and in the county court see **15.3.1.3**.

3.2.3 PRACTICAL CONSEQUENCES OF THE TIME LIMIT

3.2.3.1 Acting for a potential applicant

If instructed by a potential applicant, note that it is possible (r. 43(1) Non-Contentious Probate Rules 1987 [NCPR]) to institute a standing search at the Principal or District Registry or any sub-Registry. This will ensure that you receive notice of the issue of any grant of representation (see **12.2**).

3.2.3.2 Advising personal representatives

Personal representatives will want to know if they will be personally liable if they make payments out of the estate before the six-month time limit has expired.

If no claim within the time limit has been made, they can safely distribute the estate without being personally liable, even if the court grants leave for a late application (s. 20). However, this protection of the personal representatives is without prejudice to the right to recover the property distributed from the beneficiaries.

Does this mean that no assets can be safely distributed before the expiry of the six-month period? Not necessarily. As orders can only be made out of the net estate of the deceased (see **3.7**) then funeral, testamentary expenses and debts can safely be paid without incurring personal liability. There may be beneficiaries who would suffer severe financial hardship if they had to wait for six months from grant before any payment were made. The personal representatives must give cautious consideration to every case, but, for example, it is unlikely that a court would make an order depriving a surviving spouse with limited means of all benefits under the will. The personal representatives could therefore safely make at least some payment to such a surviving spouse.

3.3 Categories of Applicant

The onus is on applicants to show that they come within one of the categories set out in s. 1(1) in order that they can apply for an order under s. 2.

PROVISION FOR FAMILY AND DEPENDANTS

Applications under the Act are personal actions which abate on the death of an applicant. Thus in *Whyte* v *Ticehurst* [1986] 2 All ER 158, a widow was claiming under the Act against her deceased husband's estate, but died before the hearing. Her personal representatives were refused leave to continue the action for the benefit of her estate.

3.3.1 THE DECEASED'S SPOUSE (s. 1(1)(a))

Provided that the applicant can prove that there was a subsisting marriage at the time of the deceased's death, then a party to a voidable marriage or a judicially separated spouse can apply (but see **3.3.2.1**). This can even include a party to a void marriage in certain circumstances (s. 25(4)).

3.3.2 THE FORMER SPOUSE OF THE DECEASED WHO HAS NOT REMARRIED (s. 1(1)(b))

The marriage may have been dissolved or annulled by decree of a court in the British Islands, or in another country provided the dissolution or annulment is recognised by the law of England and Wales (s. 25(1)).

3.3.2.1 Orders under ss. 15 and 15A

A judicially separated or former spouse will not, however, be able to apply for financial provision if the court has made an order under s. 15 or s. 15A in the matrimonial or nullity proceedings barring an application under s. 2. The court may have done this as part of a 'clean break' order.

3.3.3 A CHILD OF THE DECEASED (s. 1(1)(c))

'Child' includes illegitimate children, children *en ventre sa mère* (s. 25(1)), legitimated children and children adopted by the deceased (but children of the deceased who have been adopted may not claim against the estate of their natural parent — *Re Collins* [1990] 2 All ER 47).

An adult child can apply, but the court will only rarely see the need to grant applications made by able-bodied children who are in employment (*Re Coventry* [1980] Ch. 461).

3.3.4 A CHILD OF THE FAMILY (s. 1(1)(d))

Any person (not being a child of the deceased) who, in the case of any marriage to which the deceased was at any time a party, was treated by the deceased as a child of the family in relation to that marriage.

This definition is similar to the definition contained in matrimonial legislation, save that the 'treatment' is by the deceased, rather than both parties to the marriage. In many cases the deceased will have married the applicant's parent during the applicant's childhood, and they will have all lived together as a family unit.

Re Leach [1985] 2 All ER 754, however, illustrates the following points:

(a) Adult step children can apply. In *Re Leach* the applicant was a 55-year-old spinster who was already an adult when her father married the deceased. She had never been maintained by her stepmother and they had never lived together in the same household.
(b) 'Treatment' for these purposes needs to be more than mere affection. What needs to be shown is that the deceased had assumed the position of parent towards the applicant, with its attendant responsibilities and privileges.
(c) This treatment must stem from the marriage, but may occur after the death of the other spouse. (In *Re Leach* the treatment after the death of the applicant's father was felt to be crucial.)

PROVISION FOR FAMILY AND DEPENDANTS

3.3.5 A DEPENDANT (s. 1(1)(e))

Any person (not being a person included in the foregoing paragraphs) who immediately before the death of the deceased was being maintained, either wholly or partly by the deceased.

3.3.5.1 Being maintained

The onus is on applicants to show that they were being maintained by the deceased. The test is set out in s. 1(3). It is in two parts:

(a) Was the deceased making a substantial contribution in money or money's worth to the reasonable needs of the applicant, and if so
(b) Was the applicant providing full valuable consideration for such contribution.

If the answer to (a) is 'yes' and to (b) 'no' then the applicant will qualify as being maintained in whole or in part.

Clearly, money payments or the provision of rent-free accommodation could be a substantial contribution for the purposes of (a). The valuable consideration provided by the applicant for (b) could be in the form of money or in the form of services for the deceased, such as housekeeping or nursing care. The court will then have to decide who provided more, the deceased or the applicant. The court will only strike out the application if the applicant had made the greater contribution or if the contributions were equal.

3.3.5.2 Example

In *Bishop* v *Plumley* [1991] 1 All ER 236, the applicant lived with the deceased in his house and was initially supported by him. Thereafter they pooled their resources and the applicant gave devoted care and attention to the deceased during his final illness. Did this mean that the application should be struck out because the applicant had provided valuable consideration? The Court of Appeal decided not: the applicant was qualified under s. 1(1)(e). Butler-Sloss LJ pointed out that comparison of substantial contribution and valuable consideration was a factual exercise. The court should apply a common-sense approach and avoid 'fine balancing computations involving the value of normal exchanges of support in the domestic sense'.

3.3.5.3 Do applicants have to prove that the deceased took responsibility for them?

In *Re Beaumont* [1980] Ch 444, Megarry VC stated that it was not sufficient that the deceased was maintaining the applicant at the date of death. It was also essential to show that the deceased had actually assumed responsibility for the maintenance and was maintaining the applicant under that assumption of responsibility. The Court of Appeal in *Jelley* v *Iliffe* [1981] 2 All ER 29, however, held that the fact of maintenance will generally raise a presumption of 'assumed responsibility', not following *Re Beaumont* on this point.

3.3.5.4 Immediately before death

Although there is no minimum period, the concept of maintenance imports recurrence or continuance. What is the position if the deceased normally maintained the applicant, but was prevented from doing so in the last few weeks before death by being hospitalised? Megarry VC considered this in *Re Beaumont* (above). He held that what mattered was not the position at the instant before death but whether there was a settled basis or arrangement whereby the applicant was maintained. If this settled basis or arrangement has been abandoned before the date of death the applicant will not be able to claim.

3.4 Reasonable Financial Provision

The Act (in s. 1(2)) sets out a two-stage process. Has the will or intestacy or a combination of both failed to make reasonable financial provision for the applicant? If so, the court considers what would amount to such reasonable financial provision.

What amounts to reasonable financial provision will depend on who is making the application, as the Act sets out two standards. One is applicable to an application by the surviving spouse, and the other for all other categories of applicant.

3.4.1 THE SURVIVING SPOUSE STANDARD (s. 1(2)(a))

If the applicant is the surviving spouse the standard is such financial provision as would be reasonable in all the circumstances, whether or not that provision is required for maintenance.

This standard is more generous than the maintenance standard applying to other applicants. The intention is that the surviving spouse will have a claim on the family assets at least equivalent to that of a divorced spouse and the court is directed to have regard to what provision would have been awarded in divorce proceedings (s. 3(2) — see **3.5.2.1** below).

3.4.1.1 Application by a judicially separated spouse

Where, however, the spouses were judicially separated and are still living apart at the date of death the lower maintenance standard (below) will apply. This is because the court may have already awarded ancillary relief to a judicially separated spouse under the Matrimonial Causes Act 1973 in the course of the decree proceedings.

3.4.1.2 Court's discretion to apply the surviving spouse standard

By s. 14 the court has a discretion to apply the surviving spouse standard to judicially separated spouses and to former spouses who have not remarried (s. 1(1)(b) applicants) if the death occurs within 12 months of the final decree in the judicial separation, divorce or nullity proceedings — and no order for financial provision has been made (or refused) in those proceedings.

3.4.2 THE MAINTENANCE STANDARD (s. 1(2)(b))

For all other categories of applicant, including a judicially separated spouse still living apart at the date of death and a former spouse who has not remarried, the standard is such provision as would be reasonable in all the circumstances for the applicant to receive for maintenance.

3.4.2.1 Level of maintenance

The proper level of maintenance has been variously described. In *Re Coventry* (above **3.3.3**), Goff LJ said it was not 'just enough to get by, on the other hand, it does not mean anything which may be regarded as reasonably desirable for [the applicant's] general benefit or welfare'. All the circumstances should be taken into account, including the standard of living of the applicant.

3.4.3 REASONABLE FINANCIAL PROVISION

The question for the court, judged objectively on the basis of facts known at the time of the hearing (s. 3(5)), is whether the will or intestacy makes reasonable financial provision for the applicant. The court is not concerned as to whether testators felt they were being reasonable, according to their own views and knowledge of the facts, in making no, or only limited, provision for the applicant.

PROVISION FOR FAMILY AND DEPENDANTS

3.4.3.1 Evidence of a testator's reasons

If a testator has a particular reason for making little or no provision for, say, a relative or dependant, then a statement of those reasons should be placed with the will. As the will is a public document these reasons should not form part of the will itself. The court can admit the statement as evidence (s. 21) and can judge as to the weight that should be given to it. If, for example, the testator made the statement shortly after a heated quarrel (as in *Williams* v *Johns* [1988] 2 FLR 349) it is likely that the court will ignore it.

3.5 The Guidelines (s. 3(1))

The court must take the guidelines into account both when determining whether the applicant has established that no reasonable financial provision has been made, and in determining what order, if any, should be made under s. 2. It is entirely in the court's discretion as to whether any order should be made. In some cases it may be that it is reasonable for no order to be made, as in *Re Coventry* (**3.3.3** above) where the applicant was an able-bodied child of the deceased. Some of the guidelines are relevant to all applicants; some only relate to a particular category of applicant.

3.5.1 GUIDELINES RELEVANT TO ALL APPLICANTS

3.5.1.1 Financial resources and needs of the applicant, any other applicant and any beneficiary whether now or in the foreseeable future

Earning capacity and financial obligations and responsibilities are included here (s. 3(6)). The court will assess the relative financial position of persons with any claim on the estate. Thus a needy applicant will have greater prospects of success if the beneficiaries are well off. In *Re Collins* [1990] 2 All ER 47, it was held that the fact that the applicant was in receipt of social-security benefits did not preclude the court from making an order out of her mother's estate.

3.5.1.2 Any (moral) obligation of the deceased to any applicant or beneficiary

In *Re Callaghan* [1984] 3 All ER 790, for example, a claim was made by an adult child of the family against his step-father's estate. The step-father died intestate and his estate passed to his three sisters whom he had not seen for ten years. The court held that the deceased's greatest obligation was owed to the applicant who had kept in close touch with him and looked after him in his last illness. The court also took into account that many of the assets of the estate came from the applicant's mother who had died some months previously, and ordered a lump sum payment of £15,000 to the applicant to enable him to buy his council house outright.

3.5.1.3 The size and nature of the net estate of the deceased

The larger the estate the easier will it be for the court to order reasonable provision for an applicant. Conversely, as costs will usually be awarded out of the estate, the court will discourage claims where the estate is small (*Re Coventry* **3.3.3** above). In *Re Fullard* [1981] 2 All ER 706, Ormorod LJ commented that judges should look very closely at the merits of each application before ordering that the estate pays the applicant's costs if the application is unsuccessful. (As to costs, see further **15.3.14**.)

The source of the deceased's estate may be relevant, as in *Re Callaghan* (**3.5.1.2** above).

3.5.1.4 Any physical or mental disability of any applicant or beneficiary

3.5.1.5 Any other relevant matter including the conduct of the applicant or any other person

Clearly the court has a wide discretion as to the matters it can take into account under this heading. As already mentioned, any statement by the deceased as to the reasons for the disposition of the

PROVISION FOR FAMILY AND DEPENDANTS

estate can be considered. In *Re Callaghan* (**3.5.1.2** above), the caring conduct of the applicant assisted his claim. In *Williams* v *Johns* (**3.4.3.1** above), the applicant's past conduct, which caused shame and substantial emotional distress to her adoptive mother, was taken into account by the court when dismissing her claim to the deceased mother's estate.

3.5.2 GUIDELINES RELEVANT TO PARTICULAR CATEGORIES OF APPLICANT

In addition to the factors set out above, the court must also take into account the following.

3.5.2.1 Where the applicant is the surviving spouse or former spouse (s. 3(2))

(a) The age of the applicant and the duration of the marriage.
(b) The applicant's contribution to the welfare of the deceased's family.
(c) Where the applicant is the surviving spouse (unless still living apart under a decree of judicial separation at the date of death) the provision which the applicant might reasonably have expected to receive if, at the date of death, the marriage had instead been terminated by divorce.

3.5.2.2 Will the provision be the same as that ordered on divorce?

According to the Court of Appeal in *Re Besterman* [1984] Ch 458, the likely provision on divorce is only a starting point; a different award may be appropriate on a financial provision application.

In *Re Bunning* [1984] Ch 480, the wife, who was some 22 years younger than her husband, lived with the husband for 15 years before she left him some four years before his death. The husband made no provision for the wife in his will, and on death his net estate was worth some £237,000. The wife, whose assets of £97,000 were derived mainly from the husband, made an application under the Act. The court considered that on divorce the wife would have received about £36,000, as this sum would have to take into account the husband's future needs. As the husband was now dead, and bearing in mind that the wife was entitled to a reasonable degree of financial security during what was likely to be a lengthy widowhood, the court awarded her the sum of £60,000. This sum, added to the wife's existing assets, would give her roughly half of the spouses' total assets.

3.5.2.3 Applying the guidelines to an application by a former spouse

Although guidelines (a) and (b) in **3.5.2.1** above apply, guideline (c) (what the divorce court would order) only applies if the court exercises its discretion to apply the surviving spouse standard (see **3.4.1.2** above). The same is true where the applicant is a judicially separated spouse still living apart at the date of death.

3.5.2.4 Likely success of applications by former spouses

In *Re Fullard* (see **3.5.1.3** above), the Court of Appeal indicated that only rarely would post-decree applications be successful. This is because the matrimonial court will have already considered the issues of maintenance and the allocation of assets between the parties. The court may however grant an application in two situations — i.e. where:

(i) periodical payments had been ordered in the matrimonial proceedings, these had been of long standing duration, and the deceased's estate could support their continuation, and
(ii) the deceased's death releases a substantial capital sum such as an insurance policy.

If the matrimonial court has made an order under s. 15 or s. 15A of the Act, the former spouse will not of course be entitled to apply (see **3.3.2.1** above).

3.5.2.5 Where the applicant is a child (s. 3(3)) *of the deceased*

Here the court must additionally consider the manner in which the applicant was being or might be expected to be educated or trained.

PROVISION FOR FAMILY AND DEPENDANTS

3.5.2.6 Where the applicant is a child of the family (s. 3(3))

As well as considering the education guideline the court must also consider:

(a) whether the deceased had assumed any responsibility for the applicant's maintenance and, if so, the extent and the basis upon which the deceased assumed responsibility and for how long;
(b) whether in assuming and discharging that responsibility the deceased did so knowing that the applicant was not his own child; and
(c) the liability of any other person to maintain the applicant.

3.5.2.7 Where the applicant was maintained by the deceased (s. 3(4))

Here the court must in addition to the general guidelines consider the extent to which and the basis upon which the deceased assumed responsibility for the applicant.

Note that the court only has to consider the extent of such responsibility. Where the applicant is a child of the family the court must also consider whether the deceased has assumed responsibility. This seems to indicate that applicants under s. 1(1)(e) of the Act must have established at the outset that the deceased had assumed responsibility for their maintenance as was held in *Re Beaumont* (see **3.3.5.3** above)

3.6 Types of Family Provision Order (s. 2)

The court must take into account the guidelines set out in **3.5** above in deciding whether to make an order under s. 2 and, if so, the type of order. The court can make any one or more of the orders set out below.

3.6.1 PERIODICAL PAYMENTS

These may be for such term as specified in the order. The amount may be set out in the order (e.g. £100 per month) or expressed to be

(a) the whole or part of the income of the estate (say, one half of the income of the estate) or
(b) the whole of the income of a such part of the estate as is directed to be appropriated or set aside for the provision of the payments (say, the rents of certain properties owned by the deceased).

Alternatively, the court may select any other way it thinks fit for determining such payments.

If the order specifies the amount of the payments it may direct that a specified part of the estate shall be set aside so that the payments can be made out of its income.

3.6.1.1 Termination on remarriage

An order for periodical payments to a judicially separated or former spouse will terminate on remarriage (s. 19(2)). Other periodical payments do not terminate automatically, for instance on the remarriage of a surviving spouse, but an application to vary the order could be made under s. 6 (see below).

3.6.1.2 Variation of periodical payments orders (s. 6)

A periodical payments order can be varied, discharged, suspended and revived.

3.6.2 LUMP SUM PAYMENT

The order may provide that the lump sum is to be paid by specified instalments. An application may be made to vary the instalments, but otherwise the order cannot be varied.

A lump sum payment will often be appropriate where the applicant is a surviving spouse but can be used in other cases. In *Re Callaghan* (**3.5.1.2** above) for example a lump sum was ordered to enable the applicant, a child of the family, to buy his council house outright.

Where the estate is small, a lump sum order may realistically be the only type of provision that can be made.

3.6.3 TRANSFER OF PROPERTY

The court could order that, for example, the former matrimonial home be transferred to the surviving spouse. The order cannot be varied.

3.6.4 SETTLEMENT OF PROPERTY

Thus property could be settled for the benefit of a minor. The order cannot be varied.

3.6.5 ORDER FOR THE ACQUISITION OF PROPERTY

The court can order that property be acquired and transferred to or settled for the benefit of the applicant. Thus the court could order that a house be purchased and transferred to the surviving spouse. Again the order cannot be varied.

3.6.6 VARIATION OF MARRIAGE SETTLEMENTS

The order cannot be varied.

3.6.7 CONSEQUENTIAL DIRECTIONS

In a case where the court makes an order and the deceased has effectively disposed of all his or her assets then the question of who will bear the burden of the award will have to be considered. The court has wide powers to make consequential directions (s. 2(4)) to give effect to the order and to ensure that it operates fairly as between one beneficiary and another. For example, if the court orders that the former matrimonial home be transferred to the surviving spouse, it may vary the disposition of the deceased's estate so that the disappointed beneficiary is compensated in some way.

3.6.8 INTERIM PAYMENTS

An interim order can be made (s. 5(1)) if:

(a) the applicant is in immediate financial need;
(b) it is not yet possible to determine what order (if any) should be made; and
(c) property forming part of the deceased's net estate is or can be made available to meet the needs of the applicant.

3.6.9 INHERITANCE TAX

How is the inheritance tax position affected if the court makes an order varying the disposition of the deceased's estate? The Act provides (s. 19(1)) that for all purposes, including inheritance tax, the variation is deemed to be effective as from the deceased's death. In effect the order is 'read back', as if the deceased had made the provision ordered by the court (see further **15.3.2**). If, for example, the court orders that provision be made for a surviving spouse, the estate's liability for inheritance tax will be reduced. This is because the property passing to the surviving spouse will be exempt from inheritance tax.

PROVISION FOR FAMILY AND DEPENDANTS

3.7 Property Available for Financial Provision Orders

The deceased's 'net estate' from which any order for financial provision orders is made is widely defined in s. 25(1). It comprises the following:

(a) All property of the deceased owned at the date of death and which could have been disposed of by will, less

    (i) funeral testamentary and administration expenses;
    (ii) debts and liabilities; and
    (iii) inheritance tax.

(b) Any property which the deceased could have appointed *inter vivos* under a general power of appointment which has not been exercised.

(c) Any property in respect of which the deceased made a statutory nomination (see **8.4.2.1**) less any inheritance tax payable by the nominee.

(d) Any property in respect of which the deceased made a *donatio mortis causa* less any inheritance tax payable by the donee.

(e) The deceased's severable share of a joint tenancy but only if the court so orders (s. 9 and see below).

(f) Any property which the court has ordered under ss. 10 or 11 (the anti-avoidance provisions — see below) to be available.

3.7.1 THE DECEASED'S SEVERABLE SHARE OF JOINT PROPERTY (s. 9)

Property owned by the deceased as joint tenant at death does not form part of the estate for administration purposes, as the deceased's share will pass to the other joint tenant by right of survivorship.

Provided, however, the application is made within the six-month time limit (**3.2.1.1** above), the court can order that the whole or part of deceased's share of such joint property shall form part of the net estate. These provisions not only affect land, but include, for instance, the deceased's share of a credit balance at death in a bank account held on a joint tenancy.

3.7.2 EXAMPLE

In *Jessop* v *Jessop* [1992] 1 FLR 591, the deceased had a wife and a long-standing cohabitee. The deceased and the cohabitee owned a house as joint tenants. The deceased died intestate with an estate of £2,500, which passed to the widow. The court found that this did not provide reasonable financial provision for the widow applicant, and ordered that the deceased's severable share of the house to the extent of £10,000 should be treated as part of the net estate.

3.8 The Anti-avoidance Provisions (ss. 10 and 11)

3.8.1 WHY SUCH PROVISIONS ARE REQUIRED

If there were no anti-avoidance provisions testators intent on defeating the family provision legislation could either dispose of their property shortly before death — thus reducing the net estate; or enter into an *inter vivos* contract to leave property by will. In the latter situation, the other party to the contract would rank as a creditor of the estate and would be entitled to take the property out of the estate before any question of provision for an applicant arises.

3.8.1.1 What powers does the court have to counter such evasion?

Section 10 deals (broadly) with *inter vivos* gifts made less than six years before death whilst s. 11 covers (broadly) contracts to leave property by will made at any time before death for less than full consideration.

In either case, if satisfied as to the requirements set out below, the court may order the 'donee' of such property to provide money or other property to satisfy a family provision claim.

3.8.1.2 Pre-requisites

Before an order can be made under either s. 10 or s. 11:

(a) the applicant must request that such an order be made;

(b) the applicant must establish that the deceased acted with the intention of defeating the application. The court must be of the opinion that (on a balance of probabilities) the deceased's intention (though not necessarily sole intention) was to prevent an order being made or to reduce the amount of provision which might otherwise have been ordered (s. 12). Subject to contrary evidence, this will be presumed in the case of an application under s. 11 where no valuable consideration has been given; and

(c) the court must be satisfied that the making of an order would facilitate the making of financial provision for the applicant.

3.8.1.3 The orders that can be made

If satisfied as to these requirements, the court may make an order against the 'donee'. It has complete discretion as to the making of an order. In exercising this discretion, the court will take into account all the circumstances — including any valuable consideration given, the relationship between the donee and the deceased and the conduct and resources of the donee.

3.8.1.4 Orders against a donee of a gift

The donee cannot be required to provide more than the amount of money or property (valued at date of death) that was received, less any inheritance tax payable by the donee.

3.8.1.5 Orders against a 'donee' of a contract

The court can make the following orders:

(a) If the money or property has already been transferred the donee may be ordered to provide not more than has been transferred, less any valuable consideration given or inheritance tax paid by the donee.

(b) If the money or property has not yet been transferred by the deceased's personal representatives, then an order preventing such transfer in whole or in part.

3.8.1.6 Example

In *Re Dawkins* [1986] 2 FLR 360, a year before his death the deceased sold the matrimonial home to his daughter for £100. The court found he did this with the intention of defeating a claim under the Act. The estate was insolvent. The court exercised its powers under the s. 10(2) and ordered the daughter to pay the widow applicant the sum of £10,000.

FOUR

INCOME TAX

You will have been introduced to the principles of income tax elsewhere, and they will not be repeated here. The purpose of this chapter is to consider the income tax position of those dealing with the estate of a deceased person (the personal representatives, whether executors or administrators — see further **Chapter 8**), and of the beneficiaries.

The personal representatives will need to know their position in relation to the finalisation of the deceased's tax affairs (**4.1**). We will then consider their responsibilities in relation to the period of the administration (**4.2**). Finally, we will discuss the position of the beneficiaries who take under the deceased's will or intestacy (**4.3**).

Statutory references in this chapter are to Income and Corporation Taxes Act 1988, unless otherwise stated.

4.1 The Personal Representatives and the Deceased's Income

4.1.1 ASSESSMENTS

Any assessment to income tax for the period prior to death must be made on the personal representatives within three years after the end of the tax year in which the death occurs. Normally, this assessment can only relate to any of the six tax years prior to that in which it is actually made. However, where there has been fraudulent or negligent conduct by the deceased, the assessment may relate to any of the six years prior to that in which the death occurs.

The amount of income tax due is an allowable deduction for inheritance tax purposes: equally, any repayment will be an asset for the purposes of that tax.

4.1.2 INCOME ARISING BEFORE DEATH

4.1.2.1 Generally

The personal representatives must make a return of income arising to (i.e. receivable by) the deceased prior to the death — any income arising thereafter is income of the estate (see **4.2** below). The deceased's statutory, total and taxable income figures will be calculated in the normal way. Thus, the personal representatives are entitled to claim deduction for any charges on income for the period prior to death. They may also claim personal reliefs available to the deceased in the tax year in question without any adjustment to take account of the death: a taxpayer who dies in (say) May is entitled to the full personal relief (or age allowance) for that tax year, together with (if appropriate) the married couples allowance. However, although there is no abatement of the appropriate personal reliefs, there may — if death occurs early in the tax year — be insufficient

INCOME TAX

income to support the full entitlement; in that event, there is no possibility of transferring the unabsorbed amount to anyone else — e.g. the personal representatives or a beneficiary.

Where the deceased was married, the tax position of the surviving spouse depends upon whether it is the husband or wife who has died. If the wife survives, she will have her own personal allowance against her income for the year and (provided she was living with her husband at the date of his death) will also be entitled to the widow's bereavement allowance (currently £1,720). She may also claim this allowance for the following tax year, provided she has not remarried before the beginning of that later year. There is no corresponding widower's bereavement allowance. A widow with dependent child(ren) may also be entitled to the additional personal allowance (sometimes called 'single parent relief'), which is currently also £1,720.

4.1.2.2 'Continuing' income

Where the income — whether actually received before or after death — derives from a source which ceases on death (e.g. the deceased's salary or business profits) it will normally be a relatively straightforward exercise to identify the income arising before the death. In other cases (e.g. dividends, interest, rents), income received after death may relate to a period partly before and partly after the death. Under s. 2, Apportionment Act 1870 such income should, for succession purposes, be apportioned on a daily basis to the pre-death and post-death periods — although, in practice, this provision is often excluded by express provision in the will (see further **13.1.2.1** and **18.4.7.7**).

Whether or not s. 2 applies for the purposes of determining the distribution of the estate, for tax purposes any dividend etc. paid after the deceased's death is treated as income of the estate and should, therefore, not be included in the return of the deceased's income — *IRC* v *Henderson's Executors* (1931) SC 681. (The only exception to this is a dividend declared due before death, but not paid until after the death — *Re Sebright* [1944] Ch 287.)

Where income received after death is apportioned for succession purposes to the pre-death period it will form part of the estate on death for inheritance tax purposes. However, as we have seen, it will be treated as income liable to income tax in the hands of the personal representatives (and ultimately the beneficiaries — see **4.3** below). An element of double taxation therefore arises; some relief from this is available to a residuary beneficiary who is absolutely entitled, but only if such beneficiary is a higher rate taxpayer — s. 699 (see further **4.3.3.3** below).

The same problem does not arise where income received before death relates to a period which wholly or partly falls after the death. Such income is taxed as the deceased's income and, in so far as not spent, forms part of the deceased's estate for inheritance tax purposes. There is no relief from this 'double taxation'!

4.1.2.3 Trust income

Similar problems arise with trust income where the deceased was a life tenant. Any income accrued due to the life tenant but not paid until after death will (for tax purposes) be treated as income of the estate, rather than of the deceased — *Wood* v *Owen* [1941] 1 KB 42. However, it will also form part of the deceased's estate for inheritance tax purposes; s. 699 (above) may again afford some relief. For the effect on the tax position of the trustees, see **7.1**.

4.1.2.4 Delay

In practice, it will often take a long time to finalise the deceased's income tax position — particularly if the deceased was in business as a sole trader or partner. As we shall see in **Chapter 6** and **Chapter 10**, personal representatives cannot obtain a grant — and therefore cannot do much to administer the estate — until they have paid any inheritance tax due, interest upon which will begin to run after six months from the end of the month in which the death occurs. To avoid delay, it is common for personal representatives to estimate the deceased's income tax liability (or entitlement to repayment) and pay inheritance tax on this basis. When the position is finally resolved, any necessary adjustments can be made on a corrective account (see **10.6.7**).

4.2 Personal Representatives and the Estate's Income

We are here concerned with the income arising during the 'administration period', which commences on the day following death and ends when the residue is ascertained for distribution purposes.

4.2.1 LIABILITY

During the administration period, the personal representatives are liable — at basic rate only — to income tax on all the income of the estate (other than dividends, on which they will be liable to tax at 20%). The estate income will essentially be computed in the ordinary way — including the profits of any business which they are running as part of the estate. As they are not an 'individual' for tax purposes, they are not entitled to claim personal reliefs — but by the same token are not liable at the higher rate on the estate income. They are not entitled to any deduction for the costs or expenses of the administration.

4.2.2 LOAN TO PAY INHERITANCE TAX

They may claim tax relief (usually for 12 months only) for interest on a loan which they have raised to allow them to pay inheritance tax so that they can obtain the grant — but only in so far as this relates to the tax on the deceased's beneficially-owned personalty which vests in them on death (or would do so if situated in the United Kingdom) — s. 384.

4.2.3 TAX DEDUCTION CERTIFICATES

Where any income taxed in the hands of the personal representatives is paid to a beneficiary, a tax deduction certificate must be provided. The beneficiary can use this as a tax credit for the tax already effectively paid (see further **4.3** below).

4.2.4 EQUITABLE APPORTIONMENTS

Where an apportionment is made under one of the rules of equitable apportionment (e.g. the rules in *Howe* v *Earl of Dartmouth* (1802) 7 Ves 137 and *Re Earl of Chesterfield's Trusts* (1883) 24 ChD 643 — see **13.1.2.2**) no income tax liability attaches to the personal representatives (or to the income beneficiary) since the apportionment concerned is of capital, not income.

4.3 The Beneficiaries

As we have seen, all the income of the estate will suffer tax (either by deduction at source or by direct assessment) at the basic rate (20% in the case of dividends) in the hands of the personal representatives. Any of this income (after the payment of any expenses met from it) which is then distributed to a beneficiary will affect the tax position of the recipient beneficiary. Basically, such beneficiaries will have to include it in their own returns of income, but may use the tax credit for the tax effectively already paid in one of three ways, according to their individual circumstances:

(a) if not liable to Basic Rate Tax, to support a repayment claim;
(b) if a basic rate taxpayer, to indicate to the Revenue that the beneficiary's liability has already been effectively discharged (even in the case of dividends where the tax credit is only 20%); or
(c) if a higher rate taxpayer, as a credit for the basic rate element, the 'excess' above that only being still due. In the case of dividends, however, a higher rate taxpayer will be liable for a further 20%.

INCOME TAX

The problem for the beneficiaries is to know in which year(s) such income is to be taxed. This will depend upon the nature of their interests in the estate.

4.3.1 SPECIFIC LEGATEES OR DEVISEES

As we will see in **13.3.2.1**, once the personal representatives vest the property concerned in the beneficiary entitled, any income produced by the property which arose during the administration period 'retrospectively' becomes income of the beneficiary for tax purposes, liable to tax in the year(s) when it arose. This may mean (depending upon the circumstances) that it will be taxed in a year other than that in which it is actually received by the beneficiary, or it may be 'spread' over more than one year. In either case, an earlier assessment on the beneficiary may have to be re-opened — though extra tax will, of course, only become payable if the beneficiary is already (or becomes as a result of this extra receipt) a higher rate taxpayer.

4.3.2 GENERAL/PECUNIARY LEGATEES

The general rule is that such legacies do not carry interest, though there are important exceptions to this rule (see **13.3.2.4**). Where interest is payable and paid, it will be received gross by the beneficiary — who will be directly assessed under Case III Schedule D in the year of receipt.

4.3.3 RESIDUARY BENEFICIARIES

A residuary beneficiary may have a limited interest (i.e. be entitled to the income only), or an absolute interest (i.e. be entitled — once residue is ascertained — to both capital and income). In either case, the amount of income to which such a beneficiary is entitled during the administration period cannot finally be established until (in effect) the administration is completed. How is the total due to the beneficiary — some of which may already have been received by way of interim payments — to be taxed in the beneficiary's hands? A further problem in the case of the absolute interest is to distinguish between income and capital, only the former being liable to income tax.

4.3.3.1 Limited interest (s. 695)

Any sums received by the beneficiary during the administration period will have already suffered basic rate tax in the hands of the personal representatives. The grossed-up amount must be returned as part of the beneficiary's income in the year of receipt — with a tax credit for the tax already paid by the personal representatives.

However, the resulting assessment is, in effect, only provisional. At the conclusion of the administration, the beneficiary's total entitlement (i.e. the net amounts already paid over plus the net balance then payable) is spread over the whole of the administration period on an even daily basis. The beneficiary is then 'reassessed' on the basis of this new allocation of the income, though liability to pay extra tax will only arise if the beneficiary is already (or becomes as a result of the allocation) a higher rate taxpayer.

For example, Dennis died on 6 March 1992 and the administration of his estate is completed on 19 July 1993 (500 days). His will leaves the residuary estate to his brother Ernest for life, with remainder to Ernest's children absolutely.

During the course of the tax year 1992/93, the personal representatives make interim distributions to Ernest totalling £2,250, which he must include in his return for the year of — grossed-up at the basic rate in force in that year — claiming the tax credit for the tax already paid by the personal representatives.

At the end of the administration period, the total amount (net of basic rate tax) due to Ernest, including the amounts already paid to him, is found to be £5,000. The income will therefore be deemed to have accrued at the rate of £10 per day, and be allocated to the various tax years as follows:

1991/92	(30 days)	£300
1992/93	(365 days)	£3,650
1993/94	(105 days)	£1,050

These amounts, grossed up at the basic rate in force in each of the respective years to which the income has now been allocated, must be included in Ernest's returns for those years and taxed accordingly.

4.3.3.2 Absolute interest (s. 696)

The initial issue here is to determine whether payments to the beneficiary are of income or capital.

Sums paid to the beneficiary in any given tax year are treated as income (net of basic rate tax, and thus to be grossed-up for the purposes of the beneficiary's return) up to the amount of 'net residuary income' (i.e. after basic rate tax) available in that year for distribution to that beneficiary. 'Residuary income' is broadly the residuary income less certain charges and management expenses properly chargeable to income. There is no statutory definition of what is 'properly' so chargeable; in another context (see **7.1.1.2**) it has been held that 'properly means properly under the general law and not properly under the terms of the particular trust' — *Carver* v *Duncan*; *Bosanquet* v *Allen* [1985] AC 1082.

Any payment in excess of (that beneficiary's share of) net residuary income is deemed to be capital.

At the conclusion of the administration, the 'provisional' assessments thus made are revised for any year in which it is found that the beneficiary has received less than the full (share of the) net residuary income available for distribution — so that at the end of the day the beneficiary is taxed as if in receipt of the full amount available in each year.

For example, assume that Diana dies on 25 June 1993, leaving her residuary estate to her sister Esme absolutely. The administration of the estate is completed on 15 August 1995. The net residuary income (NRI) and payments made to Esme during this period are:

Tax year	NRI	Payments to Esme
1993/94	£7,500	£1,500
1994/95	£2,250	£15,000
1995/96	£1,500	£45,000

In each tax year, Esme will include (grossed-up at the appropriate basic rate) amounts received from the personal representatives up to the NRI for that year, any excess being treated as capital. At the end of the administration, Esme will be reassessed for any tax year in which she received less than the NRI — in her case there was such a shortfall in 1993/94. The result is that the payment of £45,000 received in 1995/96 will be treated as comprising:

NRI for 1995/96	£1,500
Balance NRI for 1993/94	£6,000
Capital	£37,500

The revised assessment (for 1993/94 in this case) must be made within three years of the end of the tax year in which the administration is concluded — here before the end of the tax year 1998/99 (s. 700).

4.3.3.3 Section 699

We encountered this provision briefly when we were considering the deceased's income (in **4.1.2.2** above). It is designed to give some relief from an element of double taxation where income accrued due in the lifetime is not received until after the death. Such income (as we saw) is part of the estate

INCOME TAX

for inheritance tax purposes, but is for income tax purposes treated as income of the estate. A residuary beneficiary who is absolutely entitled and who is a higher rate taxpayer may claim a reduction in residuary income equivalent to the amount of inheritance tax chargeable (at the 'estate rate' — see **6.4.1.1**) on that income, grossed up at the basic rate.

For example, suppose that Desmond died on 30 June 1993. His residuary estate is left to his niece Nicola, and includes a secured loan in respect of which the personal representatives receive an interest payment at the end of September amounting to £1,000 gross. Assume that half of this amount accrued before the date of death and is thus part of the estate for inheritance tax purposes. The whole amount, however, will be taxed as income of the estate. If Nicola is a higher rate taxpayer she may claim relief under s. 699 as follows (assuming an estate rate for inheritance tax purposes of 20%):

Gross interest attributable to pre-death period ($\frac{1}{2}$)	£500
Less: basic rate	£125
	£375
The relief is:	
£375 × 20% (inheritance tax estate rate)	£75
Add: basic rate	£25
	£100

The grossed up amount (£100) is deducted from the residuary income so as to reduce Nicola's liability to higher rate tax.

FIVE

CAPITAL GAINS TAX

Again, you will have already encountered the general principles of capital gains tax. It is not the object here to reiterate those principles, for which reference will need to be made elsewhere. This Chapter considers the position of the personal representatives (both in relation to the deceased's tax liability and their own liability during the administration period), and of the beneficiaries.

Statutory references in this chapter are to Taxation of Chargeable Gains Act 1992, unless otherwise stated.

5.1 The Personal Representatives and the Gains of the Deceased

5.1.1 ASSESSMENTS

As with income tax, any assessment to capital gains tax for the period prior to death must be made on the personal representatives within three years after the end of the tax year in which the death occurs. Again, this assessment can normally only relate to any of the six tax years prior to that in which it is made. However, in the case of fraudulent or negligent conduct by the deceased, the assessment may relate to any of the six years prior to that in which the death occurs.

5.1.2 GAINS

The personal representatives are responsible for settling any outstanding liability arising from disposals made in the deceased's lifetime. The calculation of any such liability is done in the ordinary way, so that they will be able to claim any exemptions and reliefs to which the deceased may have been entitled (including the annual exempt slice — currently £5,800 — for the year in which the death occurs). Any net gain will then be charged at the normal rate(s) appropriate to the deceased, and the tax payable is an allowable deduction for inheritance tax purposes.

5.1.3 LOSSES

It may be that the deceased has allowable losses for the tax year in which the death occurs, for which relief cannot be obtained because there are insufficient gains for that year to absorb them. Such losses may, under s. 62(2), be carried back and set against any chargeable gains realised by the deceased in the three tax years prior to that in which the death occurs, taking the latest year first. The result will be that, if any tax was paid in those years, a repayment may be claimed (which will then form part of the estate for inheritance tax purposes!). If, however, this process does not give full relief for the deceased's losses, there is no way in which the unabsorbed amount can be transferred to the personal representatives to be set against any gains they may make during the administration period.

CAPITAL GAINS TAX

5.2 Personal Representatives and Gains of the Estate

5.2.1 THE POSITION ON DEATH

The death of the taxpayer is not a chargeable event for capital gains tax purposes. However, the personal representatives are at that date deemed to acquire the deceased's assets, at their then market value.

This value will be the same as that used for inheritance tax where that tax is payable (s. 274). Where land or quoted securities are sold by the personal representatives within a prescribed period after the death for less than their market value at death, it may be possible to obtain a repayment of inheritance tax by substituting the lower sale price — the so-called 'loss on sale relief' more fully explained in **6.5.2.7**. In that event, the same lower figure is substituted for the purposes of capital gains tax, with the result that any possible loss relief claim for capital gains tax purposes is eliminated.

Thus, if the deceased's holding of shares in XYZ plc is valued on death at £10,000 and they are sold within 12 months for £6,000, this lower figure may be taken as (effectively) the value at the date of death and the inheritance tax paid on the difference reclaimed. If this relief is claimed, the same adjustment will be made to the value for capital gains tax purposes, so that the personal representatives will now be deemed to have acquired them at the value of £6,000 — the same as the price at which they are sold.

As with income tax, the personal representatives are treated as a single and continuing body for capital gains tax purposes, quite independently of their tax position as individuals. They pay tax at a rate equivalent to the basic rate of income tax (currently 25%).

5.2.2 DISPOSALS BY THE PERSONAL REPRESENTATIVES

5.2.2.1 Chargeable event

Sales of the deceased's assets in the course of the administration may give rise to a chargeable gain or an allowable loss in the ordinary way. The gain or loss is calculated by reference to the personal representatives' acquisition — i.e. the market value at the date of death.

In addition to the normal permitted deduction in respect of incidental selling expenses, a proportion of the costs of valuing the estate for probate purposes may also be claimed — *IRC* v *Richards* [1971] 1 All ER 785.

5.2.2.2 Gains

In establishing the amount of any chargeable gain, personal representatives are entitled to an annual exempt slice of the same amount as may be claimed by individuals (currently £5,800). This is available to be set against disposals made by them in the tax year in which the death occurs — i.e. in this tax year the personal representatives have the benefit of two such reliefs (one for the deceased's disposals and one for any disposals made by them after the death). They may also claim the exemption for disposals made by them in each of the two following tax years, again at the same level as may be claimed by individuals in those years.

By concession, the main residence exemption available to individual taxpayers may also be claimed where the personal representatives dispose of a house which, both before and after the deceased's death, has been used as their main residence by persons entitled under the will or the intestacy to the whole (or substantially the whole) of the proceeds of sale of that property.

CAPITAL GAINS TAX

5.2.2.3 Losses

Any allowable losses can only be relieved by setting them against chargeable gains arising on other disposals by the personal representatives. If at the end of the administration they have unrelieved losses, these cannot be offset against gains realised in the deceased's lifetime or be passed on to the beneficiaries.

5.2.3 TRANSFERS TO LEGATEES

5.2.3.1 Definition

By s. 64(2), a legatee is defined (in effect) as anyone taking (beneficially or as a trustee) under the terms of a will or codicil, or under the intestacy rules; or under a *donatio mortis causa*. A person in whose favour the personal representatives appropriate assets in total or partial satisfaction of a pecuniary legacy or share of residue is also treated as a legatee.

5.2.3.2 Transfer not a disposal

When the personal representatives transfer an asset to a legatee, there is no disposal by them for capital gains tax purposes (s. 62(4)). Therefore, if the asset has risen in value since the date of death, there will be no chargeable gain; if it has gone down in value there will be no allowable loss.

5.3 The Beneficiaries

Beneficiaries are treated as acquiring assets transferred to them by the personal representatives at their market value at the date of death, together with the benefit of any indexation allowance between the date of death and the date of such transfer. A proportion of the costs of valuing the estate for probate purposes, and the expenses of transferring the asset to the beneficiary will also be taken into account. The resultant amount will constitute the beneficiary's 'base cost' by reference to which any tax liability on a future chargeable disposal by the beneficiary concerned will be calculated.

Thus, suppose Delia in her will left shares, which she had acquired for £500, to Belinda. The shares were valued on death at £1,000 and are worth £1,250 at the date of their transfer to Belinda. Assume an indexation allowance (for the period between death and the date of transfer) is available and is worth £50, and that the proportionate cost of the probate valuation attributable to these shares is £25. Belinda will be deemed to acquire the shares at £1,075; any gain or loss on a future disposal by her will be calculated by reference to this figure.

As to the capital gains tax position on disclaimers or variations of the deceased's dispositions, see **15.1.2.3** and **15.2.2.3**.

SIX

INHERITANCE TAX

It is not the purpose of this chapter to rehearse in detail the basic principles of inheritance tax, for which reference will need to be made elsewhere. Our aim here is to consider those basic principles in the context of the most important chargeable event for the purposes of inheritance tax — the death of the taxpayer. However, as you will already be aware, because of the cumulative nature of the tax the position on death can very much depend upon events which have taken place in the deceased's lifetime. Equally, the death may materially affect those who have received *inter vivos* gifts from the deceased.

This chapter will look at the issues from the point of view of the estate (the personal representatives and the beneficiaries) and the recipients of *inter vivos* gifts: the position where there are trust interests involved is considered in more detail in **Chapter 7**.

Statutory references in this chapter are to Inheritance Tax Act 1984 (as amended) unless otherwise stated.

6.1 Lifetime Dispositions

You will already be aware that inheritance tax is (so far as lifetime transfers are concerned) mainly — though not exclusively — a threat to gifts. Such gifts may be exempt (a reminder of the principal exemptions and reliefs will be found in **6.3** below) and thus not be chargeable or affect the taxpayer's cumulative total. A non-exempt transfer is a 'chargeable transfer' (s. 2(1)), and will fall into one of two categories.

6.1.1 POTENTIALLY EXEMPT TRANSFER (PET)

In practice, most non-exempt lifetime transfers will fall into this category. There is no question of any tax being payable at the time the PET is made — it is in effect treated for the time being as if exempt. However, if the transferor dies within seven years it then becomes a chargeable transfer (as to the calculation of the tax due in such event, see **6.4** below).

By s. 3A(1), a PET is defined as a transfer of value (on or after 18 March 1986) made by an individual which, apart from the section, would (wholly or in part) be a chargeable transfer and which is a transfer to another individual, into an accumulation and maintenance trust or a 'disabled trust' or (where the transfer is made on or after 17 March 1987) into a settlement with an interest in possession. (These trusts are discussed further in **Chapter 7**.)

6.1.2 LIFETIME CHARGEABLE TRANSFER CHARGEABLE IMMEDIATELY (LCT)

An LCT is a non-exempt lifetime transfer which does not fall within the definition of a PET. In the main, they are transfers into and out of discretionary and accumulation trusts which are not

INHERITANCE TAX

PETs. There may also be an LCT where the transfer does not result in property becoming comprised in the estate of another, such as where one person purchases a service for another — though in many instances where this occurs an exemption may in practice be available.

Where there is an LCT, the rate(s) of tax applicable will be one half those applicable on a transfer on death (see **6.2** below). There is further the possibility that a supplementary charge will arise if the transferor then dies within seven years — see **6.4** below.

6.2 Transfers on Death

By virtue of s. 4(1), on death there is a deemed transfer by the deceased immediately prior to the death of all the property at that time in the deceased's estate. This has to be cumulated with chargeable transfers (both LCTs and former PETs which have now become chargeable) made within the previous seven years in order to calculate the tax position of the estate. In addition, as a result of the death, a supplementary charge may arise in respect of such LCTs and the former PETs may now attract a tax charge for the first time. The calculation of the tax on and arising from the death is considered more fully in **6.4** below.

6.2.1 ESTATE

By s. 5(1), a person's estate is essentially the aggregate of all the property to which that person is beneficially entitled. On death, this will include (because the transfer is deemed to occur immediately before the death) the deceased's interest as an equitable joint tenant which automatically passes by operation of law on the death to the surviving joint tenant(s). It will also include property which had been the subject of a *donatio mortis causa* by the deceased (since such a gift is not 'fully effective' until death).

6.2.1.1 Excluded property

By s. 3(2), the estate on death does not include excluded property, so that such property is effectively exempt. 'Excluded property' comprises:

(a) most foreign property owned by a person who is not domiciled in the United Kingdom, and some property situated here but owned by a person with a foreign domicile;

(b) settled property situated abroad where the settlor was domiciled outside the United Kingdom at the date of the settlement;

(c) reversionary (i.e future) interests in settled property, wherever situate and regardless of the domicile of the settlor or the owner of that interest. Thus, if property is settled upon Anne for life with remainder to Briony absolutely, Briony's future interest is excluded property — and on her death during Anne's lifetime would not form part of her estate. However, such an interest is not excluded property where it has been acquired for money or money's worth, nor where the person beneficially entitled to it is the settlor or the settlor's spouse.

6.2.1.2 Gifts with a reservation (s. 102 and sch. 20, Finance Act 1986)

The rules apply to lifetime gifts made on or after 18 March 1986 and have the effect of causing the property subject to the reservation at the date of death (not merely the value of the benefit reserved) to be, in effect, still treated as part of the deceased donor's estate for inheritance tax purposes. Thus, it will be taxable on the basis of its then value (rather than (if it had fallen to be treated as a PET) at the value at the date of the gift). Further, its inclusion may increase the 'estate rate' (see **6.4.1.1** below) charged on the rest of the estate.

For the reservation rules to apply, there must be:

(a) a completed *inter vivos* gift of property; and either

(b) possession and enjoyment of the gifted property is not bona fide assumed by the donee at/before the start of the 'relevant period'; or

(c) at any time in the 'relevant period' the property is not enjoyed to the entire exclusion (or virtually the entire exclusion) of

(i) the donor, and
(ii) of any benefit to the donor by contract or otherwise.

The 'relevant period' means the seven years prior to the death, or (if shorter) the period between the date of the gift and the date of death. If the reservation is released during the relevant period, there is a PET at the date of the release.

Under (c)(i), the donor must be excluded both in law and fact from the gifted property itself. The old estate duty cases drew a (not always very clear) distinction between partial gifts (that which was retained never having been 'given' and thus not caught), and entire gifts with the retention of, or subsequent receipt of some benefit from, the gifted property (such as continued occupation or enjoyment of the property). However, under sch. 20, para. 6(1), continued (or resumed) occupation of land or the possession of a chattel for full consideration in money or money's worth is disregarded. Any occupation of land is also disregarded where it constitutes reasonable provision by the donee (being a relative of the donor or the donor's spouse) for the care and maintenance of an elderly or infirm donor whose circumstances have changed since the gift.

The terms of (c)(ii) are sufficiently widely drafted so as to catch purely collateral benefits not taking effect out of the gifted property itself. Thus, suppose land is given by Dan to Derek who, at the same time, enters into a covenant to pay Dan an annuity of £5,000 per annum; the land is property subject to a reservation — *A-G* v *Worrall* [1895] 1 QB 99 (CA). Any benefit obtained by 'associated operations' would be caught — sch. 20, para. 6(1). The estate duty cases suggested that the expression 'or otherwise' should be construed *ejusdem generis* with contract, so requiring some legally enforceable obligation; the court's attitude today is expected to be different!

Schedule 20 contains complex rules for the identification of property subject to a reservation, including where the donee has disposed of the property during the relevant period.

6.3 Exemptions and Reliefs

A transfer which is within an exemption is not liable to inheritance tax, nor does it affect the transferor's cumulative total for tax purposes.

We have already encountered an effective exemption in the shape of 'excluded property' (**6.2.1.1** above). There are certain lifetime dispositions which are specifically not transfers of value — and thus effectively exempt. These include dispositions 'lacking donative intent' (s. 10) and dispositions for the maintenance of the family (s. 11). Other exemptions and reliefs include the following, only briefly summarised here as you will have already considered them in more detail elsewhere.

6.3.1 APPLYING TO LIFETIME TRANSFERS ONLY

6.3.1.1 Annual exclusion (s. 19)

Transfers of value, not otherwise exempt, by any one transferor in any one tax year are exempt if they do not exceed in total £3,000 — and if the total for the year does exceed this figure, only the excess is chargeable. If the full exemption is not utilised in one year, the unused balance may be carried forward to the next tax year but no further. This 'limit' is achieved by the requirement that, in effect, the annual exclusion for any given year is first utilised and only then any unused balance from the previous year. Thus, if in year 1 a taxpayer makes gifts (not otherwise exempt) totalling

INHERITANCE TAX

£2,500, the annual exclusion available to that taxpayer in year 2 is £3,500. If the total transfers in year 3 amount to £3,000, this will absorb the whole of the annual exclusion for year 3 and the 'surplus' brought forward from year 2 is unused: in year 4, only year 4's exemption (£3,000) will be available.

The annual exclusion applies to outright gifts and to gifts into a settlement. It also applies to lifetime terminations of a life interest under a settlement (see further 7.3.2.2). It does not apply to gifts with a reservation. Where a PET becomes chargeable because the donor dies within seven years, it seems that any available annual exclusion not used by any LCTs in the year in question may be claimed against the (otherwise) chargeable amount in respect of the PET — see further **6.4** below.

6.3.1.2 Small gifts (s. 20)

Gifts in any one tax year by any one donor to any one donee not exceeding £250 in total are exempt. If this figure is exceeded, the whole of the gift is chargeable — unless otherwise exempted. The exemption is available for outright gifts and for gifts which would otherwise be caught as gifts with a reservation; it does not apply to gifts into or out of a settlement.

6.3.1.3 Normal expenditure (s. 21)

This provision does not apply to gifts with a reservation or to transfers out of settlements, but it does apply to other outright gifts and to transfers into settlements. The transfer in these cases is exempt if, and to the extent that, three conditions are met:

(a) it was made as part of the normal (i.e. habitual) expenditure of the transferor;
(b) taking one year with another it was made out of income;
(c) after allowing for all other transfers qualifying for this exemption the transferor is left with sufficient income to maintain his/her usual standard of living.

6.3.1.4 Gifts in consideration of marriage (s. 22)

The exemption (which is available even if the gift is one with a reservation) covers either an outright gift to one of the parties to the marriage or a settlement primarily for the benefit of the parties, their issue and the spouses of such issue. To qualify, the transfer must either be made before or contemporaneously with the ceremony, or (if afterwards) pursuant to a legal obligation incurred prior to the marriage. The exemption applies in respect of any one donor in relation to any one marriage up to the appropriate limit, and if this is exceeded the excess is chargeable. The limits are:

(a) £5,000 in the case of transfers by a parent of a party to the marriage;
(b) £2,500 where the transferor is a remoter ancestor, or one of the parties to the marriage;
(c) £1,000 in all other cases.

6.3.2 APPLYING TO LIFETIME TRANSFERS AND ON DEATH

6.3.2.1 Transfers between spouses (s. 18)

Generally, such transfers are wholly exempt — but if the donee spouse is domiciled outside the United Kingdom the exemption is limited to £55,000. The transfer may be outright, or into a settlement where the donee spouse becomes beneficially entitled to an interest in possession (in practice usually a life interest — see further 7.3.2). It does not matter whether the spouses are living together or not — provided they are still married. The exemption is lost on decree absolute of divorce or nullity; it cannot apply if the marriage is void *ab initio*. It is possible, without affecting the availability of the exemption, to make the gift conditional upon the donee spouse surviving the donor spouse for a specified period not exceeding 12 months — in practice, for other reasons, such a survivorship clause should not exceed six months, and is most usually 28 or 30 days: see **7.3.4.3** and **18.4.6.3**. If any other condition is attached, the spouse exemption will be lost if the condition is not satisfied within 12 months.

6.3.2.2 Gifts to charities etc. (ss. 23 to 26)

Gifts to charities, and to bodies such as the National Trust, universities, local authorities and government departments, are fully exempt — as are gifts to qualifying political parties. There are provisions denying relief if the vesting of the gift in the charity etc. is postponed, or is conditional, or the gift is made for a limited period or could be applied (e.g.) for non-charitable purposes.

6.3.2.3 Heritage property (ss. 30 to 35)

A conditional exemption is available in the case of transfers of assets designated by the Treasury as being of national, scientific, historic or artistic interest. An undertaking has to be given to keep the property in the United Kingdom, for its preservation, and for Treasury and public access. If the property is subsequently sold, the undertaking is broken, or there is a subsequent transfer and the undertaking is not 'replaced', tax will normally become payable.

6.3.2.4 Business property relief (ss. 103 to 114 as amended by Finance (No. 2) Act 1992)

In the case of transfers on or after 10 March 1992, the relief takes the form of a reduction of the value of 'relevant business property' for the purposes of charging tax. The reduction is either 100% or 50% depending upon the category of property concerned. (In the case of transfers prior to 10 March 1992, the reliefs were 50% and 30% respectively, and the categories were slightly different.)

Briefly, the present position is:

(a) 100% reduction (i.e. effectively, exemption):

   (i) a business or interest in a business (e.g. a partnership share);
   (ii) unquoted shares or securities in a company provided the transferor had control of the company immediately before the transfer;
   (iii) minority holdings of unquoted shares where immediately before the transferor had more than 25% of the voting power.

(b) 50% reduction

   (i) other unquoted shareholdings;
   (ii) quoted shares and securities which gave the transferor control;
   (iii) land, buildings, machinery and plant belonging to the transferor but used immediately before the transfer wholly or mainly for a business in which the transferor was a partner, or used for the business of a company which the transferor controlled immediately before the transferor.

To qualify for either reduction, the property must normally have been owned by the transferor for at least two years immediately prior to the transfer. There are special rules covering 'replacement property' and the case where a spouse has succeeded to relevant business property on death.

Where tax on a PET, or extra tax on an LCT, becomes payable because of the death of the transferor within seven years, such tax (or extra tax) is calculated on the basis that business property relief is not available unless the transferee still owns the original (or replacement) property at the date of the transferor's death (or, if earlier, the date of the transferee's death) — and the property is 'relevant business property' immediately prior to the transferor's death (ignoring the two year ownership rule).

INHERITANCE TAX

Business property relief is not available in so far as the property qualifies for agricultural property relief (**6.3.2.5** below) — i.e. anything which does not qualify for that relief may be eligible for business property relief.

For the position where relevant business property is held in a settlement, see **7.3.2.3**.

6.3.2.5 Agricultural property relief (ss. 115 to 124, as amended by Finance (No. 2) Act 1992)

In the case of transfers on or after 10 March 1992, a reduction is available of either 100% or 50% in the 'agricultural value' of 'agricultural property'. (In the case of earlier transfers the reliefs were 50% and 30% respectively.)

'Agricultural property' is essentially agricultural land or pasture in the United Kingdom and the farm buildings (including farmhouses and cottages) used with such land. 'Agricultural value' means the value of such property on the assumption that it is subject to a perpetual covenant prohibiting its use otherwise than as agricultural property. Thus any value attributable to development potential does not qualify — though this (and any other assets — such as farm machinery and livestock — of the farming business which are not eligible for this relief) may be covered by business property relief (above).

In order to qualify for relief, the agricultural property must normally have been either

    (a) occupied by the transferor for the purposes of agriculture throughout the two years immediately prior to the transfer; or
    (b) owned by the transferor throughout the seven years immediately prior to the transfer and throughout that period occupied by someone for the purposes of agriculture.

There are provisions which relax these requirements in respect of 'replacement property', succession on death from the transferor's spouse and succession from a donor.

Transfers of shares or securities in a farming company may also qualify for relief.

The reduction which is appropriate in a given case depends upon the nature of the transferor's interest. Relief at 100% (i.e. effectively, exemption) is available if the transferor was the owner or tenant in possession, or where the transferor's interest carries the right to obtain vacant possession within 12 months (this would be the case where the tenant in possession does not have the protection of the Agricultural Holdings Acts (e.g.) because they have grazing rights only). Relief at 50% is available in other cases.

As with business property relief, where tax on a PET (or extra tax on an LCT) becomes payable because of the death of the transferor within seven years, such tax is calculated on the basis that agricultural property relief is not available unless the transferee still owns the original property (or replacement property) at the time of the transferor's death (or at the date of the transferee's death if earlier) and the property qualifies for agricultural property relief at the date of the transferor's death.

Again, for the position where agricultural property is held in a settlement, see **7.3.2.3**.

6.3.3 APPLYING ON DEATH ONLY

6.3.3.1 Woodlands (ss. 125 to 130)

Where the deceased's estate includes land which does not qualify for agricultural property relief, the value of any timber growing on that land may be left out of account (i.e. is, in effect, exempt) on the death, provided (normally) the relief is claimed within two years of the death and the land concerned had not been purchased by the deceased within five years of the death. The land itself is chargeable, subject to any business property relief which may be available.

INHERITANCE TAX

The exemption is, however, a qualified one in that tax will become payable if subsequently the timber is disposed of (with or without the land) otherwise than on a death upon which the relief is also claimed. When such a chargeable event occurs, the person making the disposal is liable to tax on the sale proceeds, or the net value of the timber at the date of disposal where this is not by way of sale for full consideration in money or money's worth. Tax is charged as if the appropriate amount had been included in the value transferred on the last death upon which the relief was claimed, and had formed the highest part of that value.

Where the chargeable event is itself a chargeable transfer (e.g. a gift *inter vivos*), not only is the deferred charge triggered but the gift itself may be subject to tax (subject to the availability of business property relief). In such event, the taxable amount in relation to the gift is reduced by the amount of the triggered charge to tax.

6.3.3.2 Quick succession relief (s. 141)

When someone dies not more than five years after a chargeable transfer to them (whether that earlier transfer was made *inter vivos* or occurred on a death) a reduction in the tax payable on the (later) death may be available. This is so whether or not the deceased still owns the property received by the earlier transfer.

The available percentage relief depends upon the time which has elapsed since the earlier chargeable transfer:

1 year or less	100%
1 – 2 years	80%
2 – 3 years	60%
3 – 4 years	40%
4 – 5 years	20%

The amount of tax payable on the (later) death is reduced by an amount found by applying the appropriate percentage to the tax paid on the occasion of the earlier transfer on the net amount received by the deceased on that occasion.

For example, assume Duncan dies, leaving an estate of £300,000. His will leaves a tax-free legacy to Bertram of £150,000: the total tax payable on Duncan's death (assuming no previous transfers and that current rates apply) is £60,000. Bertram dies 2½ years later, leaving an estate of £250,000. The relief is calculated as follows:

Tax payable on Duncan's death attributable to net legacy received by Bertram is

$$\frac{£150,000}{£300,000} \times £60,000 = £30,000$$
$$\text{QSR } 60\% \times £30,000 = £18,000$$

This is the amount which will be deducted on Bertram's death from the tax otherwise payable. Thus (again assuming current rates and no previous transfers):

Tax on £250,000	£40,000
Less: QSR reduction	£18,000
Tax payable	£22,000

Again, suppose Beatrice received a gift of £50,000 from Delia and paid tax (on Delia's death within seven years) of £10,000. On Beatrice's death six months later the calculation will be:

$$\frac{£40,000}{£50,000} \times £10,000 \times 100\% = £8,000$$

INHERITANCE TAX

This is the sum deductible from the tax payable on Beatrice's death. If the amount of quick succession relief exceeds the amount of tax which would be payable on the death, no tax will be payable on that occasion — but no repayment can be claimed from the Revenue!

6.3.3.3 Death on active service (s. 154)

This exemption entirely relieves from charge to tax the transfer deemed to take place on death (including under any *donatio mortis causa*), but not any PETs which then become chargeable (nor the supplementary charge arising on any LCTs made within the previous seven years).

The exemption applies where death can be shown to be as a result of active service or service of a war-like nature whilst a member of the armed forces or ancillary services. It may apply even where the death occurs many years after (e.g.) a wound inflicted whilst on active service; the wound must have been a cause of death, but need not have been the only or direct cause.

6.4 Calculation of Tax on Death

6.4.1 THE DEATH ESTATE

6.4.1.1 Generally

The chargeable transfer deemed to take place on death has to be cumulated with the deceased's existing cumulative total of chargeable lifetime transfers — all LCTs and PETs made within the previous seven years. The transfer on death is the highest part of this total. Tax is calculated according to the rates applicable at the date of death. Currently, these are:

First £150,000 of chargeable transfers	Nil
Excess	40%

Each chargeable item of property in the death estate then bears tax at the 'estate rate' — in effect, an average rate of tax.

Thus, suppose the deceased's cumulative total of lifetime transfers is £50,000 and the death estate amounts to £200,000. Tax on this will amount to £40,000 (£100,000 @ Nil, £100,000 @ 40%). The estate rate will be $\frac{£40,000}{£200,000} \times 100 = 20\%$.

6.4.1.2 *Commorientes*

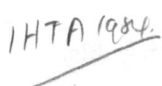
IHTA 1984

We have already noted (in **1.4.3.3** and **2.2**) the effect of s. 184, Law of Property Act 1925 (as amended) for succession purposes. However, even though the rule may operate to determine the succession to property, it will not for inheritance tax purposes, because s. 4 deems the younger and the elder to have died 'at the same instant'. There will be no question, therefore, of a double charge to inheritance tax on the property deemed to pass from the elder to the younger under the rule. However, this provision only deals with those cases to which s. 184 applies; where there is evidence as to the order of death a survivorship clause will be needed (see further **18.4.6.3**).

6.4.2 LIFETIME TRANSFERS

6.4.2.1 LCTs

Any LCTs within the seven years prior to the death will already have been chargeable to tax when made at half the rates applicable on a death at that time — currently, this would be at nil or 20%. As a result of the death, it is now necessary to recalculate tax (usually on the value of the property when it was transferred — but see **6.4.2.3** below) at the rates applicable at death (subject to any taper relief — see **6.4.2.4** below). Credit is then given for the tax already paid and the difference is the amount of the supplementary charge. If the amount of tax already paid exceeds the amount under the recalculation, no supplementary charge arises — but no repayment can be claimed!

6.4.2.2 PETs

Where the deceased has died within seven years of a PET this now becomes a chargeable transfer. Subject to what is said in **6.4.2.3** and **6.4.2.4** below, this charge is calculated on the value of the property given at the date of the gift — at the rates of tax in force at the date of death. The tax on each former PET will have to be calculated separately, cumulating it with chargeable transfers (including former PETs now chargeable) made within (in each case) the previous seven years. The tax on any LCT made after a (now chargeable) PET will also require recalculation to take account of the (now changed) cumulative total at the time it was made.

6.4.2.3 The value charged

For both the supplementary charge on LCTs and the charge on former PETs, what value is to be taken for the purposes of the above calculations? If the property given was cash, the sum given is always the amount taken, whatever has since happened to it. In other cases, it is normally the value of the property concerned at the date of the LCT or former PET which is material — and not its value at the date of death. Where the value of the property has fallen, it is possible to 'substitute' the lower value at the date of death provided the property concerned is not tangible moveable property and a wasting asset. Thus, if shares have fallen in value, their lower value can be used: but if the subject matter of the gift was a car, its value at the date of the gift will have to be taken.

There are detailed rules to cover the situation where the transferee no longer has the property originally given.

6.4.2.4 Taper relief

Where the transferor has died within three years of the LCT or former PET, the full rate(s) at the date of death are applicable. Where death occurs more than three years thereafter, tax is calculated (or recalculated) at the following percentage of the full rate(s) at the date of death:

Transfer made 3 – 4 years before death	80%
4 – 5	60%
5 – 6	40%
6 – 7	20%

Again, there is no question of the application of this relief allowing a claim for repayment of tax.

6.4.3 DISCLAIMERS AND VARIATIONS

For the tax implications of post-death changes brought about by disclaimers or variations, see **15.1.2.1** and **15.2.2.1**.

6.5 Valuation

6.5.1 THE GENERAL RULE

The value of any property for inheritance tax purposes is its open market value — the price it might reasonably be expected to fetch if sold on the open market (s. 160). This is a question of fact.

INHERITANCE TAX

Any special purchaser must be taken into account, and a sale shortly after a transfer of value may lead to an adjustment (up or down) as being evidence of the value at the time of the transfer. If property is subject to restrictions on its disposal, the value has to be found on the assumption that it can be offered freely on the market — but that the transferee will be bound by the same restrictions.

On death, the hypothetical sale is deemed to take place immediately before the death, though certain changes in value brought about by the death are taken into account — (s. 171). No reduction is allowed because all the property is deemed to be placed on the market at the same time.

6.5.2 SPECIAL RULES

6.5.2.1 Related property (s. 161)

The related property rules apply to property held by husbands and wives. Their purpose is to prevent tax advantage being gained by husbands and wives 'asset splitting' so that they own separate assets, the sum of whose value is less than the value of the whole. For example, suppose that Harold owns a valuable pair of antique candlesticks and he gives one of them to his wife Wendy (an exempt transfer). Valued individually and independently they are each worth (say) £5,000: as a pair, they might be worth £20,000. Again, each of them might own 40% of the issued share capital in their family company. Each holding is, by itself, a minority holding — but when related to the other's holding the asset is in fact a controlling holding.

The rules require valuation on this related basis where it would have the effect of producing a higher value than if valued independently. Thus, in the examples, the candlesticks would each have to be valued as one of a pair, and the shareholdings as (each) half of an 80% controlling holding.

6.5.2.2 Quoted securities

These are to be valued by reference to the Stock Exchange Daily Official List for the day on which the transfer took place. If the Stock Exchange was closed on that date, it is necessary to use the List for the nearest trading day before or after the date of the transfer (at the option of the transferor or the personal representatives). However, in such a case, where several quoted securities are included in the transfer — as might well be the case, for example, on death — it is essential that they are all valued on the same day.

The value to be taken is usually the lower of the two quoted prices for the relevant day plus one quarter of the difference between the two. So, if the quotation is 98–100, the value for tax purposes will be 98¼. As an alternative, if it would produce a lower valuation, the halfway figure between the highest and lowest prices at which bargains were marked on the relevant day may be used.

6.5.2.3 Unquoted securities

The valuation in such cases is a complex matter. Basically, it is necessary to ascertain the open market value, the hypothetical purchaser being assumed to be in possession of all the relevant information which a prudent purchaser might require from a willing vendor. A number of factors will have to be taken into account, including the value of the company's assets, its profitability and its dividend record. If the shares are subject to rights of pre-emption, it is assumed for valuation purposes that the shares can be sold on the open market but that the purchaser will be bound by the same rights — *IRC v Crossman* [1937] AC 26.

6.5.2.4 Land

The general open market value rule applies. Any tenancy will have to be taken into account. When valuing the interest of co-owners, a discount (of the order of 10%) is in practice allowed to reflect the difficulty of selling such an interest on the open market. However, because of the related property rules (**6.5.2.1** above), no such allowance can be claimed where the co-owners are spouses.

6.5.2.5 Life assurance policies

On a lifetime transfer, the value for inheritance tax purposes will be the greater of its surrender value or the premiums paid to the date of the transfer. On death, the policy proceeds are taxable (unless the deceased was not beneficially entitled).

6.5.2.6 Liabilities (s. 5)

Generally, the value of the transferor's estate for tax purposes is its net value after the deduction of liabilities. In the case of an LCT, these include the liability to pay inheritance tax — i.e. the principle of grossing-up applies (avoided if the transferee pays).

A liability is taken into account if it is imposed by law, or (if incurred by the transferor) to the extent that is was incurred for consideration in money or money's worth. No deduction is allowed if there is an enforceable right of reimbursement.

Incumbrances on any property reduce the value of that property so far as possible. Thus a mortgage on Blackacre reduces the value of Blackacre for tax purposes.

On death, allowance is available for reasonable funeral expenses (including by concession the reasonable costs of a tombstone). However, the costs of administering the estate are not allowed, except where there are foreign assets involved; in such cases, the extra expense in administering them may be claimed, up to 5% of the value of the assets concerned. As we have seen, the deceased's unpaid income tax and capital gains tax liabilities are allowable deductions; the same is true of inheritance tax liability provided it is paid by the estate.

There are provisions designed to prevent the deduction of 'artificial debts' in valuing the deceased's estate on death. For example, suppose Jack gives Jill a valuable antique ring and subsequently buys it back from her at its full market value, but leaves the purchase price outstanding until the date of his death. The gift to Jill is a PET and will escape tax if Jack survives for seven years. The debt owed to Jill is incurred for full consideration and is therefore prima facie fully deductible on Jack's death.

Section 103, Finance Act 1986 denies deduction where, and to the extent that, the consideration for the debt was either derived from the deceased (so that in the above example no deduction would be allowed); or from any person to whose resources the deceased had contributed — unless it can be shown that there is no causal connection between the deceased's contribution and the subsequent transaction creating the debt. If a debt which would be caught on death by s. 103 is repaid *inter vivos* the repayment is treated as a PET, so that deathbed repayments are ineffective to avoid the provision.

6.5.2.7 Changes in value

We have already noted (in **6.5.1**) that a sale shortly after a transfer may be argued (by either the Revenue or the taxpayer) to reflect more accurately the value at the date of that transfer.

There are three special cases where a valuation on death may be altered if the asset is sold within a prescribed period for less than the valuation at death. In these cases, the sale proceeds (usually) are substituted for the purposes of inheritance tax and capital gains tax (thus preventing any loss relief claim in respect of the latter). The three cases are:

(a) Related property sold within three years of death (s. 176). Where property valued on death on a related property basis (see **6.5.2.1**) is sold (otherwise than in conjunction with a sale of the

INHERITANCE TAX

related property) for less within three years (by the personal representatives or a person in whom the property concerned vested immediately after the death) in an arm's length sale, the property can be revalued on death as if the related property rules did not apply. Thus, if in the example in **6.5.2.1** the value of Harold's holding on a related property basis was £200,000, and this is sold (otherwise than with Wendy's holding) within three years for £150,000, the holding will be revalued ignoring the related property rules — i.e. as a 40% minority holding. Its value immediately before death is required; the sale price may be evidence of what this was.

(b) Quoted shares and securities sold within 12 months (ss. 178ff.). The lower sale price may be substituted provided the aggregate consideration for all such sales by 'the appropriate person' — usually the personal representatives — within the specified period is lower than the (aggregate) valuation on death.

(c) Land sold within four years of death (ss. 190ff. as amended). The terms of this provision are similar to those applying in (b). Again, the election to substitute the lower sale price relates to all sales of land within the specified period.

6.6 Liability

The question here is, in essence, from whom can the Revenue recover the tax due? The answer will depend upon the circumstances of the transfer.

6.6.1 LCTs (s. 199)

The person primarily liable for the tax on an LCT of unsettled property is the transferor (where the LCT is of property already in a settlement see **6.6.4** below). In certain cases, to prevent avoidance of tax, the transferor's spouse may be liable (s. 203).

If the Revenue fails to collect from the transferor (or the transferor's spouse), the following may then be held (secondarily) liable:

(a) The transferee. The limit of the transferee's liability is tax (at the rate(s) appropriate to the transferor) on the value of the gross transfer after deducting the unpaid tax. Thus, suppose Sebastian makes a gross transfer to the trustees of a discretionary trust of £50,000 on which tax at the rate appropriate to him (say 20%) would be £10,000. If the Revenue fails to recover this tax from him, the limit of the trustees' liability is 20% of £40,000 (gross transfer less unpaid tax) — i.e. £8,000.

(b) Anyone in whom the property is vested (beneficially or otherwise) after the transfer. This category would include (as well as the trustees of the settlement) anyone to whom they in turn have transferred the property — including beneficiaries and, in principle, a purchaser (though see further **6.6.4** below). The liability of trustees and beneficiaries is limited to the value of the purchased property.

(c) Beneficiaries under a discretionary trust to the extent that they have received income or had any of the property applied for their benefit (less any income tax).

6.6.2 TAX ON FORMER PETs AND SUPPLEMENTARY CHARGE ON LCTs (s. 199)

Primarily, the liability for such tax (or the payment of the supplementary charge) falls upon those mentioned in **6.6.1** above as having secondary liability — i.e. the donee, trustees, etc. However, if any of the tax remains unpaid 12 months after the end of the month in which the death occurs, the deceased transferor's personal representatives may be liable — to the same extent as they are liable in relation to the deceased's free estate on death (see **6.6.3** below). The personal representatives do not have a statutory right of recovery of any such tax paid by them.

Similar rules apply to the tax attributable to property deemed to be part of the estate on death as a gift with a reservation (see **6.2.1.2**), save that in this case, there is a statutory right of recovery given by s. 211(3).

6.6.3 TRANSFER ON DEATH (s. 200)

Here, the following have concurrent liability (limited by the terms of s. 204):

(a) The personal representatives. They are liable — to the extent of assets which they have received (or should have received but for their own neglect or default) — for the tax on the deceased's free estate. As well as the property beneficially owned and vested solely in the deceased's name, the free estate includes property held by the deceased as a beneficial joint tenant or tenant in common, and property the subject of a statutory nomination or a *donatio mortis causa*. The personal representatives are also liable for the tax on settled land which devolves on them (i.e. where the land ceases to be settled land on the death of the life tenant, or only becomes comprised in a strict settlement under the terms of the deceased's will).

An executor *de son tort* (someone who has become executor by intermeddling in the estate — see **Chapter 8**) is similarly liable for tax to the extent of assets which have come into such executor's hands.

(b) The trustees of a settlement (i.e. already existing at the date of death). They are liable for the tax attributable to the property comprised in such settlement immediately prior to the death, limited (in effect) to the value of such assets as they have received or should have received but for their own neglect or default.

(c) Anyone in whom property is vested (beneficially or otherwise) or who has a beneficial interest in possession is liable for the tax attributable to, and to the extent of the value of, such property. This category will include those entitled under the will or the operation of the intestacy rules, and anyone to whom they in turn had transferred the property.

(d) beneficiaries under a discretionary trust (i.e. created prior to the death). Their liability is limited to the amount of the income or property received from the trustees (less any income tax).

6.6.4 PURCHASERS

Purchasers may in principle be liable for inheritance tax attributable to any property as persons 'in whom the property is vested'. However, bona fide purchasers without notice for consideration in money or money's worth (including a lessee or mortgagee) or anyone deriving title through them are not liable for tax in relation to the purchased property unless that property is subject to an Inland Revenue charge (i.e. for the unpaid tax) — (s. 237). Such a charge attaches to all property included in a chargeable transfer, though in relation to the transfer on death does not attach to the deceased's personal or moveable property in the United Kingdom. Further, in relation to land situated in the United Kingdom, the charge is void against a bona fide purchaser for value of the legal estate unless registered as a Land Charge Class D(i) or protected by notice on the Register (s. 238).

6.7 Burden

The Revenue is only concerned with the question of liability. It has no interest in where the burden of the tax ultimately falls. In the case of lifetime transfers, this is essentially a matter for agreement between the transferor and transferee. The decision (because of the requirement of 'grossing-up' where the transferor pays) may affect the amount of tax payable — and also affects the value of the net transfer to the transferee!

6.7.1 THE GENERAL POSITION ON DEATH

6.7.1.1 Provision in the will

On death, the question of burden can (and should) be the subject of express provision in the will (see **17.4.6**). Any such provision prevails, except to the extent that the will purports to impose the

INHERITANCE TAX

burden of the tax attributable to a chargeable share of residue upon an exempt share of residue (see further **6.7.2** below).

6.7.1.2 No provision in the will

In such cases, tax attributable to the deceased's free estate in the United Kingdom — whether realty or personalty — which vests in the personal representatives is a testamentary expense. In practice, this means that it is usually payable from the residue (see further **14.3.4**). The burden of the tax on all other property (i.e. interests under joint tenancies, foreign property, settled land devolving upon the personal representatives, property the subject of a statutory nomination or a *donatio mortis causa*) is effectively borne by the property concerned.

6.7.1.3 Recovery of tax paid

The personal representatives will have paid the tax in order to obtain the grant (see further **10.4.10.3**). Where they have paid tax which — whether under the terms of an express provision in the will or under the general law — is not a testamentary expense, the personal representatives have the right to recover the amount paid from the person(s) in whom the property is vested (s. 211). A problem can arise in this context in the case of property where an election can be made to pay the tax by instalments (see **6.8** below). If the personal representatives do not exercise this election and pay the amount due in full, the person from whom they may be entitled to recover may elect to repay them by instalments (s. 213). In such cases, therefore, it is important to consult with the beneficiary before they make a decision as to the payment of the tax!

6.7.2 PARTIALLY EXEMPT TRANSFERS (ss. 36 to 42)

A partially exempt transfer arises where some of the property comprised in a transfer passes to exempt beneficiaries and other property passes to non-exempt beneficiaries. Thus, for example, a will leaves some property to the testator's spouse (or perhaps a charity) and other property to the children. The gift to the children is taxable; where does the burden of this fall?

Where the non-exempt gifts are residuary gifts or (either by the terms of the will or the general law) bear their own tax, there is no particular difficulty: the burden falls upon the non-exempt beneficiaries (**6.7.1** above). However, there are two situations where the question of burden is more complicated; the basic principles applicable in these cases are discussed in **6.7.2.1** and **6.7.2.2** below.

6.7.2.1 Tax-free legacy to non-exempt beneficiary, residue to exempt beneficiary

The legacy may be tax free because the will so provides or because it is not one which bears its own tax under the general law (6.7.1 above). To ascertain the amount of tax attributable to the legacy it must be 'grossed-up', and if there is more than one such legacy they are aggregated *inter se* for this purpose. (At current rates, the amount of tax is relatively easily found: it will be two-thirds of the amount by which the tax-free legacies exceed the nil rate band upper limit — after taking into account any cumulative total of lifetime transfers.) The tax so payable will then effectively reduce the amount of the residue passing to the exempt beneficiary.

For example, suppose Tom (who has made no lifetime transfers) leaves a net estate of £500,000. By his will he leaves shareholdings (worth £105,000 each) to his two children, and the residuary estate to his widow, Wilma. Unless the will otherwise provides, the tax on the legacies to the children (which total £210,000) will be payable from the residuary estate, and will be £40,000 (two-thirds of the amount by which the aggregate legacies exceed £150,000). The exempt residue passing to Wilma is therefore £250,000.

If Tom had a cumulative total of lifetime transfers of £30,000, only £120,000 of his nil rate band would have been available on his death. The legacies to the children would now exceed the

INHERITANCE TAX

available nil rate band by £90,000, so that the tax attributable to them would be £60,000. The exempt residue passing to Wilma would now be £230,000.

The calculations are more complex if some of the legacies in the will bear their own tax.

6.7.2.2 Part of the residue exempt, part chargeable

Here, the object of the rules is to prevent the exempt share of residue bearing the burden of the tax attributable to the non-exempt share.

Suppose Theresa leaves a net estate of £500,000 and her will directs that (after payment of tax) the residue shall be divided equally between her only daughter and her favourite charity. The rules require:

(a) calculate the shares ignoring tax — here £250,000 each;
(b) calculate the tax on the daughter's non-exempt share as if it were a separate transfer; here, assuming no lifetime cumulative total, this would be £40,000;
(c) deduct this from the daughter's share, so that she will receive £210,000. The charity will receive its £250,000 intact.

The calculations are more complex where the will also contains other gifts (whether tax free or tax bearing).

6.8 Accounts and Payment of Tax

6.8.1 DUTY TO ACCOUNT

In the case of lifetime transfer, an account need only be submitted if the transfer is an LCT. It should be submitted by the transferor, as the person primarily liable for the tax, within (generally) 12 months after the end of the month in which the transfer takes place. In the case of former PETs and the supplementary charge in respect of LCTs, the duty to account (normally within 12 months after the end of the month in which the death occurs) lies primarily with the transferee (i.e. the donee and the trustees respectively).

In respect of the transfer on death, the deceased's personal representatives are under a duty (where the estate is not an excepted estate — see **10.2**) to deliver an account within 12 months of the end of the month of death of all property forming part of the deceased's estate immediately before the death. This will include property in which the deceased had a beneficial interest in possession (such as a life interest under a settlement — see further **7.3.2**). It will also include property over which the deceased had a general power of appointment because, since it could be appointed to the deceased, it is effectively the deceased's property unless the power is exercised to appoint it to someone else.

6.8.2 PAYMENT

6.8.2.1 General rule

Inheritance tax is, subject to the instalment option election (**6.8.2.2** below), normally due in full six months after the chargeable event giving rise to the liability. Thus, for example, on death the tax should be paid within six months after the end of the month in which the death occurs. However, where an LCT is made between 6 April and 30 September inclusive in any year, tax is not due until the end of the following April. Thus, the tax on an LCT made on 6 April 1993 is not due until 30 April 1994.

Interest on outstanding tax runs from the due date and does not qualify for income tax relief.

INHERITANCE TAX

6.8.2.2 Payment of tax by instalments (ss. 227 and 228)

In certain situations, tax may — at the option of the person paying the tax — be paid in ten equal annual instalments, the first being due when the tax would otherwise be payable in full. For this election to be possible, both the transfer and the property must qualify.

(a) The transfer must be either

   (i) a transfer on death; or
   (ii) an LCT where the transferee pays; or
   (iii) a former PET chargeable on the death of the transferor within seven years where the donee pays the tax and still owns the gifted property (or replacement property) at the date of the transferor's death. (A similar rule applies to the supplementary charge in relation to an LCT.); or
   (iv) certain transfers relating to settlements.

(b) The property to which the tax is attributable must be:

   (i) land (of any description);
   (ii) shares or securities in a company which gave the transferor control immediately before the transfer;
   (iii) non-controlling shareholdings in an unquoted company (i.e. not quoted on a recognised stock exchange) worth more than £20,000 at the time of the transfer, being at least 10% of the nominal value of all the issued shares in the company or (if ordinary shares) being at least 10% of the nominal value of the issued ordinary shares in the company;
   (iv) non-controlling holdings of shares or securities in an unquoted company where the Revenue is satisfied that the tax cannot be paid in full without undue hardship;
   (v) (on a transfer on death only) where the tax on non-controlling holdings of shares or securities in an unquoted company and any other property qualifying for the instalment option comprises at least 20% of the tax due from a particular person (in the same capacity — e.g. as personal representative);
   (vi) a business or interest in a business (e.g. a partnership share);
   (vii) timber (where the event triggering the charge to tax is itself a chargeable transfer — see woodlands relief, **6.3.3.1** above).

If the instalment option is available but not exercised, tax is due in full in the ordinary way. If the option is exercised, the outstanding tax may be paid in full at any time during the instalment period — and must be so paid immediately in the event of a sale of the asset(s) concerned.

Apart from easing cashflow, another attraction of taking the instalment option where it is available is that, in most cases, no interest is payable provided the instalments are paid on time — and even if late, interest is only charged on the late instalment(s).

However, in the case of land (not qualifying for business property or agricultural property reliefs) interest on the outstanding tax is payable even where the instalments are paid on time.

SEVEN

TAXATION OF TRUSTS AND SETTLEMENTS

It is the purpose of this chapter to consider the tax implications of settlements from the viewpoint of both trustees and beneficiaries. Settlements may be created *inter vivos* or by will, or arise under the intestacy rules. The meaning of the term 'settlement' for tax purposes may be different from that used in other contexts, and in the tax context no distinction is drawn between strict settlements and trusts for sale.

7.1 Income Tax

Statutory references in this section are to Income and Corporation Taxes Act 1988 (as amended) unless otherwise stated.

As we will see, income arising under a trust will normally suffer tax in the hands of the trustees in a manner not dissimilar (in general terms) to that applicable to personal representatives discussed in **Chapter 6**. Beneficiaries under the trust may have to include trust income in their tax returns, thus perhaps (according to their circumstances) enabling them to make a repayment claim or causing them to be liable to higher rate tax.

However, in relation to certain *inter vivos* trusts there are anti-avoidance provisions which effectively require the income from the settlement still to be taxed as part of the settlor's income. These provisions (found in ss. 660 to 694) affect (broadly) the following categories of settlement, a term which is for these purposes very widely defined:

    (a)   where the settlor has made a settlement under which the settlor's minor children benefit;
    (b)   where the settlor or the settlor's spouse have retained an interest in the settlement, whether or not actual benefits are received by them;
    (c)   where the settlor, the settlor's spouse, or minor child have received a capital payment or benefit from the settlement.

These provisions, which do not apply to trusts arising on death, are complex and are not further discussed in this book.

7.1.1 LIABILITY OF TRUSTEES

7.1.1.1 Generally

Trustees (who are for tax purposes a single and continuing body) are liable to income tax at the basic rate on all of the income arising to the trust (other than dividends where the rate is 20%),

TAXATION OF TRUSTS AND SETTLEMENTS

without any deduction for any trust expenses. Their statutory income is calculated in essentially the same way as that of individual taxpayers; they cannot, however, claim personal reliefs — but are not liable to higher rate tax.

7.1.1.2 Trustees special rate (s. 686, as amended)

This is currently 35% and is payable on income which (under s. 31, Trustee Act 1925 or the trust instrument) is to be accumulated, or is payable at the discretion of the trustees or some other person — and (in either case) is not to be treated (before distribution) as the income of either the settlor (see above) or a beneficiary (see **7.1.2** below).

In practice, the liability to pay tax at this special rate applies to those cases where there is an accumulation and maintenance settlement for inheritance tax purposes, and to most other cases where there is for the purposes of that tax a settlement without an interest in possession (see **7.3.3** and **7.3.4** below).

The special rate is in effect only levied on the amount of trust income actually available for accumulation or for the exercise of the discretion, since the trustees are able to deduct expenses 'properly' chargeable to income under the general law (whatever the trust instrument may actually provide). Such expenses must, however, be claimed against dividends in priority to other income.

Where any of the net income of the trust is paid to, or applied for the benefit of, a beneficiary, the trustees must provide a tax deduction certificate for the tax paid by them.

7.1.2 BENEFICIARIES WITH A RIGHT TO TRUST INCOME

In cases where beneficiaries have a vested interest in the income of the trust it will be taxed as part of their income when it arises, whether it is accumulated, applied for their benefit, or distributed to them.

A beneficiary who has a vested interest in the capital will (unless the trust instrument otherwise provides) normally also have a vested interest in the income — even if under 18. A beneficiary whose right to capital is contingent on attaining an age greater than 18 will (unless s. 31, Trustee Act 1925 has been excluded or modified by the trust instrument) effectively receive a vested interest in the income at 18. From that age until either the capital vests or the interest fails (e.g. because the beneficiary dies before fulfilling the contingency), the trustees (under s. 31) must pay the income to the beneficiary. It must be returned, therefore, as part of the beneficiary's statutory income.

Where beneficiaries have vested interests, it is their share of the income (after trustees' expenses have been met) grossed up at basic rate which must be included in their returns. They have tax credits for the tax paid by the trustees.

Capital payments by the trustees will, in principle, not be liable to income tax. However, where the beneficiary is entitled to have income augmented from capital such 'topping-up' payments will be taxed in the hands of the beneficiary — *Brodie's Will Trustees* v *IRC* (1933) 17 TC 432; *Cunard's Trustees* v *IRC* [1946] 1 All ER 159.

7.1.3 BENEFICIARIES WITH NO RIGHT TO TRUST INCOME

This situation arises where the beneficiary's entitlement to the income depends upon the fulfilment of a contingency, or the exercise of a discretion in the beneficiary's favour.

In these cases, the trust income will be taxed at 35% in the hands of the trustees as it arises. If such income is simply accumulated, it is not taxable as part of the beneficiary's income; and the accumulations, when finally paid over to the beneficiary, are effectively capital and therefore not then liable to income tax. The fact that such accumulating income cannot (where the beneficiary is only contingently entitled) be treated as the beneficiary's income is really the reason why this special rate is payable in such cases. By taxing the income at an effective rate of 35% the Revenue makes such contingent accumulation trusts less attractive compared with those cases where (because the income is to be treated as belonging to the beneficiary) they have the chance to tax the income at the higher rate of 40%.

However, if any of the income is advanced to, or applied for the benefit of, the beneficiary the amounts so paid or applied (grossed-up at the rate paid by the trustees) are then treated as part of the beneficiary's income for tax purposes — with the benefit of a tax credit for the total tax effectively already paid by the trustees.

7.2 Capital Gains Tax

Statutory references in this section are to Taxation of Chargeable Gains Act 1992 unless otherwise stated.

As we shall see, the creation of a settlement is a disposal for the purposes of the tax. Thereafter, so long as the property remains within the definition of 'settled property' — with the possibility of an 'exit charge' when it ceases to do so — it is subject to a special charging regime. Disposals (actual or notional) by the trustees of the trust property may trigger a charge to tax; disposals by the beneficiaries of their beneficial interests generally do not.

The Act does not define the term 'settlement'; rather, it talks of 'settled property', which is defined (s. 68) as 'any property held in trust' except in those situations excepted from the definition by s. 60. This excludes from the definition property held by a person:

(a) as nominee for another person; or
(b) as trustee for another person who is absolutely entitled as against the trustee (i.e. someone who has the exclusive right — subject only to the payment of trust expenses — to direct how the property should be dealt with). Such a situation (sometimes called a 'bare trust') might arise where a remainderman has become absolutely entitled on the death of the life tenant, or a beneficiary has fulfilled a contingency; or
(c) as trustee for any person who would be absolutely entitled as against the trustees but for infancy or other disability. This must be the only reason why the person concerned is not able to call immediately for the property to be 'handed over' — i.e. that person's interest must be vested. If a contingency (e.g. attaining 18) still has to be fulfilled, the property remains settled property.

Where one of the three exceptions applies, the trust property is for tax purposes dealt with as if it were vested in the beneficiary concerned, and acts of the nominee or trustee are treated as those of the beneficiary.

If two or more persons hold property as joint tenants or tenants in common, the property is not 'settled property' for the purposes of capital gains tax provided they are together absolutely entitled to the property.

7.2.1 SETTLOR'S LIABILITY

This will depend upon whether the settlement is created *inter vivos* or on death.

7.2.1.1 Settlement created *inter vivos*

Whenever property is transferred to trustees, there is a disposal for capital gains tax purposes by the settlor to the trustees. This is so whether the settlement is revocable or irrevocable, and even if the settlor (or the settlor's spouse) is a trustee (even the sole trustee) or a beneficiary.

TAXATION OF TRUSTS AND SETTLEMENTS

The disposal (and corresponding acquisition by the trustees) is at the then market value of the property concerned. Any gain or loss will essentially be computed in the ordinary way. However, as the settlor and the trustees are connected persons (s. 18(3)) any loss can only be relieved by setting it against gains made on subsequent disposal(s) to the trustees. If hold-over relief (s. 165) is available (either because the assets are put into the trust by a transfer which is an LCT for inheritance tax purposes, or are business assets), it may be claimed by the election of the settlor alone.

7.2.1.2 Settlement created on death

Here, there will be no disposal (in line with the general scheme of the Act that death is not a chargeable event for capital gains tax purposes). The deceased's personal representatives will (as we saw in 5.2.1) be deemed to acquire the assets concerned at their market value at the date of death, and this will also be the value at which the trustees will be deemed to have acquired them, subject to the benefit of any indexation allowance available to the personal representatives at the date of handover to the trustees.

7.2.2 LIABILITY OF TRUSTEES

As in the case of income tax, trustees are a single and continuing body for tax purposes; thus a change of trustees is not a chargeable event for capital gains tax purposes. Normally, trustees pay capital gains tax at a rate equivalent to the basic rate of income tax, but where for income tax purposes trustees are liable at the basic and additional rates (i.e. in the case of discretionary and accumulation trusts) their capital gains tax rate is also effectively 35%. There are anti-avoidance rules (in ss. 77 and 78) whereby if the settlor or the settlor's spouse has any interest in a settlement, any gains are taxed as gains of the settlor and not of the trustees.

7.2.2.1 Actual disposals

Where the trustees sell trust assets, any chargeable gain or allowable loss is calculated in the normal way. The exemptions and reliefs to which they may be entitled include:

(a) Annual exempt slice (s. 3 and sch. 1). This is available normally at half the rate to which an individual is entitled in the year in question (currently it is therefore £2,900). However, where the same settlor has created more than one settlement, the available exempt slice is divided equally between them — subject to the proviso that each trust is entitled to a minimum exemption of 10% of the exemption available to individuals (currently, therefore, £580).

(b) Main residence (s. 225). Trustees may claim this exemption on the disposal of a property which has been the only or main residence of a person entitled to occupy it under the terms of the settlement.

(c) Retirement relief (s. 164). Trustees of an interest in possession settlement which includes a business or shares in a family company may claim this relief on a 'material disposal' provided the various conditions are met by reference to the life tenant.

(d) Roll-over relief (s. 152). This will only be available if the trustees are carrying on an unincorporated business.

Where trustees incur a loss on the disposal, it can be relieved against any gains which they have in the same tax year, with any surplus being carried forward to future years.

7.2.2.2 Notional disposals (s. 71)

When someone becomes absolutely entitled to (any part of) the trust property as against the trustees (or would become so entitled but for infancy or other disability) such property (or part) ceases to be 'settled property'. This may occur, for example, where the trustees exercise a power of advancement — though not where cash is advanced, since sterling is an exempt asset for tax purposes; when a beneficiary obtains a vested interest on fulfilling a contingency; where the

TAXATION OF TRUSTS AND SETTLEMENTS

remainderman becomes absolutely entitled on the *inter vivos* termination of a life interest (e.g. on the surrender of the life tenant's interest).

On the happening of any such event, the trustees are deemed to dispose of the property concerned and immediately reacquire it (as nominee of the beneficiary) at its then market value. Any chargeable gain or allowable loss is calculated in (essentially) the ordinary way. Hold-over relief may be claimed in appropriate circumstances on a joint election by the trustees and the beneficiary; in this case, the disposal is deemed to be not at market value but at the trustees allowable expenditure at the date of disposal.

If the trustees incur an allowable loss for which they are unable to obtain relief, the loss may effectively be transferred to the beneficiary who becomes absolutely entitled.

Where the event causing the property to cease to be 'settled property' is the death of the life tenant, there is no chargeable disposal; but (as is generally the case for capital gains tax purposes on death) there is nonetheless a deemed disposal and reacquisition by the trustees at the then market value of the property (s. 73). The effect is that the remainderman acquires the property at this value. However, tax must now be paid on any gain held-over when the property was put into the settlement.

If on the death of the life tenant the property remains settled property (e.g. because another life tenant becomes entitled, or because a remainderman is only contingently entitled), the position is governed by s. 72. There is again no chargeable disposal, but there is a deemed disposal and reacquisition of the property by the trustees which will form the basis of any future charge. However, tax will again be payable on any gain held-over when the property was put into the settlement.

7.2.3 THE BENEFICIARIES

The tax position of the beneficiaries will depend upon whether the trust property is within the definition of 'settled property' or not.

7.2.3.1 Settled property (s. 76)

On the disposal by a beneficiary of the beneficial interest there is no chargeable event — unless that beneficial interest was acquired by the beneficiary or a predecessor in title for consideration in money or money's worth (other than consideration consisting of another interest under the settlement).

7.2.3.2 Bare trust

If the property has ceased to be 'settled property', the beneficiary is effectively treated as already the 'owner' of the property. The result is that any subsequent disposals by the trustees are treated and taxed as if made by the beneficiary.

7.3 Inheritance Tax

Statutory references in this section are to Inheritance Tax Act 1984 (as amended) unless otherwise indicated.

For the purposes of inheritance tax, the term 'settlement' is defined by s. 43(2). It includes a disposition whereby property is for the time being:

(a) held in trust for person's in succession (e.g. 'to Lesley for life, remainder to Rosalind');
(b) held for a person subject to a contingency (e.g. 'to Charles provided he attains the age of 25');

TAXATION OF TRUSTS AND SETTLEMENTS

(c) held on trust to accumulate the whole or part of the income, or to make payments from income at the discretion of the trustees or some other person;
(d) charged or burdened with the payment of an annuity.

There is no settlement for inheritance tax purposes where property is held behind a trust for sale as beneficial joint tenants or tenants in common, nor where it is held in a bare trust.

The charging regime for settlements basically draws a distinction between those settlements where there is a beneficial interest in possession (**7.3.2**) and those where there is not (**7.3.3**). Certain 'privileged' trusts where there is no interest in possession are excepted from the charging rules described in **7.3.3**; the most important example is the accumulation and maintenance settlement, which is considered in **7.3.4**.

Where chargeable events occur, the primary liability for the payment of the tax lies with the trustees — the burden falling upon the trust property. In appropriate cases, the instalment option will be available if the charge arises on a death or, in other situations, if qualifying property remains settled.

7.3.1 CREATION OF A SETTLEMENT

Prima facie, this constitutes a transfer of value by the settlor and its chargeability will be determined in the normal way. Unless covered by an exemption, therefore, when property is put into a settlement *inter vivos* there will be either a PET or an LCT. If this is done on death (either by the terms of the will or the operation of the intestacy rules) the property involved is part of the transfer deemed to take place on death and so chargeable (unless, again, covered by an exemption).

7.3.2 SETTLEMENTS WITH A BENEFICIAL INTEREST IN POSSESSION

There is no statutory definition of an interest in possession. The basic test is the immediate right to the income from, or the use or enjoyment of, the property. Thus, the following clearly do not have such an interest:

(a) remaindermen;
(b) minors;
(c) beneficiaries whose interests are contingent only. In this context, however, it is important to bear in mind the terms of s. 31, Trustee Act 1931. Under this section (which may be excluded or modified by the trust instrument), a beneficiary whose interest in capital does not vest at 18 nonetheless effectively obtains at that age a vested interest in the income. Thus, if the disposition is 'to Anna provided she attains the age of 21', Anna is entitled to receive the income from age 18 — at which point she has, therefore, a beneficial interest in possession.

Generally, it will not be difficult to identify the existence of an interest in possession. A life tenant prima facie has such an interest (unless a minor or only contingently entitled), whilst in the case of a discretionary trust no one has any right to income. A power to accumulate income will generally be interpreted as a power to withhold it (so that no interest in possession can exist). On the other hand, a power of revocation or appointment — which, if exercised, would determine the interest, but if not exercised does not affect the beneficiary's immediate entitlement to income — does not prevent the interest from being an interest in possession.

7.3.2.1 Charging basis (s. 49)

A beneficiary who has a beneficial interest in possession is treated as if beneficially entitled to the property in which that interest subsists. In other words, if Lincoln is the life tenant entitled to the income from a trust fund whose capital is valued at £500,000, that capital value is treated as part of his estate for tax purposes. (If he were entitled to half of the income from the fund then £250,000 would be deemed to be part of his estate.)

TAXATION OF TRUSTS AND SETTLEMENTS

This, incidentally, is why a reversionary interest (a remainderman's future interest) is normally excluded property for inheritance tax purposes. All the value of the property is for tax purposes attributed to the life tenant's estate; the future interest is therefore 'ignored' in considering the remainderman's estate.

7.3.2.2 Chargeable events

These occur whenever, and to the extent that, the interest in possession terminates — since this will (effectively) be treated as a disposition of the property by the person with the interest in possession.

Thus, the deemed transfer on the death of the life tenant includes the trust property. The trustees are primarily liable for the tax attributable to this part of the estate, and the burden of that tax will fall upon the trust property. However, the tax payable on both the unsettled and settled estate will be affected by the need to cumulate both with any chargeable lifetime transfers made by the life tenant in the seven years prior to the death to fix the rate(s) of tax payable.

The termination may occur during the lifetime of the life tenant — e.g. on the sale, gift or surrender of the life interest, or the consent by the life tenant to the advancement of the remainderman. Normally, unless exempt, such lifetime terminations will be treated as PETs made by the life tenant and thus only actually chargeable to tax if the life tenant dies within the next seven years.

Notice that a tax charge may arise on a sale of the life tenant's interest. A transfer of value will occur even if the sale has been for the full market value of the life tenant's interest — because the life tenant has been treated as 'owning' the property, whereas the value of the life interest will be determined on an actuarial basis.

Suppose that Lisa is the life tenant of a fund of £100,000 and she sells her life interest to Penelope for £25,000 (its full actuarial value). There will be a transfer of value (normally a PET) of the amount by which her estate goes down in value — £75,000. (This demonstrates the fact that inheritance tax is not merely a tax on gifts or transactions at an undervalue.)

If on the termination of the interest in possession the life tenant becomes absolutely entitled to the settled property, no charge will arise. This is because the value of the life tenant's estate does not change, and so there can be no transfer of value. Thus, suppose that the trustees advance £10,000 from capital to the life tenant under a power given to them by the trust instrument (this would not, of course, be possible under the general law). Prior to the advancement, this sum would have been deemed to be part of the life tenant's estate; it now is the life tenant's absolutely. A similar result will follow from a partition of the settled property to the extent of the property taken by the life tenant under the arrangement. Thus, suppose Lucas is the life tenant and Roger the remainderman of a settled fund worth £500,000, and they agree to break the settlement on terms that Lucas will take £100,000 absolutely and Roger the remaining £400,000. The amount taken by Lucas does not affect the value of his estate; however, there is a transfer of value (normally a PET) by Lucas of the amount taken by Roger.

However, if the life tenant purchases a reversionary interest, special rules apply to prevent avoidance of tax. Suppose Lois is the life tenant under a settlement of £500,000. Ronald is the remainderman, and she agrees to purchase his reversion for its full actuarial value of (say) £100,000. Her estate both before and after the transaction includes the value of the settled property, but the estate of Lois has now been depleted by the £100,000 paid to Ronald. She has, in effect, bought something which was already regarded as hers for tax purposes and reduced the value of her estate in the process. By s. 55 she is prevented from gaining any tax advantage from such a deal: she will be deemed under this provision to have made a transfer of value (normally a PET) of the amount paid to Ronald.

TAXATION OF TRUSTS AND SETTLEMENTS

7.3.2.3 Exemptions and reliefs

In the main, the availability of exemptions and reliefs will be determined by reference to the circumstances of the life tenant, the 'deemed owner' of the property for tax purposes. Thus, if on the termination of the interest in possession the former life tenant's spouse then becomes entitled (either absolutely or to a life interest), the spouse exemption will apply. On a lifetime termination, although the small gifts and normal expenditure exemptions are not available, the life tenant may claim any available annual exclusion and marriage exemption.

Where the settlement includes property which might qualify for business property or agricultural property reliefs, their availability will be determined by whether the life tenant fulfils the various conditions.

There is a special version of quick succession relief (s. 141) which operates in a broadly similar manner to the general quick succession relief described in **6.3.3.2**.

There is also an exemption in certain circumstances where, on the termination of the interest in possession the property reverts to the settlor (s. 141). Thus, if Stanley settles property on Lancelot for life but fails to deal with the remainder interest, the property will revert to Stanley's estate on Lancelot's death — with no charge to tax. The exemption will also apply if the property were to revert to the settlor's spouse or widow (if the settlor is dead) provided this occurs within two years of the settlor's death. However, the exemption will not be available if the settlor or the settlor's spouse had acquired the reversionary interest for consideration in money or money's worth. Thus, if Stanley had settled the property on Lancelot for life with remainder to Roberta, the exemption would not apply on the death of Lancelot if Stanley or his wife had meanwhile purchased Roberta's interest.

7.3.2.4 Reversionary interests

As we have already seen, in **6.2.1.1**, these are normally excluded property for inheritance tax purposes. The effect is that a disposition of any such interest cannot lead to a charge to tax.

However, there are certain situations where, to prevent avoidance of tax, reversionary interests are not excluded property. We have already encountered one of these — where the reversionary interest is sold to the life tenant (s. 55 — see **7.3.2.2** above). The other cases include (s. 48):

(a) where the reversionary interest has at any time been acquired for a consideration in money or money's worth. Suppose Romeo sells his reversionary interest under a settlement to Xavier (who is not another beneficiary under the trust) for £50,000. Romeo is disposing of excluded property so that no tax liability can arise. Xavier has replaced a chargeable asset (£50,000) with excluded property which would not be taxable as part of his estate on his death — and which he could give away *inter vivos* without fear of a tax charge. By removing the reversion's excluded property status once it has been the subject of a sale, s. 48 prevents such potential avoidance of tax.

(b) where either the settlor or the settlor's spouse is, or has been, beneficially entitled to the reversionary interest. Were it not for this rule, it would be possible to avoid tax by this sort of device. Suppose Sarah settles property worth £500,000 on her mother Mildred (aged 90). Sarah retains the reversionary interest which she then gives to her daughter Doreen. The settlement giving Mildred the life interest would be a PET of (in practice) a relatively small sum (the loss to Sarah's estate being the difference between the value of the property settled and the value of the reversionary interest in it subject to the life interest of an elderly life tenant). The subsequent gift of the reversionary interest escapes tax as a disposition of excluded property. However, by s. 48 its excluded status is effectively removed so that there is a transfer of value (a PET) on that occasion. There will also, of course, be a charge to tax on the settled property on the death of Mildred!

TAXATION OF TRUSTS AND SETTLEMENTS

7.3.3 SETTLEMENTS WITHOUT AN INTEREST IN POSSESSION

Discretionary and accumulation trusts clearly fall into this category, but remember that for inheritance tax purposes it also includes any case where the beneficiary is a minor, or is only contingently entitled. Unlike those cases where there is an interest in possession, there is no one to whom the value of the settled property can be readily attributed for tax purposes. Rather, it is the property itself which is effectively taxed, though the basic intention of the charging regime is to achieve some sort of parity with what happens where there is an interest in possession (and indeed in the case of unsettled property) — i.e. the equivalent of one full tax charge every generation.

Tax is charged on 'relevant property', which is defined (s. 58) as settled property (other than excluded property) in which there is no qualifying interest in possession — one to which (normally) an individual is beneficially entitled. Certain special cases — including accumulation and maintenance settlements (see **7.3.4** below) — are excepted.

It is not our purpose here to discuss the charging scheme in all its complexity; rather, we will only attempt an outline explanation so as to assist a clearer understanding of the special treatment afforded to accumulation and maintenance settlements and other favoured trusts excepted from the scheme.

7.3.3.1 Creation of the settlement

This will generally be a transfer of value by the settlor. As we saw in **6.1.2**, the *inter vivos* creation of a discretionary settlement is an LCT, chargeable at half the rate(s) which would have applied on a death at that time, with the possibility of a supplementary charge should the settlor then die within seven years. Grossing-up will apply on creation, unless the settled fund pays the tax. There are special rules which apply where a settlor creates 'related settlements' (basically, several settlements on the same day) and where property is subsequently added to the settlement.

If the settlement with no interest in possession is created by the terms of the settlor's will, the property concerned will be part of the estate deemed to be transferred on the settlor's death.

7.3.3.2 Subsequent chargeable events

These basically fall into two categories.

   (a) The periodic charge. This is imposed at ten-yearly intervals, the first occasion of the charge normally being the tenth anniversary of the creation of the trust. Basically, the charge is upon the value of 'relevant property' in the settlement at the time.
   (b) The 'exit charge'. This is imposed when capital 'leaves' the settlement during the first ten years or between periodic charges (e.g. because the trustees exercise a discretion to distribute capital; or a beneficiary fulfils a contingency and becomes absolutely entitled; or someone becomes entitled to an interest in possession in the settled property). The value to be charged is the value leaving the settlement. However, no exit charge will apply where the capital leaves the settlement within three months of the creation of the trust or of a periodic charge (s. 65); or if it does so within two years of the creation of the settlement where this happened on death (s. 144).

7.3.3.3 Rates of tax and cumulation

The periodic charge is levied at 30% of the lifetime rate of inheritance tax — i.e. at a maximum rate of 6% (30% of 20%). The exit charge is levied at a proportion of the charge which would have been levied on a periodic charge had it occurred at the time — the precise method of calculation depending upon whether the exit charge arises before the trust's first ten-year anniversary or subsequently.

TAXATION OF TRUSTS AND SETTLEMENTS

In all cases, in calculating the tax payable the settlor's cumulative total of chargeable lifetime transfers in the seven years prior to the creation of the settlement is the starting point of the settlement's cumulative total. This is so however long the settlement has been in existence.

7.3.4 ACCUMULATION AND MAINTENANCE SETTLEMENTS AND OTHER FAVOURED TRUSTS

These are all trusts without an interest in possession but to which the usual charges do not apply.

7.3.4.1 Accumulation and maintenance settlements (s. 71)

Such a settlement must satisfy all of the following conditions:

(a) One or more of the beneficiaries, on or before attaining a specified age not exceeding 25, will become entitled to, or to an interest in possession in, the settled property or part of it.

It is not necessary that the beneficiaries should attain a vested interest in the capital by the specified age; the acquisition of an interest in possession is sufficient. Thus, this condition is met in the case of a gift of capital at age 30 because the beneficiary becomes entitled under s. 31, Trustee Act 1925 to the income (and thus an interest in possession) at 18, notwithstanding that the capital does not then vest.

There may be difficulties in satisfying the condition that beneficiaries 'will' attain such an interest where the settlement gives the trustees overriding powers of advancement or appointment. However, as long as such powers can only be exercised amongst the existing beneficiaries and cannot postpone entitlement (to income at least) beyond 25, the condition is met. Thus, for example, there is no problem if the trust provides for property to be held for a class of beneficiaries in equal shares contingent upon their attaining the age of 25, with a power given to the trustees (expressed to be exercisable until a beneficiary attains 25) to appoint the fund to one or more of the class as they think fit. The trust property will vest either in the beneficiaries (or those selected by the trustees) no later than age 25.

(b) No interest in possession subsists in the settled property (or part) and the income therefrom is being accumulated so far as not applied for the maintenance, education or benefit of a beneficiary who will become entitled on or before age 25.
(c) either

(i) not more than 25 years have elapsed since the creation of the settlement (or, if later, since the (latest) time when conditions (a) and (b) were satisfied); or
(ii) all the beneficiaries are/were either grandchildren of a common grandparent or are the children or widow(er)s of such grandchildren who were beneficiaries but who died before attaining an interest in possession.

The inheritance tax consequences on the creation of an accumulation and maintenance settlement are determined in the ordinary way (remember that the lifetime creation of such a settlement is a PET). Thereafter, there is generally no periodic or exit charge. However, tax will become payable (on a special basis) if at the end of 25 years the settlement still satisfies conditions (a) and (b) but the beneficiaries are not all within (c)(ii).

7.3.4.2 Charitable and similar trusts

Trusts for charitable and similar purposes and those for the benefit of mentally disabled persons and those in receipt of an attendance allowance are not subject to the rules described in **7.3.3** above. Nor are pension fund trusts (s. 151), employee trusts (s. 86), or protective trusts even after forfeiture (ss. 73 and 88).

7.3.4.3 Survivorship clauses

These are commonly included in wills for a variety of tax and succession reasons (see further **17.4.4** and **18.4.6.3**). A standard provision of this kind is 'To Benedict provided he survives me for 28 days but if he fails to do so then to Clarissa'.

Because Benedict's interest is contingent, a settlement with no interest in possession arises on the death of the testator. At the end of the survivorship period (or on Benedict's earlier death) this will come to an end because Benedict (or Clarissa) becomes absolutely entitled to the property. In principle, therefore, an exit charge should then arise. However, provided the survivorship period does not exceed six months, this will not happen (s. 92).

EIGHT

GRANTS OF REPRESENTATION

In this chapter we begin our consideration of the practice and procedure relating to the issue of a grant of representation to the personal representatives of someone who has died. Such grants are court orders and are evidence of the personal representative's title to deal with the deceased's estate.

We will begin by examining the court's jurisdiction in probate matters (**8.1**) and the responsibilities of solicitors instructed to act in the administration of an estate (**8.2**). We will then consider the effect of grants (**8.3**) and those cases where a grant is not necessary (**8.4**). The various types of grant will then be examined (**8.5**), and the issues of amendment and revocation (**8.6**). The concluding sections (**8.7** to **8.10**) will look at various aspects of the position of personal representatives.

8.1 Background

8.1.1 PROBATE JURISDICTION

The probate jurisdiction of the court is concerned with three issues:

(a) whether a document may be admissible to probate;
(b) who is entitled to a grant of representation;
(c) should a grant already made be revoked.

Most probate business is non-contentious (in the probate lawyer's jargon, 'common form') business and is exclusively the province of the Family Division of the High Court. Where there is a dispute concerning any of the above issues, the matter becomes contentious. Contentious (or 'solemn form') business is conducted in the Chancery Division, the county court having a concurrent jurisdiction where the value of the estate is below the county court limit at the date of death (currently this is £30,000). (Solemn form procedure is considered in outline in **12.5**.) However, even in these cases, once the dispute is resolved the grant issues from the Family Division.

A grant is normally made by the English courts where the deceased left property situate in England and Wales, though the court has a discretion to issue a grant even where this is not the case — s. 2, Administration of Justice Act 1932. Sometimes it will not be necessary to obtain a separate English grant where a 'foreign' grant has already been made — see further **8.3.3** below.

8.1.2 NON-CONTENTIOUS BUSINESS

Common form business is mostly conducted in either the Principal Registry of the Family Division in London (headed by a senior district judge and a number of district judges) or in one of the District Probate Registries (or sub-Registries attached to most of them), each headed by a registrar.

GRANTS OF REPRESENTATION

The jurisdiction of the Registries is not restricted to any geographical area. On the death of someone living (say) in Bristol there is no reason why the grant should not be applied for in Newcastle upon Tyne — or indeed anywhere else. However, in practice, it will normally be more convenient to use the local Registry. Application for a grant may be made by a personal representative in person or through a practising solicitor.

Non contentious business is regulated by the Non Contentious Probate Rules 1987, as amended by the Non-Contentious Probate (Amendment) Rules 1991. For convenience, these are hereafter referred to as 'the Rules' or 'NCPR'.

8.2 Responsibilities of Solicitors Instructed by Personal Representatives

It is not essential for personal representatives to instruct solicitors to act for them in obtaining a grant or in the administration of the estate. However, where a solicitor is instructed it is important to appreciate that the personal representatives are the solicitor's clients. Clearly, there is a potential for a conflict of interest if the solicitor also advises members of the family or the beneficiaries — especially if any hint of a dispute emerges.

It is also important to remember that the personal representatives will often be close relatives of the deceased and therefore (particularly initially) experiencing a degree of distress. The solicitor acting must be sensitive to this in dealings with the client, tempering efficiency with sympathy and understanding of the client's feelings.

8.2.1 INITIAL DUTIES

On receiving instructions, the solicitor's first responsibilities will relate to the obtaining of the grant. There are basically three types of grant, which are discussed in detail in **8.5** below:

(a) *Probate*. This normally only issues to an executor duly appointed by the will or a codicil.
(b) *Letters of administration with will annexed*. This grant is appropriate where there is a will but for some reason it is not possible to make a grant of probate to an executor.
(c) *Letters of administration*. This grant, often called 'simple administration', is issued where the deceased died intestate.

Whichever is the appropriate grant, details will be required of the various assets and liabilities of these estate so that their value can be established. If there is a will, this will need to be obtained and its validity and admissibility to probate considered. Any application for a grant has to be supported by certain papers which will have to be prepared. These include the appropriate oath (see **Chapter 9**) and (where required) an Inland Revenue account (see **Chapter 10**). In some cases, it may be necessary to furnish further affidavit evidence in support of the application (see **Chapter 11**).

Once all the documentation is complete and any tax has been paid, application for the grant is made by lodging the various papers (including any will and codicils) at the selected Registry, either in person or by post, together with a cheque for the appropriate court fees.

On receipt by the Registry, the papers are examined to check that they are in order and any testamentary documents are photocopied. The court records are searched to check that no caveat has been entered (see **12.3**); that no grant has already been made; and that no application has been made to another Registry. If all is in order, the grant is prepared, signed by a duly authorised signatory and sealed with the seal of the Family Division or of the District Registry. The grant is then sent, together with any office copies requested on making the application, to the 'extracting solicitor' — usually some 10 to 14 days after the application is lodged.

8.2.2 LATER DUTIES

Once the grant has been obtained, it will be necessary to advise the personal representatives as to their powers and duties (**Chapter 13**). The various assets will need to be realised and the liabilities discharged. There may be a need to advise on a variety of matters, including beneficial entitlement, interim distribution and possible changes in the disposition of the estate, before the estate can be finally wound up. These matters are considered in **Chapters 14 to 16** inclusive.

8.3 The Effect of the Issue of a Grant

A grant of representation issued by the court is conclusive evidence as to the terms and due execution of any will (and codicil), or that the deceased died intestate. However, this is subject to the possibility of its being revoked (see **8.6.2** below).

From the viewpoint of the personal representatives, the effect of the grant depends upon whether they are executors or administrators.

8.3.1 EXECUTORS

An executor's title to act derives from the will (or codicil). The deceased's property vests in the executor on death, and the executor has full authority to deal with it without a grant. An executor may even commence court proceedings prior to the issue of a grant — though if the action depends upon the executor's title to act as such, it will be necessary to obtain a grant before judgment.

The grant of probate, then, merely confirms the executor's title to act. However, a grant (or an office copy) is the only acceptable proof of the executor's title, and except in cases considered in **8.4** below will in practice always be required to enable the executor to deal with the deceased's property.

8.3.2 ADMINISTRATORS

Whether the grant is with will annexed or of simple administration, the issue of the grant actually confers authority to act upon the administrator; prior to this not even the person with the best right to a grant has any authority to act in the administration. It is only on the issue of the grant that the deceased's property vests in the administrator; in the interim it has been vested in the President of the Family Division of the High Court. What is more, the grant once made does not relate back to the date of death so as to confirm any action taken in the interim — except for the limited purpose of protecting the deceased's estate from wrongful injury in that period.

The test as to whether this doctrine of 'relation back' will be applied (so as to validate the administrator's pre-grant action) is whether, at the date of the grant, it would (judged objectively) be beneficial to the estate for the general rule not to apply — *Mills* v *Anderson* [1984] QB 704. In that case, the parents of a child killed in a road accident reached an agreement with the insurers prior to the issue of a grant. Subsequently, a newly reported case caused the parents' solicitors to advise against pursuing the settlement pending the outcome of an appeal. The court held, applying the test laid down, that the parents as personal representatives would not be held to their pre-grant agreement because the damages were too low so that the agreement was not beneficial to the estate.

8.3.3 FOREIGN GRANTS

If a grant of representation has been made by the courts of a jurisdiction outside England and Wales, a separate English grant may not always be necessary to enable the personal representatives to deal with any English property.

GRANTS OF REPRESENTATION

8.3.3.1 Recognition of Scottish confirmations and grants issued in Northern Ireland

Under s. 1, Administration of Estates Act 1971, automatic recognition is given in England and Wales to grants of representation (in Scotland called 'confirmations') issued by the Scottish and Northern Irish courts where the grant contains a statement that the deceased died domiciled in Scotland and Northern Ireland respectively. By ss. 2 and 3, similar recognition is given to English grants in Northern Ireland and Scotland, provided the English grant states that the deceased died domiciled in England and Wales.

The Scottish confirmation issued to an 'executor nominate' has broadly the effect of a grant of probate, whilst that issued to an 'executor dative' is treated as a grant of administration. In Northern Ireland a grant is either of probate or administration.

8.3.3.2 Resealing

The English court has a discretion to reseal (with the seal of the Family Division) a grant of representation made in any country to which the Colonial Probates Acts 1892 and 1927 have been applied — in practice, most of the countries in the Commonwealth, plus South Africa. Once resealed, the grant has the same effect as if issued by the English court.

8.4 Grant not Necessary

It may sometimes be possible for property to be obtained or dealt with by the personal representatives without the need for a grant. There are also a number of situations where property passes on death directly to those entitled and not through the hands of the personal representatives; in these cases, since the personal representatives do not need to make title to the assets, a grant is again not necessary.

8.4.1 SMALL SUMS DUE TO THE ESTATE

Under the Administration of Estates (Small Payments) Act 1965, it may be possible for the personal representatives to obtain payment of sums due to the estate without the need to produce a grant — a copy of the death certificate being sufficient. However, where orders have been made under this Act, there is an upper limit (currently £5,000) in respect of each item — and if this is exceeded a grant will be necessary to establish title to the whole sum, not just the excess. The Act allows such payment to be made to the person appearing to be entitled to the grant or to be beneficially entitled to the asset concerned; however, the Act merely permits payment — it is not obligatory.

Monies which are covered by orders under this Act include:

(a) Money held in the National Savings Bank, Trustee Savings Bank, National Savings Certificates or Premium Savings Bonds. In practice, if there is more than £5,000 in total held in the deceased's name in the National Savings Bank, National Savings Certificates and Premium Savings Bonds the Director of Savings will require the production of a grant before making payment.
(b) Monies payable on the death of a member of a trade union, Industrial or Provident Society or a Friendly Society.
(c) Civil servants' salaries, wages or superannuation benefits.
(d) Service pensions, police and firemen's pensions.

Similar provisions apply under Building Societies Act 1986 to funds invested in a building society.

It will sometimes be a prerequisite of such a payment that the Capital Taxes Office provide a certificate that inheritance tax has been paid or is not payable.

8.4.2 PROPERTY NOT PASSING TO THE PERSONAL REPRESENTATIVES

As was mentioned in **Chapters 1** and **2**, not all property in the deceased's estate passes on death under the terms of the deceased's will or the operation of the intestacy rules. Such property can be dealt with without the need for a grant; a copy of the death certificate as proof of death will suffice.

8.4.2.1 Property in the deceased's estate

In this category, the property in the deceased's estate effectively passes outside of the will or the operation of the intestacy rules, but remains nonetheless part of the estate for inheritance tax purposes.

(a) Joint tenancy. Where the deceased was a beneficial joint tenant of any property, the deceased's interest accrues automatically on death to the surviving joint tenant(s). (If the deceased was a beneficial tenant in common, the deceased's interest is part of the estate passing under the will or the intestacy rules.)

(b) Nominated property. In the case of certain investments, a person who is aged 16 or over may pass the property concerned on death under a statutory nomination made in writing and attested by one witness. Such a nomination is revoked by subsequent marriage, a later nomination, or if the nominee predeceases the nominator: however, it is unaffected by any subsequent will.

It is now only possible to make such a nomination of monies deposited in Friendly Societies and Industrial and Provident Societies, up to a limit in each case of £5,000. It used to be possible to nominate funds in Trustee Savings Banks (withdrawn 1 May 1979) and National Savings Certificates and the National Savings Bank (withdrawn 1 May 1981). However, nominations made before these dates remain effective (unless revoked).

If property capable of nomination in this way is not so nominated, it forms part of the property passing on death under the terms of the deceased's will or the intestacy rules.

(c) *Donationes mortis causa*. Property passing under a valid *donatio mortis causa* passes directly to the donee on death. To be valid, four conditions must be satisfied:

(i) The gift must have been made in contemplation of death.
(ii) The gift must be conditional on death.
(iii) There must have been delivery of the subject matter of the gift or the means of obtaining it.
(iv) The subject matter of the gift must be capable of passing by a *donatio mortis causa*. The Court of Appeal has held that land is capable of so passing — *Sen* v *Headley* [1991] 2 All ER 636.

8.4.3 PROPERTY NOT PART OF THE DECEASED'S ESTATE

Property in this category does not form part of the deceased's estate for succession purposes and so is not affected by the terms of the will or the intestacy rules. A grant is therefore not relevant in establishing title. In addition, because the deceased has no beneficial interest in the property concerned it is not part of the taxable estate either.

(a) Trust policies. Policies of life assurance may be held for the benefit of someone other than the life assured as a result of an express assignment or trust, or as a result of being written under s. 11, Married Women's Property Act 1882. The latter case is only applicable if the intended beneficiaries are the life assured's spouse and/or children; in other cases, an express assignment or trust of the policy will be required.

In either case, the policy 'belongs' to the beneficiaries and the policy monies are payable directly to them (or trustees for them) on proof of death.

GRANTS OF REPRESENTATION

It is very important to appreciate that by no means all life policies are 'trust policies'. Where the policy 'belongs' to the deceased, its proceeds will be payable on death to the personal representatives as part of the estate passing under the will or the intestacy rules.

(b) Pension scheme benefits. Many occupational pension schemes are drafted in such a way that a lump sum payable on death 'in service' does not form part of the estate of the deceased member of the scheme. This is achieved by making any such sum payable entirely at the discretion of the trustees of the scheme — though usually the member is allowed to make a (non-binding) 'nomination' of his/her preferred recipient — not to be confused with the sort of nomination discussed in 8.4.2.1 (b) above. The deceased has no interest in such lump sum, and the trustees of the scheme only require proof of death.

Again, it must be stressed that not all pension schemes operate in this way; frequently, any 'death in service' benefit is part of the estate of the deceased passing under the terms of the will or the intestacy rules.

8.5 Types of Grant

We have already identified the three types of grant. Entitlement to these will now be more fully considered, along with a number of special and limited grants appropriate to particular situations.

8.5.1 PROBATE

This grant can only be made to an executor, who is usually expressly appointed by the will or a codicil. If a firm of solicitors is appointed, unless the will clearly provides to the contrary, it will be the partners at the date of the will (or codicil containing the appointment) who are entitled to act (see further **18.4.4.2**). The appointment of an executor may be implied (in which case the appointee is described as 'executor according to the tenor of the will') where the will shows an intention that a particular person should perform the functions of an executor. These are, essentially, the collection of the deceased's assets, the payment of debts and other liabilities and the distribution of the net estate. Such an intention was shown, for example, in *In the Goods of Baylis* (1865) LR 1 P & D 21, where trustees were appointed to pay the debts and to hold the residue on trust for the deceased's children. However, an appointment of a trustee without any direction to pay debts is not enough (*In the Estate of McKenzie* [1909] P 305).

Occasionally, a will appoints someone to nominate an executor. The court also has power to appoint executors in certain circumstances. These include the power to appoint a substituted executor in place of any or all of the existing executors under s. 50, Administration of Justice Act 1985; and a power to appoint an additional executor(s) during the subsistence of a minority or life interest under s. 114, Supreme Court Act 1981.

Appointments of executors are usually 'unlimited' as to property and time. However, it is possible for the appointment to be limited in either of these respects: for example 'I appoint X to be executor as to my business of . . .'; 'I appoint Y to be executor until my son Z attains his majority'. A grant issued to any such executor will be similarly limited. An appointment may be conditional (e.g. 'I appoint A if he has attained the age of 25 at the date of my death') or substitutional (e.g. 'I appoint B but if she shall have predeceased me or be unable or unwilling to act then I appoint C').

8.5.2 LETTERS OF ADMINISTRATION WITH WILL ANNEXED

This grant is appropriate where there is a valid will but it is not possible to make a grant of probate in favour of an executor. It may be that the will fails to appoint an executor, or that those appointed are dead or are unwilling or unable to act. Other situations where this grant will issue include cases where an executor has been cited but has not applied for a grant (see **12.4**); the appointed executors

GRANTS OF REPRESENTATION

are minors or otherwise incapable of taking a grant (see **8.5.4** below); where a grant to an attorney is sought (see **8.5.7.5** below); and where an executor has been 'passed over' by order of the court under s. 116, Supreme Court Act 1981 (see **8.7** below).

8.5.2.1 Rule 20, NCPR

This governs the order of entitlement to a grant where the deceased died domiciled in England and Wales and left a valid will. At the head of the list is an executor (who as we have seen is entitled to a grant of probate). Where such a grant is not possible, the Rule lays down the order of entitlement to a grant of letters of administration with will annexed. For a person in a later category to establish title to the grant it will be necessary to satisfactorily account for all those (including executors) who would have a better right — see **9.3.3**.

Under r. 20 the full order is:

(a) An executor.
(b) A trustee of the residuary estate.
(c) Any other residuary beneficiary (including one for life), or (where there is a partial intestacy because the residue is not wholly disposed of by the will) anyone entitled to share in the undisposed of residue. Normally, a residuary beneficiary whose interest is vested will be preferred to one whose interest is contingent only.
(d) The personal representative of anyone in (c) other than a life tenant of residue.
(e) Any other beneficiary (including a life tenant or one holding as a trustee) or a creditor. Again, a person with a vested interest is normally preferred to one whose interest is contingent only.
(f) The personal representative of anyone in (e) other than a life tenant or person holding as a trustee.

As can be seen, the order mainly depends upon entitlement to the deceased's property under the terms of the will, with the residuary interest being treated as the principal interest — whatever its value in relation to the other gifts under the will.

8.5.2.2 Rule 21, NCPR

Where a gift in a will fails by virtue of s. 15, Wills Act 1837 (because the beneficiary or the beneficiary's spouse has witnessed the will — see **1.4.3.4**), that beneficiary loses the right to a grant under r. 20 as a beneficiary named in the will — though may still claim in any other capacity (e.g. as a person entitled on intestacy or as a creditor).

8.5.2.3 Deceased having foreign domicile

If the deceased was domiciled outside England and Wales, r. 30, NCPR governs the order of entitlement to any English grant.

8.5.3 LETTERS OF ADMINISTRATION

A grant of 'simple administration' is appropriate where there is no valid will.

Where the deceased died domiciled in England and Wales, the order of entitlement to the grant is governed by r. 22, NCPR, which as will be seen broadly follows the order of entitlement to share in the estate of the intestate (discussed in **Chapter 2**). Again, for anyone in a lower category to be able to establish title to the grant it will be necessary to satisfactorily account for all those with a better right (see **9.4.2.2**). If the deceased died domiciled outside England and Wales, r. 30 again governs the position.

GRANTS OF REPRESENTATION

8.5.3.1 Rule 22, NCPR

The order under r. 22 is:

(a) The surviving spouse.
(b) The children of the deceased and the issue of any child who has predeceased.
(c) The deceased's parents.
(d) The deceased's brothers and sisters of the whole blood and the issue of any who have predeceased.
(e) The deceased's brothers and sisters of the half blood and the issue of any who have predeceased.
(f) Grandparents.
(g) Uncles and aunts of the whole blood and the issue of any who have predeceased.
(h) Uncles and aunts of the half blood and the issue of any who have predeceased.
(i) The Treasury solicitor where the Crown claims *bona vacantia*.
(j) A creditor of the deceased, or any person who would have a beneficial interest in the estate in the event to an accretion to it (see **8.5.3.3** below).

8.5.3.2 Personal representatives

Basically, the personal representatives of a person have the same right to a grant as the deceased whom they represent. This is subject to r. 27, NCPR (**8.8** below) and to r. 22(4) which gives preference to persons in categories (b) to (h) in **8.5.3.1** over the personal representative of a surviving spouse who has died before obtaining a grant unless the spouse was beneficially entitled to the whole estate.

8.5.3.3 Beneficial interest

In categories (a) to (h) inclusive in **8.5.3.1**, entitlement to a beneficial interest in the estate is an essential prerequisite to entitlement to the grant. This may in some cases depend upon the size of the estate. Thus, for example, if the size of the estate is such that the surviving spouse alone is entitled to it all — e.g. where the estate (apart from the personal chattels) is (say) £100,000 and there are no issue — prima facie only the surviving spouse is entitled to a grant. However, if the estate had been larger, as we saw in **2.2.3** the deceased's parents (or if both dead, the brothers and sisters of the whole blood or their issue) might have been entitled to a share. So, subject to the surviving spouse being satisfactorily accounted for (e.g. by showing that the spouse had renounced the right to a grant), an application could be made (under (j) in **8.5.3.1**) by the parents (or brothers and sisters).

8.5.4 GRANTS LIMITED AS TO TIME

In addition to a grant of probate limited by the terms of the appointment in the will (e.g. because the executor has been appointed to act 'during the minority of my son Joseph'), there are other cases where a grant may be in its effect limited as to time.

8.5.4.1 Administration for the use and benefit of a minor — r. 32, NCPR

A minor is not entitled to a grant. As we shall see (in **8.7**) this does not normally pose much of a problem where the minor is appointed one of several executors, or is one of several potential administrators entitled in the same degree. However, if the only executor(s) or potential administrator(s) in the category having highest priority are minors, a grant of letters of administration (with will annexed if there is a will) is made until the minor attains 18, when it automatically terminates and a grant of probate or administration can then be made.

Normally the grant for the use and benefit of the minor is made to the parent of the minor who has (or is deemed to have) parental responsibility under Children Act 1989, or a guardian appointed under that Act. A guardian may be appointed by a district judge or registrar under r. 32(2). However, if the minor is the sole executor appointed by the deceased's will and the minor has no interest in the residuary estate, the grant will normally issue to the person entitled to the residuary estate.

8.5.4.2 Grants in case of mental incapacity — r. 35, NCPR

A similar difficulty arises where the only executor(s) or potential administrator(s) are suffering from mental incapacity. In such cases, unless a district judge or registrar otherwise directs, grant will be made for the use and benefit of the person suffering the incapacity in the following order of priority:

(a) the person authorised by the Court of Protection to apply for the grant; or if no such person
(b) the lawful attorney of the person suffering the incapacity acting under a registered enduring power of attorney; or if no such person (or if the attorney has renounced)
(c) the person entitled to the deceased's residuary estate.

Any such grant will be limited until 'further representation be granted or in such way as the district judge or registrar may direct' — usually in practice for the duration of the incapacity.

8.5.5 LIMITED AS TO PURPOSE

8.5.5.1 Administration *ad colligenda bona*

Anyone having a bona fide interest may apply for such a grant to enable the collection and preservation of estate assets prior to the issue of a general grant. The purpose is the protection of assets at risk (e.g. because of their perishable nature) and the grant does not authorise distribution of the estate. Application is made *ex parte* to a district judge or registrar under r. 52, NCPR. Any such grant ceases to have effect when the purpose for which it was issued has been achieved or when a full grant is made.

8.5.5.2 Grant *ad litem* — s. 116, Supreme Court Act 1981

Such a grant may be made where there is no personal representative of the deceased and it is necessary for the estate to be represented in legal proceedings. It is limited to bringing, defending or being a party to particular legal proceedings. Where a grant is required to enable someone to make an application under Inheritance (Provision for Family and Dependants) Act 1975, and there is no one able and willing to apply, the Official Solicitor has indicated that he will consider applying for a grant *ad litem* so that the proceedings may be brought.

8.5.5.3 Administration pending suit — s. 117, Supreme Court Act 1981

Such a grant is issued when a probate action (see **8.1.1** above and **Chapter 12**) has been commenced and terminates once such action has been concluded. It will only be granted in practice on the application of a party to the action (or any other interested person) where the court considers it proper in all the circumstances to do so (e.g. because assets need to be collected and safeguarded). The grant is not made to a party to the action unless all parties consent; normally it is issued to an independent third party who acts under the supervision of the court. The grant does not normally authorise distribution of the estate.

8.5.6 GRANTS LIMITED AS TO PROPERTY

An executor may have been appointed to deal with particular property — such as the deceased's business. The grant to such an executor will be similarly limited.

GRANTS OF REPRESENTATION

The court also has a power, under s. 113, Supreme Court Act 1981, to make a grant to any part of the deceased's estate (provided not insolvent) limited in any way it thinks fit. Applications under this provision are governed by r. 53, NCPR.

8.5.7 SPECIAL GRANTS

8.5.7.1 Settled land grants

Such a grant is necessary where the deceased was the tenant for life in whom land was vested at the date of death under a strict settlement, and the land remains settled land notwithstanding the death of the deceased — s. 22, Administration of Estates Act 1925. The grant is normally made to the trustees of the settlement (see below) to enable them to make title under the settlement. The grant will always be of administration and is issued as a separate grant (i.e. even if those entitled to it are also entitled to a grant in respect of the rest of the estate).

The order of entitlement to a settled land grant is (r. 29, NCPR):

(a) The special executors. These are, by s. 22, the trustees of the settlement at the date of the death of the life tenant.
(b) The trustees of the settlement at the time of the application for the grant.
(c) The deceased's general personal representatives (failing anyone in the above categories) are entitled to the settled land grant.

It must be appreciated that these special grants are only required for land which was settled prior to, and which remains settled after, the death of the life tenant. If the settlement then comes to an end because someone then becomes absolutely entitled to the land, it devolves upon the deceased's general personal representatives and no settled land grant is necessary.

8.5.7.2 Administration *de bonis non*

Such a grant is made to allow the completion of the administration of the deceased's estate following the death of the sole, or last surviving, personal representative to whom a grant has been issued who has died leaving part of the estate unadministered. It is also the appropriate grant following the revocation of a previous grant (see **8.6** below).

A *de bonis non* grant is not necessary where one of several proving personal representatives has died; the remaining grantees have full authority to complete the administration of the estate. Nor is it appropriate on a death before a grant has been issued; a *de bonis non* grant is always a 'second grant'.

Further, it will not be necessary to obtain such a grant where the so-called 'chain of representation' exists. This occurs where a sole, or last surviving, proving executor dies and that executor's executor duly takes a grant of probate. For example, suppose that Toby dies appointing Tabitha to be his executor. Tabitha proves the will but dies before completing the administration of Toby's estate, appointing Trevor to be her executor. By proving Tabitha's will, Trevor automatically becomes also the executor by representation of Toby and able to complete the administration of Toby's estate.

The 'chain' only operates through proving executors. If, in the example, Tabitha had failed to appoint an executor, or if Trevor had renounced or died before taking a grant to Tabitha's estate, or either Toby or Tabitha had died intestate, there would have been no chain and a grant *de bonis non* would have been needed to complete the administration of Toby's estate.

The order of entitlement to a *de bonis non* grant is governed by r. 20 (**8.5.2** above) if the original grant was of probate or administration with will annexed; or r. 22 (**8.5.3** above) where it was a grant of simple administration.

8.5.7.3 Double probate

This is also a 'second grant' which, when made, operates concurrently with the original grant — hence 'double probate'. It is issued to an executor to whom power (i.e. to apply for a grant) was reserved on the making of the original grant of probate (see further **8.6** and **8.8** below).

8.5.7.4 Cessate grants

Again, this grant is a 'second grant' — in this case following upon a grant of probate or administration which was limited as to time. Thus, it is the appropriate grant where (for example) a sole executor or administrator was unable to take a grant originally because a minor, but has now attained the age of 18 (see **8.5.4.1** above).

8.5.7.5 Attorney grants — r. 31, NCPR

Under this Rule, a grant (of letters of administration with will annexed or simple administration) may be made to the lawfully constituted attorney of a person entitled to a grant. Such grants are for the use and benefit of the donor of the power of attorney, usually until such donor seeks a grant.

8.6 Amendment and Revocation of Grants

Under r. 41, NCPR, upon good cause being shown, a grant may be amended or revoked by order of a district judge or registrar.

Normally, the person to whom the grant was issued must apply for (or at least consent to) the application for this to be done.

8.6.1 AMENDMENT

The reasons why a grant might require amendment include:

8.6.1.1 Minor errors

If a grant is inaccurate, or deficient in some way, as a result of an official error (not one by the extracting solicitor!) there is a simplified process of correcting it. Provided the original grant and all office copies are returned 'unused' within 14 days of issue, a new grant will be issued by the Registry concerned. Otherwise, the procedure described in the next paragraph will have to be followed, though an affidavit in support will not normally be required.

In the case of any other minor error, an application to correct is made by lodging at the issuing Registry the original grant with an affidavit by the grantee explaining the nature and reason for the original error, and the amendment required. If satisfied, the district judge or registrar makes an order for the appropriate amendment.

Only minor errors can be corrected by amendment; more serious errors can only be dealt with by the revocation of the offending grant and the issue of a new one.

8.6.1.2 Redemption of spouse's life interest

In **2.2.4.1** we saw that the surviving spouse may elect to redeem the life interest which arises (where the estate is large enough) when there are also issue of the deceased. We saw that when the surviving spouse is the sole personal representative, notice of such election must be given in the prescribed form to the President of the Family Division. This is done by lodging such notice at the Registry issuing the grant, along with the original grant for notation.

GRANTS OF REPRESENTATION

8.6.1.3 Appointment of additional personal representative

Where an application under s. 114, Supreme Court Act 1981 to appoint an additional executor or administrator is granted, the district judge or registrar may order that the appointment be noted on the original grant (see further **8.9.3.2** below).

8.6.1.4 Order under s. 2, Inheritance (Provision for Family and Dependants) Act 1975

The court making such an order (see **Chapter 3**) sends the grant to the Principal Registry with an office copy of its order. A memorandum of the order is prepared and placed with the original papers; a copy is attached to the original grant, which is noted to that effect (see **15.3.1.2** and **15.3.1.3**).

8.6.2 REVOCATION

8.6.2.1 Grant wrongly made

If it is subsequently discovered that a grant should not have been made, the grant will be revoked. Such a situation might arise, for example, where it is discovered that the grantee is not in fact entitled; where a will (or later will) is found, or if a will admitted to probate is established not to have been duly executed; or where the 'deceased' is found in fact to be alive.

An affidavit as to the facts of the matter, together with any other evidence as may be required, must be lodged at the Registry together with the grant to be revoked. If satisfied, the district judge or Registrar orders the revocation and the retention of the grant in the Registry.

Under s. 121, Supreme Court Act 1981, the court has at its own instance the power to call in a grant of representation where it appears that it should not have been issued, and to revoke such grant where it is satisfied that it would have been revoked on the application of an interested party.

8.6.2.2 Physical or mental incapacity of grantee

Where either of these events occurs after a grant has been issued, it must be revoked. A fresh general grant may then be issued to applicants having an equal right to that of the incapacitated grantee. Where an application is made by someone with an inferior right, the grant will be limited to the use and benefit of the incapacitated grantee for the duration of the incapacity.

8.6.2.3 Consequences of revocation

There are two issues here: the position of the personal representatives acting under the revoked grant, and that of those dealing with them.

(a) Section 27, Administration of Estates Act 1925. This protects the personal representatives in respect of payments and distributions made by them in good faith, and also those who made payments to them in good faith.
(b) Section 37, Administration of Estates Act 1925. By this section, a conveyance of any realty or personalty remains valid provided it was to a purchaser in good faith for valuable consideration.
(c) Section 39, Administration of Estates Act 1925. This provides that contracts for sale entered into by the personal representatives remain enforceable by and binding upon the estate.
(d) Section 204, Law of Property Act 1925. A purchaser in good faith for valuable consideration receives further protection from this provision, which entitles such a purchaser to rely upon the grant (as an order of the court) as being 'conclusive'.
(e) Unpaid and wrongly paid beneficiaries. For the position of such beneficiaries, see **13.4**.

8.7 Personal Representatives — Capacity

In principle, a testator is free to appoint anyone as executor. Equally, any person who under r. 20 or r. 22, NCPR (see **8.5.2** and **8.5.3**) has the right to a grant is entitled to apply for a grant of letters of administration. There is no rule automatically debarring (say) someone who is insolvent or who has a criminal record. However, there are a number of qualifications to this general principle.

8.7.1 MINORS

As we have already seen, a minor cannot take a grant. If the minor is one of several executors or potential administrators, the practice is to make a grant immediately to the adult executors or administrators — with, in the case of a grant of probate, power being reserved to the minor to apply for a grant of double probate on attaining 18. Where the minor is the only or last surviving executor or potential administrator, we saw (in **8.5.4.1** above) that a grant will be made for the use and benefit of the minor until age 18.

8.7.2 MENTAL OR PHYSICAL INCAPACITY

Again, we have noted (in **8.5.4.2** above) the position where executors or potential administrators are suffering from mental incapacity such as to render them incapable of managing their own affairs. The position is broadly similar to that applying in the case of minors, and similar rules apply to those incapacitated by physical disability.

8.7.3 CORPORATIONS

There are three possibilities:

8.7.3.1 Corporations sole

A corporation sole (e.g. a bishop) can be appointed executor and take a grant of probate in his own name.

8.7.3.2 Trust corporations

A trust corporation (as defined by s. 128, Supreme Court Act 1981 — e.g. the Public Trustee, bank executor and trustee companies) may, under s. 115 of that Act, take a grant (through one of its officers — r. 36, NCPR) in its own name, either alone or jointly with others. It may be appointed executor and thus entitled to a grant of probate; it may be entitled to a grant of administration with will annexed as (e.g.) residuary legatee or devisee. It may also take a grant of letters of administration with will annexed or simple administration in place of those prima facie entitled. In such cases, all adult potential grantees and the residuary beneficiaries must consent: the matter will have to be referred to a district judge or registrar where minors' beneficiaries are involved.

8.7.3.3 Other corporations

Other corporations cannot, under r. 36, NCPR, take a grant in their corporate name but only through a nominee or attorney who completes all the papers personally. The grant will be limited to the use and benefit of the corporation and until further representation is granted.

8.7.4 SECTION 116, SUPREME COURT ACT 1981

This section gives the court a discretion, where it considers that 'by reason of any special circumstances' it is necessary or expedient, to issue a grant to someone other than the person who is prima facie entitled under the Rules. Under r. 52, NCPR, an application for the exercise of this power is made *ex parte* to a district judge or registrar, supported by an affidavit as to the facts of the matter and any other relevant documentary evidence. A grant in these circumstances may be issued to anyone (not necessarily the person with the 'next best right'), and may be general or limited in any way in which the court sees fit.

This power has been used, for example, to pass over a potential grantee shown to be unfit to administer the estate (e.g. because bankrupt) or otherwise unsuitable or unable to act (e.g. because in prison; or missing and whereabouts unknown).

8.7.5 RULE 24, NCPR

This Rule applies where all those entitled to the deceased's estate (whether under the will or the operation of the intestacy rules) have assigned the whole of their interests. In such cases, the assignee(s) have the same entitlement to a grant of letters of administration (with will annexed if there is a will) as the assignor with the highest priority. If not all of the assignees apply, those not doing so must consent. The original deed of assignment (which will be returned after inspection) and a copy must be lodged at the Registry with the papers to lead the grant.

8.7.6 SECTION 50, ADMINISTRATION OF JUSTICE ACT 1985

This allows the court to remove any existing personal representative and appoint a substitute. Such substitute will be an executor if replacing an executor; otherwise the grantee will be an administrator.

8.8 Personal Representatives — Several Claimants

8.8.1 PROBATE

On an application for a grant of probate, all the executors appointed by the will or any codicil (and whose appointments have not been revoked by a later codicil) must in some way be accounted for. How this is achieved will be discussed in **Chapter 9**. Subject to this, the grant may issue to any one or more of them, up to the limit imposed by s. 114, Supreme Court Act 1981 (**8.9** below). Rule 27, NCPR requires that notice of the application shall normally be given to any executors to whom power is being reserved.

8.8.2 ADMINISTRATION

When a grant of letters of administration with will annexed or simple administration is applied for, all those having a better right to a grant than the applicant(s) must be 'cleared off' (i.e. accounted for). Again, we will consider how this should be done in **Chapter 9**.

Where there are several potential grantees in the same degree of priority, r. 27 allows the grant to be made (again, subject to the limits imposed by s. 114, Supreme Court Act 1981) to any one or more of them, without any requirement for notice to the others entitled in the same degree.

However, r. 27 further provides that preference should normally be given to:

(a) an adult rather than someone on behalf of a minor entitled in the same degree;
(b) a living person rather than the personal representative of a deceased person who, if living, would have been entitled in the same degree.

In the event of a dispute as to who should take the grant amongst those entitled in the same degree, this will be resolved on a summons before a district judge or registrar.

8.9 Personal Representatives — Number

8.9.1 EXECUTORS

A sole executor always has full authority to act — even in cases where minority or life interests arise (contrast the position of administrators — **8.9.2** below).

A testator can appoint any number of executors, but a grant of probate cannot issue to more than four — s. 114, Supreme Court Act 1981. Those who have not predeceased the testator or renounced have 'power reserved' to them (see further **Chapter 9**).

However, s. 114 does not prevent the possibility of a grant to a maximum of four executors in respect of part of the deceased's estate and another grant to four different executors in respect of another part. Thus, if the deceased had appointed four executors to deal with his/her business and four further executors to deal with the rest of the estate, two grants in respect of the different parts of the estate can be made to them all.

8.9.2 ADMINISTRATORS

Here, whether the grant is with will annexed or simple administration, s. 114 again provides for a maximum of four grantees.

However, in certain cases, it also requires that there should normally be a minimum of two (or a trust corporation). This minimum requirement arises whenever, under any will or on the intestacy, a beneficiary is an infant or there is a life interest. However, if a grant is made to two grantees as a result of this requirement and one of them then dies, there is no requirement for a replacement to be appointed: the survivor has full authority to act henceforth alone (though see **8.9.3** below).

The requirement for a minimum of two grantees in such cases does not apply, however, if a district judge or registrar (on an *ex parte* application) considers that it is 'expedient in all the circumstances' to appoint an individual as sole administrator. Nor does it apply to grants of administration pending suit (**8.5.5.3** above) or to settled land grants (**8.5.7.1** above).

8.9.3 ADDITIONAL PERSONAL REPRESENTATIVES

8.9.3.1 Rule 25, NCPR

A person entitled to a grant of administration may, without leave, apply for a grant with a person entitled in a lower degree, provided there is no other person entitled in priority to the person to be joined — or, if there are any such persons, they have all renounced. If the person sought to be joined does not have any (or any immediate) right to a grant, an *ex parte* application to a district judge or registrar will normally be required, supported by an affidavit, the consent of the proposed grantee and any other evidence required. However, such application is not required where the intended joinder is of a trust corporation.

8.9.3.2 Rule 26, NCPR

By s. 114, Supreme Court Act 1981 the court has power to appoint an additional administrator or executor, where at the time there is only one (not being a trust corporation), to act during a beneficiary's minority or the subsistence of a life interest. Under r. 26, application is made *ex parte* by any interested person to a district judge or registrar, supported by an affidavit as to the facts of the matter. The original grant, the consent of the proposed grantee and any further evidence required must also be lodged.

8.10 Personal Representatives — Renunciation

No one can be forced to accept office as an executor or administrator, though a person entitled to a grant can be forced to make up their mind whether to take a grant or not (see citation to take a grant in **12.4.2.2**). Executors or administrators are free to renounce their rights to a grant provided they have not accepted office.

8.10.1 EXECUTORS

An executor accepts office, thus losing the right to renounce, by taking a grant, or even before this by 'intermeddling' in the estate, i.e. by doing something which shows an intention to accept office. Acts of charity, humanity or necessity are not sufficient to constitute such acceptance. Thus, for example, arranging the funeral will not be enough; but writing to request payment of monies due to the estate will.

A renunciation must be in writing, signed by the renouncing executor, and containing a statement that the executor has not intermeddled. It becomes effective on being filed at the Registry (usually with the papers to lead the grant to some other person).

An executor cannot generally renounce part of the office. The office must be accepted in full (including any executorship by representation — **8.5.7.2** above), or renounced in full.

Under r. 37, NCPR, a renunciation by an executor of the right to a grant of probate does not operate as the renunciation of any rights that person may have to a grant of letters of administration (whether as beneficiary or creditor), unless there is also an express renunciation of those rights.

Retraction is permitted with the leave of a district judge or registrar under r. 37(3) — but only in exceptional circumstances will an executor be allowed to retract once a grant has been issued to someone entitled in a lower degree.

8.10.2 ADMINISTRATORS

An administrator accepts office only by taking a grant: no amount of 'intermeddling' prior to this will constitute acceptance.

Renunciation is again effected in writing, signed by the renouncing 'administrator' (no declaration that there has been no intermeddling being required in this case), and this is filed (usually) with the other papers to lead the grant to someone else. Rule 37(2) provides that an administrator who has renounced in one capacity (e.g. as a residuary beneficiary) can claim a grant in another (e.g. as a creditor), unless a district judge otherwise directs. Retraction is possible with leave of a district judge or registrar.

NINE

OATHS

[*Note: When studying this chapter you will find it helpful to have with you copies of the various forms being discussed.*]

9.1 Generally

Every application for a grant of representation must be supported by an oath — in effect, evidence in the form of an affidavit — sworn or affirmed by the personal representatives before a solicitor holding a current practising certificate and who is not a partner or employee of the firm preparing the oath.

The main purpose of the oath is to establish the applicant's title to the grant sought. Usually, pre-printed forms are completed and adapted to meet the circumstances of the particular case (but in any case where this cannot be conveniently done the oath should be drafted and engrossed in the appropriate form by the solicitor acting in the matter).

There are a number of different versions of pre-printed forms available from law stationers, which may vary slightly — e.g. in the order in which information is presented, or in what is actually pre-printed — but whose basic structure is essentially similar. They all contain marginal notes to assist in their completion. In cases of doubt or difficulty it is possible, on payment of the appropriate fee, to have an oath formally settled by the Registry. If this is done, the settled draft oath must be submitted with the sworn oath. Alternatively, the Registry is often prepared to peruse and give informal comments upon a draft oath; where this is done, the draft oath should again be lodged with the sworn papers.

In this chapter we will consider the completion of oaths for executors (**9.2**); for administrators with will annexed (**9.3**); for administrators (**9.4**); and for administrators *de bonis non* (**9.5**). In all cases, the heading will be the same:

> IN THE HIGH COURT OF JUSTICE
> FAMILY DIVISION
> THE PRINCIPAL REGISTRY   (or)
> THE DISTRICT PROBATE REGISTRY AT ....
> In the Estate of .... deceased [see **9.2.1** below]

Some stationers have different prints of the forms for use in the Principal and District Registries: in other cases, it will be necessary to adapt the form as appropriate.

In all cases, the details of the extracting solicitor should also be given: the Registry will then address any correspondence or queries to the solicitor rather than the personal representatives. It will be convenient (especially in the case of larger firms) for the solicitor's reference also to be given: this will then appear on the grant when issued and thus make it easier to identify who is dealing with the matter when this is received in the extracting solicitor's office.

9.2 Oaths for Executors

This is the appropriate oath where a grant of probate is sought by an executor appointed by the will or a codicil.

9.2.1 *IN THE ESTATE OF .... DECEASED*

This is, in effect, the final part of the heading. The true full name of the deceased should be entered here. In most cases, this will present no difficulty. However, sometimes it may be necessary to include an alternative 'alias' name — for example, because the will was not executed in the deceased's full name; because the deceased's name has changed since making the will; or because the deceased held property in different names. Whenever an alias is necessary, the deceased (wherever his or her name is to be mentioned in the oath) should be described by the true full name, followed by the alternative(s) — e.g. 'John Edward Smith otherwise John Smith'. To comply with the requirements of r. 9, NCPR it will also be necessary to furnish an explanation for the 'alias' (see **9.2.1.1** to **9.2.1.4** below).

9.2.1.1 The true full name

Normally, this will be the name on the birth certificate or, in the case of a married woman, the name of her husband (assuming she had adopted his surname). The same principles will prima facie apply in the case of a divorced woman.

9.2.1.2 Will in 'incorrect' name

This might arise, for example, because the deceased whose full name is Jane Elizabeth Smith has made her will in the name of Jane Smith. In such a case, she should be described as 'Jane Elizabeth Smith (otherwise Jane Smith)'.

It will also be necessary to swear, in the oath (at the end of the printed form) or in a separate affidavit, that 'the true name of the deceased is Jane Elizabeth Smith but that she made and executed her will in the name of Jane Smith'. In such a case, the grant will normally issue in the true name only.

9.2.1.3 Change of name

Where the testator's name has been changed since the making of the will (by deed poll, or by habit and repute and the former name has been abandoned), the full current name should be given, followed by the former name — e.g. 'John Smythe (formerly John Smith)'. The oath should also make reference to any deed poll evidencing the change (which should be produced at the Registry), or confirm the abandonment of the old and the adoption of the new names. Again, the grant when issued will normally only refer to the full correct name at the date of death.

9.2.1.4 Property in different names

Where the deceased held property in different names, again the full true name should be given first, followed by the 'alias'. It will be necessary, at the end of the oath form or in a separate affidavit, to indicate which is the true name and to include a statement that the deceased held property in the alternative name(s) — identifying at least one item of property held in the alternative name(s). For example, at the end of the pre-printed form might be added: 'And that the true name of the deceased was Jonathan Smith and that he held Blackacre in the name of John Smith'.

9.2.2 THE APPLICANTS

The first paragraph of the oath identifies those who are applying for the grant. The order should be the same as that in the will: if it is desired to change the order (e.g. to place a solicitor who has been appointed first), the consents of all the executors should be lodged — though even if this is not done in practice the grant will nevertheless be made showing the changed order.

9.2.2.1 Names

The true full name of each applicant should be given. If this differs from the name in the will/codicil containing the appointment, an explanation will be required.

If the discrepancy is slight, the matter is usually easily dealt with — e.g. 'Susan Jones (in the will called Sue Jones)'. If the name has been misspelt, again the solution is simple — e.g. 'Jonathan James (in the will written Jonathon James)'. If the name has changed on marriage the explanation (e.g.) 'Ann Evans, married woman (formerly and in the will called Ann Brown, spinster)' will suffice.

If the name has been changed by deed poll, this should be recited and the deed poll lodged for inspection. If the change has been by habit and repute, the statement in the oath must confirm the total abandonment of the old name.

Sometimes, the Registry may require further proof of the identity of an applicant. This might arise, for example, where the will appoints 'Mr Smith', or 'my wife' without naming her. Sometimes, the (short) further evidence needed can be incorporated into the oath (e.g. by including a statement that the applicant 'was the lawful wife of the deceased at the date of the will'). In other cases, it will be necessary to furnish an affidavit of identity, dealing with the circumstances at the date of the will and disposing of the possibility that there could be anyone else better fitting the description in the will.

9.2.2.2 Addresses

The full postal address of the true place of residence of each applicant should be given. Solicitors (and others acting in a professional capacity) may give their business addresses. Former addresses need not be given unless relevant in establishing the executor's identity (where this is an issue).

9.2.2.3 Occupations or descriptions

The occupation of each applicant, male or female, should be given (e.g. 'schoolteacher' or, if retired, 'retired schoolteacher'). If the applicant has no occupation, this should be stated: in the case of a woman, her marital status should be given.

9.2.3 ... MAKE OATH AND SAY ...

It is not necessary for the oath to be sworn. Applicants may, instead, affirm — in which event, the words 'make oath and say' whenever they appear should be deleted and replaced with 'do solemnly and sincerely affirm'. It will also be necessary to alter the jurat at the end of the form (in some prints this appears on the back of the form) by deleting the word 'SWORN' and substituting 'AFFIRMED'.

9.2.4 ... THAT [I/WE] BELIEVE THE PAPER WRITING NOW PRODUCED TO AND MARKED BY [ME/US] TO CONTAINS THE TRUE AND ORIGINAL LAST WILL AND TESTAMENT ...

In some prints of the oath this statement appears after the details of the deceased (see **9.2.5** below). Its purpose is to identify the document(s) which are being put forward as admissible to probate.

OATHS

This is achieved by 'marking' the document(s) concerned: the deponents (the applicants for the grant swearing the oath or making the affirmation) and the solicitor administering the oath or taking the affirmation sign the documents, thus exhibiting them to the affidavit evidence which the oath comprises. These signatures should ideally be placed well away from the text of the will, codicil or document to be incorporated, because if the will etc. is rendered unsuitable for photocopying the Registry will require an engrossment of the document concerned to be supplied.

If there is a codicil, after the word 'testament' there should be added 'with (one) (two, or as the case may be) codicil(s)'.

If for any reason the original will is not being proved, the word 'original' should be deleted.

9.2.5 DETAILS OF THE DECEASED

This part of the form requires basic information regarding the deceased testator.

9.2.5.1 Name

As already discussed (in **9.2.1** above) the deceased's full true name should be given again here, with any alias.

9.2.5.2 Address

The last residential (postal) address of the testator should be given. If this is different from the address in the will or codicil, the previous address should be added after the words 'formerly of . . .' (any intervening changes of address are ignored). If the addresses are the same, the words 'formerly of ' should be deleted.

9.2.5.3 Date of death

Usually, the death certificate will give the date of death, which should be inserted here. (It will not normally be necessary to submit a copy of the death certificate.)

Sometimes, although there is no doubt that the deceased is indeed dead, it is not possible to give an exact date of death: in such a case, the wording of the oath must be adapted to read 'who was known to be alive on . . . and whose dead body was found on . . .'. Where it is believed that death has occurred but no body has been found, leave may be given by the Registry to 'swear death'. Here, the oath should specify that the deceased died 'on or since' the date indicated in the order and give details of such order, following its wording closely.

9.2.5.4 Age

The testator's age should be stated — the best estimate being sufficient where this is uncertain.

9.2.5.5 Domicile

Unless otherwise directed by a district judge or registrar, the deceased's domicile at the date of death must be included in the oath. Where the deceased died domiciled in England or Wales, domicile should be sworn as 'England and Wales'. The sworn domicile will appear in the grant: this may have important consequences in relation to the recognition of grants within the different jurisdictions in the United Kingdom (see **8.3.3.1**).

In some prints of the form, domicile 'in England and Wales' is pre-printed; in others this information will have to be added.

9.2.6 SETTLED LAND

The personal representatives must state whether there is/is not any settled land — it is quite wrong simply to delete the whole paragraph where there is no such land in the estate. In fact, the only permissible deletion is of the word '(no)' where there is, in fact, such land for which a separate grant will be needed. In this event, it is enough to disclose in the oath its existence: it is not necessary to give details of the settlement.

Note also that the statement is about the existence (or otherwise) of settled land which was settled prior to the death (and not by the deceased's will/codicil) and remains settled notwithstanding the death of the deceased tenant for life. Thus, if the land only becomes settled land under the terms of the deceased's will, or on the death of the deceased it ceases to be settled land, the correct statement to be included in the oath is that there is 'no' such land; the paragraph should therefore be left as printed.

9.2.7 EXECUTOR'S TITLE

This purpose of this part of the form is to establish the 'capacity' in which the proving executors claim to be entitled to the grant. The discussion which follows is not intended to be exhaustive, but simply to highlight some of the more commonly met situations.

9.2.7.1 Relationship to the deceased

As we have seen (in **8.3.1**) an executor's 'title' essentially depends upon appointment as executor by the will or codicil, the grant only being strictly required as evidence of that title. The fact that an executor is related to the deceased is therefore normally immaterial and need not be stated. However, it will be necessary to state the applicant's relationship to the deceased where identity is an issue: for example, if the will appoints 'my daughter' without naming her. If the will appoints 'my wife' or 'my husband' without naming the spouse concerned, the oath should include a statement to the effect that the applicant is the lawful widow(er) and was lawfully married to the deceased at the time of the making of the will.

9.2.7.2 Where all appointed are applying

The wording to be used to describe the title of the proving applicant(s) will obviously depend upon the circumstances of the particular case. For example:

Only one appointee	*the sole executor/executrix*
All male, or male and female	*the executors*
All female	*the executrixes*
Implied appointment	*the executor according to the tenor*

9.2.7.3 Not all applying

Again the wording to be used to describe the entitlement of those applying will depend upon the circumstances. For example:

Some have died	*the surviving executor(s)/executrix(es)*
Some have renounced	*one (or two etc.) of the executors/executrixes*

In this case it is not necessary to recite the fact of renunciation by the other executor(s), but it helps the Registry if this is done.

However, the renunciation itself must be filed with the papers to lead the grant.

Power is to be reserved	*one (or two etc.) of the executors/executrixes*

OATHS

In this situation, the name(s) of the executor(s) to whom power is to be reserved should be entered in the space provided in the margin. Further, unless a district judge or registrar dispenses with this requirement, the oath must also state (r. 27, NCPR) that notice of the application for the grant has been given to the executor(s) to whom power is being reserved. This is done at the end of the printed form: some forms have the necessary statement pre-printed — in which case it should be deleted if not required.

9.2.7.4 Partners in a firm

Where partners in a firm (e.g. of solicitors) are appointed by name and some have predeceased or renounced, or power is to be reserved to one or more of the named partners, the procedures described in **9.2.7.3** above should be followed.

Where, however, the appointment is of partners in a firm without naming them (e.g. 'the partners at the date of my death in Solicitor & Co.') and not all of them wish to apply, it is sufficient for the oath to contain a statement that the applicant is/was a partner (or the applicants are/were partners) at the appropriate date. Power can be reserved to 'the other partners' without naming them, and notice need not be given to those not wishing to act (r. 27(1A), NCPR).

9.2.8 DUTIES OF THE PERSONAL REPRESENTATIVES

In practice, little needs to be done with this paragraph of the oath, except where there is settled land (see **9.2.6** above), when it will be necessary to insert the words 'save and except settled land'.

9.2.9 VALUE OF THE ESTATE PASSING UNDER THE GRANT

There are two paragraphs relating to the value of the gross and net estate passing under the grant. One of these must be completed and the other deleted.

9.2.9.1 The estate passing under the grant

This is the deceased's free estate in the United Kingdom (in England and Wales only if the deceased died domiciled outside England and Wales) in respect of which the grant is needed as evidence of the personal representatives' title. Property which does not pass to the personal representatives as such is not relevant here, for example:

(a) joint property passing by survivorship;
(b) nominated property;
(c) gifts *inter vivos* (including gifts with a reservation);
(d) *donationes mortis causa*;
(e) settled property interests (other than reversionary interests).

9.2.9.2 First paragraph

This should be completed (and the second paragraph deleted) only if the estate is an excepted estate for inheritance tax purposes (see **10.2**). Where it is appropriate to complete this paragraph, the gross and net figures are not stated precisely, but rather as not exceeding the upper limit of the appropriate band. In respect of a death on or after 1 April 1991, the limit for the gross estate will be £125,000, and the net estate should be stated to be not exceeding (as the case may be) £10,000, £25,000, £40,000, £70,000, £100,000 or £125,000. Thus, for example, if the estate is an excepted estate and the value of the estate passing under the will is £105,000 (gross) and £90,000 (net), the figures to be inserted in the first paragraph would be £125,000 (gross) and £100,000 (net).

These bands of the net estate also serve to fix the court fees payable on lodging the papers at the selected Registry. Where the net estate does not exceed £10,000, no fee is payable. Thereafter, the fees are currently:

Net estate not exceeding	Court fee
£25,000	£40
£40,000	£80
£70,000	£150
£100,000	£215
£125,000*	£300

*The fixed fee of £300 is payable, in fact, on net estates up to and including £200,000 (see **9.2.9.3** below).

9.2.9.3 Second paragraph

This paragraph should be completed (and the first one deleted) in all other cases — i.e. whenever an Inland Revenue account is required. In such cases, the figures to be shown in the oath are the gross and net figures from the probate summary on the appropriate form of account — on page 4 of the Form IHT 202 and on page 11 of the Form IHT 200.

The fixed fees as described in **9.2.9.2** are payable on a net estate not exceeding £200,000. Where the net estate exceeds £200,000, the fees payable on the excess above that figure are £50 for every additional £100,000 or part thereof.

9.2.10 OTHER MATTERS

The blank space at the end of the printed form can be used to provide any further information which might be required — e.g. as to an alias (see **9.2.1** above); as to the notice required under r. 27, NCPR — if not pre-printed — (see **9.2.7.3** above); or as to the identity of the applicant (see **9.2.2** above). If the matter cannot be dealt with concisely, it will be necessary to file a separate affidavit.

9.2.11 JURAT

Each deponent must swear, or affirm, the oath before an independent solicitor (or Justice of the Peace). It is not necessary for the names of all the deponents to be inserted if they are all swearing or affirming at the same time. Otherwise, a separate jurat should be drawn and completed for each deponent.

9.3 Oaths for Administrators with Will Annexed

As we saw in **8.5.2**, a grant of letters of administration with will annexed is appropriate whenever there is a will and a grant is for some reason not going to be made to an executor (because, perhaps none were appointed, or those appointed are all dead, or have renounced).

Many of the points discussed in **9.2** above regarding the completion of an oath for executors apply equally to the oath for administrators with the will. In this section we will concentrate upon the points of difference.

9.3.1 THE APPLICANTS

Entitlement to apply for a grant of administration with will annexed is determined by r. 20, NCPR (see **8.5.2.1** above). The order in which the applicants' names appear in the oath should follow that order.

9.3.2 MINORITY AND LIFE INTERESTS

We have already seen (in **8.9.2**) that if a minority or life interest arises, a grant of letters of administration (whether or not with will annexed) will normally only issue to two grantees (or a

OATHS

trust corporation). An oath for administrators with will annexed must contain a statement as to whether or not there are minority or life interests arising — either under the terms of the will, or under the intestacy rules where the deceased died partially intestate. This part of the oath form must, therefore, always be appropriately completed.

9.3.2.1 Minority interest

If the only minor beneficiary at the date of death has attained 18 by the time of the swearing or affirmation of the oath, the statement may be made that 'no' minority interest arises.

9.3.2.2 Life Interest

If a life interest arose on the death but has since come to an end (e.g. because the life tenant has since died) the statement in the oath may be made that 'no life interest now arises' and the circumstances causing the cessation of the life interest will need to be explained (by an additional statement at the end of the printed form).

9.3.2.3 Life interest under intestacy rules

Where there is a partial intestacy, the intestacy rules (discussed in **Chapter 2**) govern the entitlement to the property undisposed of by the will. In deciding whether, under those rules, a minority or life interest arises, certain deductions may be made (discussed in detail in **9.4.3** below). These deductions may effectively 'eliminate' an apparent minority or life interest (because when the deductions have been claimed the estate is in fact less than the amount of the spouse's statutory legacy). In such a case, the oath may properly state that no such interests arise but should include an explanation (at the end of the printed form) to justify this.

9.3.3 CLEARING

The oath must always 'clear off' — in effect, account for — all those who under r. 20, NCPR (**8.5.2.1**) have a 'better right' to the grant than the applicant(s). There is no need to account for anyone else in the same category as the applicant(s), nor to give notice of the application to any such person(s).

All oaths for administration with will annexed therefore have to account for the fact that no executor is applying by showing (as the case may be) that no executors were appointed, or that they are all dead or have renounced.

What further clearing is required will then depend upon how far down the list the applicant comes. Where there is a partial intestacy and an applicant is seeking a grant as a person entitled to share in the undisposed of property under the intestacy rules, anyone under those rules having a 'better' claim than the applicant will also have to be cleared.

9.3.4 CAPACITY

The oath must then state the precise capacity in which the applicant claims to be entitled to the grant. This, remember, depends essentially upon entitlement to share in the estate rather than relationship to the deceased. Thus, for example:

(a) 'the residuary legatee and devisee under the said will';
(b) 'the daughters of the deceased and two of the persons entitled to share in the undisposed of estate of the said deceased';
(c) 'one of the specific legatees and devisees named in the said will'.

9.3.5 DUTIES OF THE PERSONAL REPRESENTATIVES

Where the grant is to be issued 'for the use and benefit' of (e.g. a minor or person suffering from mental incapacity — see **8.5.4.1** and **8.5.4.2** above) the appropriate limitation should be inserted in the space at the end of the first duty listed in the printed form. Thus, for example:

(a) 'for the use and benefit of . . . until he/she shall attain the age of 18 years'; *limited in time*
(b) 'for the use and benefit of . . . and during his/her incapacity'.

9.4 Oaths for Administrators

The grant of simple administration is appropriate where the deceased died wholly intestate. The entitlement to the grant essentially depends (as we saw in **8.5.3**) upon the applicant's relationship to the deceased.

Many of the comments made in explanation of the practice in completing the oath for executors (**9.2** above) and the oath for administrators with will annexed (**9.3** above) are equally relevant in this case also. Again, we will here concentrate upon the differences.

9.4.1 THE APPLICANTS

The order in which the names of the applicants are set out in the form should follow the order of priority in r. 22, NCPR (see **8.5.3.1**), but can in practice be changed at the request of all the applicants.

In the case of simple administration, no question of a discrepancy with the will can, of course, arise.

9.4.2 CLEARING OFF

Following the words '. . . *domiciled in . . . Intestate*' it is necessary to account for those with a better right to the grant than the applicant. Specifically, three matters must here be addressed.

9.4.2.1 Status of the deceased

The deceased's marital status must first be indicated:

(a) 'a bachelor/spinster'
(b) 'a married man/woman'
(c) 'a widow/widower'
(d) 'a single man/woman' (where the deceased's marriage had been ended by a decree absolute of divorce). The details of the divorce (including the name of the court and the date of the decree) must be recited and it must also be sworn or affirmed that the deceased had not remarried. If the decree was made outside England and Wales an office copy of the decree must be lodged.

Where the deceased's marriage has been annulled, the deceased should be described as having the status which he/she had immediately before the 'marriage' concerned. Again, the circumstances should be explained in the oath, and where a decree of nullity was made by a court outside England and Wales an office copy of the decree lodged.

If the deceased was still married but there was at the date of death a decree of judicial separation in force, the deceased should be described as 'a married man/woman' and details of the decree and a statement that the separation continued up to the date of death should be included.

OATHS

9.4.2.2 Clearing of those entitled under r. 22, NCPR

It is not necessary to clear anyone entitled under this Rule in the same category as the applicant (nor is it necessary to give notice of the application to any such person). Thus, for example, if the deceased had four children, an application may be made by one of them (two if a minority or life interest arises) without reference to the others.

However, it is essential to account for all those who might have a better right to the grant. This is, in effect, done by showing that the deceased was not survived by any relative(s) in the categories higher than that of the applicant(s), or that any survivors have since died or renounced, or have failed to appear to a citation (see **12.4**).

In the simplest case — i.e. where there are no surviving relatives with a better right to the grant — the wording used is as follows:

To clear	*Swear that deceased died*
Spouse	a bachelor, spinster, widow(er), single man/woman
Children/issue	without issue
Parents	(or) parent
Brothers/sisters/their issue	(or) brother or sister of the whole [or half] blood or issue thereof
Grandparents	(or) grandparent
Uncles/aunts/their issue	or uncle or aunt of the whole [or half] blood or issue thereof

Where a relative in a higher category has survived but is not seeking a grant (e.g. having renounced) the wording of the oath must deal with this: e.g. '... Intestate leaving ... his lawful widow and the only person entitled to his estate him surviving who has since duly renounced letters of administration'. The renunciation must be lodged with the papers to lead the grant.

9.4.2.3 Clearing of 'any other person entitled in priority ... by virtue of any enactment'

These words are designed to clear any illegitimate, legitimated and adopted children and remoter issue of the deceased: they cannot be used as a 'short cut' formula for clearing those entitled under r. 22.

If the application is being made by the surviving spouse or children/issue of the deceased, these words should normally be deleted.

Where, however, a spouse is applying as the person solely entitled (because there are no issue) and the deceased's net estate exceeds £75,000 but not £125,000, the oath should state that the deceased died '... without issue or any other person entitled ... by virtue of any enactment' so as to establish that the applicant is indeed solely entitled.

Similarly, where the net estate exceeds £125,000 and the spouse is claiming the whole estate (because there are no issue, parents or brothers or sisters of the whole blood or their issue), the oath should state that the deceased died 'without issue parent brother or sister of the whole blood or their issue thereof or any other person etc.'.

If the applicant is from any category in r. 22 below children or other issue, the words 'or any other person entitled ... by virtue of any enactment' must always be left in.

9.4.3 MINORITY AND LIFE INTERESTS

The oath for administrators must (as with the application for a grant with will annexed) contain a statement as to whether or not any such interests arise. A minority interest may of course arise whenever a beneficiary entitled to a share under the intestacy rules is under 18. A life interest will arise under the intestacy rules where the deceased is survived by a spouse and issue and the value of the estate is greater than the spouse's statutory legacy (see **2.2.2.1**).

In most cases, it will be clear whether any such interests arise. However, this will not be so where the gross estate does not greatly exceed the £75,000 statutory legacy to which the spouse is entitled. In such a case, whether or not a minority or life interest arises will depend upon how much is ultimately available to the administrators for actual distribution (i.e. after all the deceased's debts and the estate's expenses etc. have been met). Further, it is strictly the value of the estate at the time of the payment of the statutory legacy which will determine the matter. How should the statement required in the oath be completed in such cases?

The value at the date of death clearly has to be used, and the following deductions are allowed in determining the net value of the estate:

(a) the value of the personal chattels (as defined by s. 55(1)(x), Administration of Estates Act 1925);
(b) debts;
(c) any inheritance tax payable out of the estate (without any right of recovery from any other person or property);
(d) fair and reasonable costs
(e) probate court fees.

If after claiming deduction for these amounts the net figure is below £75,000, it may be sworn that there are no minority or life interests, but the oath must contain an explanation (see **9.4.5** below).

9.4.4 CAPACITY IN WHICH GRANT SOUGHT

Essentially, as we have seen, the applicant's title depends upon the relationship to the deceased and entitlement to the estate. The oath must contain a precise statement as to both these matters.

9.4.4.1 Relationship

Some of the more commonly met descriptions to be used here are:

Spouse	*lawful husband/lawful widow*
Child	*son/daughter* — note that this is the appropriate description whether the child's parents were (or were not) married at the time of its birth
Adopted child	*lawful adopted son/daughter* — note that the oath should contain a statement giving details of the adoption order and that it is still subsisting
Grandchild	*grandson/granddaughter* — note that the oath will have to show that the grandchild's parent had predeceased so as to give the grandchild a beneficial interest under the statutory trusts
Brother or sister	*brother/sister of the whole [or half] blood*
Nephew or niece	*nephew/niece of the whole [or half] blood* — again, it will be necessary for the oath to show that the applicant's parent has predeceased so as to give the applicant a share of the estate
Parent	*father/mother*
Grandparent	*grandfather/grandmother*
Uncle or aunt	*uncle/aunt of the whole [or half] blood*
Cousin	*cousin german of the whole [or half] blood* — again, the oath must show that the applicant's parent has predeceased so as to give the cousin a share of the estate.

OATHS

9.4.4.2 Entitlement to the estate

The oath must show the applicant(s) entitlement to the estate. For example:

(a) 'the only person(s) entitled to the estate';
(b) 'one [two etc.] of the persons entitled to share in the estate'.

9.4.5 GROSS AND NET ESTATE

One of the two paragraphs should (as before) be completed and the other deleted. The following points should, however, be additionally noted.

9.4.5.1 Excepted estate

Where the net estate falls within the range £70,000 to £100,000, the normal practice would be to swear the net estate as not exceeding £100,000. If it is in fact less than £75,000 so that the spouse is solely entitled, it should be sworn as not exceeding £75,000 — thus 'confirming' the spouse's sole entitlement.

9.4.5.2 Marginal cases

Where the gross estate exceeds the amount of the statutory legacy but (after claiming the permitted deductions identified in **9.4.2.3** above) the net estate does not, the oath should show (by the inclusion of an additional statement at the end of the pre-printed form) that 'after deduction of the value of personal chattels, debts, inheritance tax, costs amounting to £... and probate fees the net value of the estate is £...'.

9.5 Oaths for Administrators *de bonis non*

We have already discussed (in **8.5.7.2**) the circumstances in which a grant of administration *de bonis non* may be required. We saw there that if the original grant was of probate or administration with will annexed, the *de bonis non* grant will be with will annexed. Where the deceased whose estate has not been completely administered died wholly intestate, the *de bonis non* grant will be of simple administration.

The following are principal points to note regarding the oath required to lead the appropriate *de bonis non* grant.

9.5.1 PRIOR GRANT

The oath must give details of the deceased's death and of the issue of the original grant. Where the deceased left a will, normally an office copy of the original issued by the Registry is 'marked' (an 'unofficial' copy is not acceptable unless a district judge or registrar gives leave). If the present application is to a Registry other than that which issued the original grant, an office copy of the original grant should also be lodged with the papers to lead the *de bonis non* grant.

9.5.2 REASON FOR PRESENT APPLICATION

A statement must be included explaining the necessity (e.g. the death or incapacity of the original grantee) for the *de bonis non* grant. If the original grant was of probate, this explanation must show that the chain of representation has been broken (e.g. because the sole executor has died intestate).

9.5.3 MINORITY AND LIFE INTERESTS

It must be sworn or affirmed whether there is (at the date of the *de bonis non* application) any such interest — in which event there will normally have to be two applicants.

9.5.4 CAPACITY

The applicant's title to the grant is determined by r. 20, NCPR (**8.5.2.1**) where the original grant was of probate or administration with will annexed, and r. 22 (**8.5.3.1**) where the original grant was of simple administration. Those having a better right under the appropriate Rule must be cleared off.

9.5.5 VALUE OF THE ESTATE

The gross and net values to be shown in the oath are of the estate remaining unadministered.

TEN

INLAND REVENUE ACCOUNTS

[*Note: When studying this chapter you will find it helpful to have with you copies of the various forms being discussed.*]

10.1 Generally

Unless the estate is an 'excepted estate' (see **10.2** below), it will not normally be possible for the personal representatives to obtain a grant of representation until they have submitted an Inland Revenue account, giving details of all the property in the deceased's taxable estate and its value, and (subject to the instalment option) paid any inheritance tax for which they are liable — s. 109, Supreme Court Act 1981. As we have seen (in **6.8.1**) the personal representatives are under a duty to deliver an account (normally) within 12 months after the end of the month of death. However, they will in practice want to be in a position to do so much earlier than this, because interest will begin to run six months after the end of the month of death.

In this chapter, we will examine in detail the completion of the two forms of account in most common use in practice — IHT 202 (**10.3**) and IHT 200 (**10.4**). Where tax is payable, we will examine (in **10.5**) some of the ways in which payment may be funded. We will then examine briefly the Corrective account (CAP D-3) needed where for some reason the original account is 'incorrect' and Form CAP A5-C which is required in cases where a second grant to an estate is necessary (**10.6**).

In order to complete the appropriate account, it will be necessary for the solicitor acting for the personal representatives to obtain details of the various assets and liabilities in the estate, including property which passes on the death otherwise than through them (such as property of which the deceased was a beneficial joint tenant; property in which the deceased had an interest under a settlement; nominated property; property passing under a *donatio mortis causa*). The value of all such assets and liabilities must be established. This is a straightforward-enough process in many cases, simply involving correspondence (e.g. with the bank, building society, insurance company, etc.) to ascertain the amount due to the estate. In other cases, expert assistance may be required (e.g. from a surveyor or stockbroker) in order to establish the open market value of the property concerned at the date of death.

In ascertaining the extent and value of the taxable estate, the personal representatives (and thus the solicitor acting for them) are required to make the fullest enquiries that are reasonably practicable in the circumstances — failure to do so may lead to penalties being imposed. Where an account is required, this must be completed to the best of the personal representatives' knowledge and belief. Again, there may be penalties (and even the liability to prosecution) for failure to disclose property on which tax may be payable.

INLAND REVENUE ACCOUNTS

The account forms are essentially for 'self-assessment' of the taxable estate and any tax payable. The values shown in the account will ultimately have to be 'agreed' with the Capital Taxes Office (in the case of land with the local district valuer), but this is usually done after the grant has been issued. The solicitor acting for the personal representatives must calculate the tax (if any) and, if tax is payable, send the account (with a cheque for the amount of the tax and any interest due from the personal representatives) to the Financial Services Office in Worthing for receipting. Alternatively, it may be taken (not posted) for immediate receipting to Somerset House in London. A preliminary check of the calculations is made at this time, but a fuller examination of the form will be carried out after the issue of the grant. Once the account has been receipted, it may be lodged at the selected Registry with the other papers to lead the grant.

If no tax is payable, which as we shall see must be the case if IHT 202 is correctly used and may be so even where IHT 200 is appropriate, there is no need to submit the account to Worthing. The account must, however, exceptionally be sent to the Capital Taxes Office for assessment before applying for the grant if:

(a) it is claimed that the deceased died domiciled outside the United Kingdom;
(b) exemption is claimed for any heritage property;
(c) tax is to be paid from monies in a National Savings Bank account, or from the proceeds of National Savings Certificates, National Savings Income Bonds, Premium Bonds or certain government securities;
(d) the grant is required for settled land (i.e. settled prior to the death and which remains settled after the death).

10.2 Excepted Estates

If the estate is an 'excepted estate' there is no requirement to file an account in order to obtain a grant of representation. However, an account must be filed in two situations:

(a) if the Capital Taxes Office so requires by notice in writing within 35 days of the issue of the grant; or
(b) if it is subsequently discovered that the estate is not, after all, an excepted estate — in which event an account must be filed within six months of that discovery.

An 'excepted estate' is (in the case of someone dying after 1 April 1991) one where the following conditions are all met:

(a) the deceased died domiciled in the United Kingdom;
(b) the estate comprises only property which passes under the deceased's will or under the intestacy rules, or by a statutory nomination, or beneficially by survivorship;
(c) the total gross value of such property did not exceed £125,000;
(d) not more than £15,000 of that gross value is attributable to property situated outside the United Kingdom;
(e) the deceased made no lifetime transfers (including PETs) chargeable to tax within the seven years prior to the death.

Thus, if the estate of the deceased includes trust property, or the deceased has an existing cumulative total at the date of death, the estate cannot be an excepted estate. Nor, strictly, can it be such an estate if there is property passing under a *donatio mortis causa* — though it seems that if the other conditions are all met the Revenue will not, in practice, press the point. In deciding whether condition (c) is met, where the deceased was a beneficial joint tenant only the value of the deceased's interest is taken into account.

INLAND REVENUE ACCOUNTS

10.3 Form IHT 202

Where the estate is not an excepted estate, this shorter account (Form IHT 202N if the grant is being sought in Northern Ireland) should be used whenever possible. Only where IHT 202 cannot properly be used should the longer account IHT 200 (see **10.4** below) be used.

10.3.1 WHEN IHT 202 IS APPROPRIATE

The following conditions must all be met:

(a) the deceased must have been domiciled in the United Kingdom at the date of death;
(b) the estate comprises only property passing by will or on intestacy, or by a statutory nomination, or joint property passing beneficially by survivorship;
(c) all such property was situated in the United Kingdom;
(d) the deceased had made no gifts with a reservation, nor any LCTs or PETs within seven years of death;
(e) the deceased did not within seven years of death enjoy any interest in settled property;
(f) the net estate (after exemptions and reliefs have been claimed) does not exceed the inheritance tax threshold at death (i.e. currently does not exceed £150,000);
(g) the gross estate (before exemptions and reliefs are claimed) does not exceed twice the inheritance tax threshold at the date of death (i.e. currently does not exceed £300,000).

10.3.2 THE FORM

The latest version — IHT 202 (1993) — is a four-page document, with two inserts (IHT 37 and IHT 40 (see **Appendix**) — discussed in detail in the context of IHT 200 in **10.4** below): these are discarded if not required in a particular case. If there is insufficient space provided on the form, the details required should be supplied in a schedule, headed with the full name and date of death of the deceased.

The Inland Revenue have issued guidance notes on the completion of Inland Revenue accounts (IHT 210) and there are various marginal notes in IHT 202 which make reference to this document. Many of these are discussed in detail in **10.4** below in the context of IHT 200.

Apart from questions which must be answered, the form should be left blank where there is nothing to be recorded under a particular heading.

10.3.2.1 Page 1

This page deals with a number of formal matters and its completion should normally present few difficulties.

10.3.2.2 Page 2 — *Nominated and Joint Property*

The first two questions must be answered by ticking the appropriate boxes: if either of the answers is 'Yes' further information is required, as indicated.

The first question concerns any statutory nominations which may have been made by the deceased. The particulars of any such property should be shown in the space below.

The second question — concerning joint property interests — has a number of 'supplementaries' to be dealt with in the event of a 'Yes' answer, including the response to two further questions. If the deceased was a beneficial joint tenant, the interest will pass by survivorship and details should be provided in this part of the form. If, on the other hand, the deceased's interest was as a beneficial

INLAND REVENUE ACCOUNTS

tenant in common it will pass as part of the free estate and be shown later on Page 2 or on Page 3 as appropriate.

In showing the value of any of the deceased's assets or liabilities on the form, pence are ignored — simply show the £s figure: thus, for example, an asset or a liability of £5.75 would both feature on the form as £5.

Only liabilities relating to the property disclosed in this part of the form should be shown here — e.g. the deceased's share of the mortgage charged upon property of which the deceased was a beneficial joint tenant.

The 'Net value' figure at [A] is carried to Page 4 — *Tax Summary*.

[The heading on Page 2 — *Section 2A — Nominated and Joint Property — Without the Instalment Option* — appears to be an 'error'.]

10.3.2.3 Pages 2 and 3 — *Free Estate*

In this part of the form it is necessary to disclose (again, in £s only) the details of the property in respect of which the grant is required by the personal representatives — i.e. the property passing under the terms of the deceased's will or on intestacy.

Note that the form effectively identifies two categories of such property; *Property without the Instalment Option* and *Property with the Instalment Option*. (We discussed the circumstances in which inheritance tax can be paid by instalments in **6.8.2.2**.) The gross value at the date of death of any items in the deceased's estate falling in the respective categories are first listed, and then the liabilities. Thus, for example, the value of the house Blackacre which was beneficially owned by the deceased, should be shown on Page 3 (and further details given on IHT 37), with any mortgage shown at the bottom of Page 3 (and not halfway down that page).

The various totals [B], [E], [C] and [F] are then carried to Page 4.

10.3.2.4 Page 4 — *Probate Summary*

The totals at [B] and [C] from Page 3 are added together to give at [D] the gross estate for Probate purposes. The 'liabilities totals' at [E] and [F] from Page 3 are then aggregated to give total [G], which is then deducted from [D] to give — at [H] — the net estate for probate purposes. The totals [D] and [H] will be the gross and net estate figures needed to complete the appropriate form of oath (see **Chapter 9**). They will also appear on the grant in due course.

10.3.2.5 Page 4 — *Tax Summary*

In this part of the form, the gross and net estates for tax purposes are identified. The gross estate [J] comprises the net value of the nominated and joint property (total [A] from Page 2) and the net estate for probate purposes (total [H] above). From this must be deducted any exemptions and reliefs (e.g. spouse or charity exemptions; business or agricultural property reliefs) totalled at [K]. Total [J] less total [K] gives — at [L] — the net estate for tax purposes. If IHT 202 has been properly used, the figure at [L] must currently be below £150,000.

10.3.2.6 Page 4 — *Declaration* and *Warning*

It is necessary to indicate the grant being sought by the personal representatives and complete the various declarations by them. They should then sign and date the form, which can then be lodged with the other papers to lead the grant at the selected Registry.

INLAND REVENUE ACCOUNTS

10.4 Form IHT 200

Where an estate is not an excepted estate and Form IHT 202 is not appropriate, the Form IHT 200 (IHT 200N if the grant is being sought in Northern Ireland) must be completed if the deceased died domiciled in the United Kingdom. Where the deceased died domiciled outside the United Kingdom, Form IHT 201 should be used; this form (which is substantially similar to the Form IHT 200) is not further considered in this book.

Essentially, the purpose of the Form IHT 200 is to identify the taxable estate on death (including settled property interests and gifts with a reservation) and any cumulative total of lifetime transfers. After any available exemptions and reliefs have been claimed, the tax payable (if any) is calculated. Where tax is payable the completed form (after signature by the personal representatives and the solicitor acting for them) is submitted with a cheque for the tax to the Capital Taxes Office for receipting; having been receipted it is then lodged at the chosen Registry with the other papers to lead the grant.

The current version of the form is IHT 200 (1993). There are 12 pages and the form is supplied with the two inserts — IHT 37 and IHT 40 — for use if required. Again, there are marginal references to various notes in Form IHT 210. If there is insufficient room on the printed form to give the information required, schedules should again be prepared. These should be headed with the full name and date of death of the deceased and, to assist cross-referencing, sequentially identified in the main body of the form and in the schedule itself.

As with IHT 202, the value of the various assets and liabilities should be shown in £s only — though when it comes to the calculation of any tax due, pence are not ignored! Again, as with IHT 202, except where a question is required to be answered, it is not necessary to make any entry unless there is something to be recorded under any given Section or heading.

10.4.1 PAGE 1

This deals with essentially formal matters — details of the solicitors acting, and information regarding the deceased and those intending to apply for the grant.

10.4.2 PAGE 2 — SECTION 1 — LIFETIME GIFTS OR TRANSFERS OF VALUE

All the questions in Section 1 must be answered — and if in the affirmative further information will have to be supplied.

10.4.2.1 Question 1

The purpose of this question is to establish whether the deceased had made any LCTs or PETs within the seven years prior to the death. A 'yes' answer is not required if the only gifts made in this period were covered by the spouse exemption (**6.3.2.1**); or were gifts of money not exceeding £3,000 in any one tax year and the personal representatives are satisfied that they are within the normal expenditure out of income exemption (**6.3.1.3**); or were within the small gifts exemption (**6.3.1.2**); or were gifts of money or quoted shares/securities which (together with any other gifts not included in the present list) are covered by the annual exclusion (**6.3.1.1**).

Where the deceased had made LCTs and/or PETs within the seven years prior to death, a list (in chronological order) should be given in the space provided lower down the page (see **10.4.2.5** below).

10.4.2.2 Question 2

This is intended to establish whether the deceased had (within seven years of the death) paid premiums on a policy of life assurance (whether upon the life of the deceased or someone else)

INLAND REVENUE ACCOUNTS

which did not 'belong' to the deceased or the deceased's spouse. If the policy proceeds are payable to the deceased's personal representatives they are part of the deceased's estate and should be included in Section 3A of the form on Page 4. The policies to which the question relates are essentially trust policies not forming part of the deceased's estate or that of the deceased's spouse. If there are any such policies, full details should be given in a schedule.

10.4.2.3 Question 3

If the deceased had, again within seven years of the death, ceased to be entitled to a beneficial interest in possession in settled property (e.g. by virtue of an advancement to the remainderman, or by partial/total surrender of the life interest) there would at that time have been a PET (unless an exemption was applicable). This would therefore become chargeable upon the life tenant's death within seven years. If the answer to this question is 'yes', full details of the settlement and of the circumstances in which the deceased ceased to be entitled must be given in a schedule.

10.4.2.4 Question 4

The purpose of this question is to establish whether the deceased at any time on/after 18 March 1986 (and even if more than seven years prior to the death) had made any gifts with a reservation (see **6.2.1.2**). If so, and the benefit is still 'reserved' at the date of death, the value of the property at that date (not at the date of the gift) must be shown in Section 5 on Page 8. If the reservation ceased within the seven years prior to the death there will have been a PET at that time, and the appropriate details should be given.

10.4.2.5 Details of lifetime gifts

Here it is necessary to list in chronological order any LCTs, PETs and gifts with a reservation. The chargeable value for each should be entered — i.e. after taking into account any available exemptions and reliefs, including any available annual exclusion (**6.3.1.1**). The total value of chargeable gifts made within seven years of the death — the deceased's lifetime cumulative total — should be carried to Page 10 Box A. However, if the property was subject to a reservation still effective at the date of death its value should instead be shown in Section 5 on Page 8 (**10.4.2.4**).

A separate schedule should identify any LCTs made within the seven years prior to the earliest transfer listed on the form but more than seven years before the death. Such an LCT is not itself liable to the supplementary charge (because outside the cumulation period) but does affect the cumulative total in respect of any LCTs and PETs now chargeable made within seven years thereafter. The total of any such gifts is not to be carried to Page 10: the Revenue only needs this information so as to be able to check the tax payable in respect of the chargeable transfers made within seven years of death.

10.4.2.6 Superannuation benefits

The question is concerned with pension etc. arrangements which may have been made by or on behalf of the deceased — apart from the sate retirement pension. If the answer is 'yes', a further question must be answered concerning any lump-sum benefit which might be payable on the death. If any such benefit is payable to the deceased's personal representatives as of right, or if the deceased could have nominated or appointed to any person, then this question must be answered in the affirmative and the details given in Section 3A on Page 5 (under the heading 'Other personal property'). However, if the payment is a matter for the discretion of the trustees of the scheme the answer is 'no' even where the deceased may have given a (non-binding) indication of his/her wishes.

10.4.3 PAGE 3 — SECTION 2 — NOMINATED AND JOINT PROPERTY

The questions at the top of the page must both be answered — and if in the affirmative details must be supplied as indicated.

10.4.3.1 Nominated property

The question relates to property which has been the subject of a statutory nomination (see **8.4.2.1**(b)). If there has been such a nomination, the details must be supplied in Section 2A. If not, the property concerned will be part of the deceased's estate to be disclosed in Section 3A.

10.4.3.2 Joint property

The question relates to the deceased's joint property interest as a beneficial joint tenant or tenant in common. In many cases, any such interest will have been enjoyed with the deceased's spouse: in this event, the separate statement relating to the history of the joint ownership need not be provided. However, in all cases the remaining questions relating to the joint property should be answered, and if in the affirmative the details provided as directed:

(a) if the property was situated outside the United Kingdom, in Section 4;
(b) if the property was held under a beneficial joint tenancy and situated in the United Kingdom, in Section 2
(c) if the property was held under a beneficial tenancy in common, so that the deceased's interest passes under the will or the intestacy rules, in Section 3.

In each case, if the property concerned does not qualify for the instalment option, its value should be shown in Part A of the appropriate Section; if qualifying for the instalment option (it does not matter whether this is being exercised) it should be shown in Part B.

10.4.3.3 *Section 2A — Particulars*

The gross value of any nominated or joint property not qualifying for the instalment option should first be disclosed. In the case of joint property, the value of the deceased's fractional share should be entered. This will include the deceased's share of any mortgage protection policy (unless this was in the sole name of the deceased in which event it should appear in Section 3A on Page 4). In the case of property producing income, the deceased's share apportioned to the date of death should be included.

So far as liabilities are concerned, the deceased's share should be deducted and the net value figure carried to Page 10 Box 1.

10.4.3.4 *Section 2B — Particulars*

Again, the gross value of the deceased's fractional share of property qualifying for the instalment option should be included. Where there was an outstanding mortgage, the deceased's share will then be deducted and the net value figure carried to Page 10 Box 8.

Finally, the question as to whether the instalment option is to be exercised in relation to the Section 2B property must be answered.

10.4.4 PAGES 4 AND 5 — *SECTION 3A*

Section 3 of the form is concerned with the deceased's free (i.e. unsettled) estate situated in the United Kingdom. This is property which will pass under the terms of the will or the intestacy rules and in respect of which the personal representatives need the grant as evidence of their title.

Normally, all such property should be shown in Section 3. However, there are certain exceptions:

(a) if there is a limitation to the proposed grant (e.g. a literary executor is seeking a grant) any property which would otherwise be shown in Section 3 but is to be excluded from the grant sought should be entered in Section 5 on Page 8. Similarly, if the grant is required only for settled land,

INLAND REVENUE ACCOUNTS

the settled land details should be entered in Section 3B on Page 6 and the value of all the property passing under the deceased's will or intestacy shown in Section 5 on Page 8.

(b) if there is property over which the deceased had — and had exercised — a general power of appointment by will, the value of such property should again be shown in Section 5 on Page 8.

In Section 3A, only the free estate in the United Kingdom which does not enjoy the instalment option for inheritance tax purposes should be disclosed (see **10.4.5** where this option is available in respect of assets in the free estate). In most cases, the headings are reasonably self-explanatory, but the following points should be noted.

10.4.4.1 Stocks and Shares etc.

Separate lists for quoted and unquoted shares etc. should be made on Form IHT 40 and the totals (in £s only) should be entered on Page 4. Note that shares etc. should not be entered here if they have the benefit of the instalment option (see **6.8.2.2**): in that event, they should be shown in Section 3B on Page 6.

If a professional valuation has been obtained and is attached to the Inland Revenue account, IHT 40 can be dispensed with.

In the case of shares etc. quoted on the London Stock Exchange, they should be listed in the order in which they appear in the Stock Exchange Daily Official List. If you are undertaking the valuation yourself, remember the valuation rules discussed in **6.5.2.2**. You will also need to be careful with the unit of quotation — that in use at the date of death may differ from that shown on the share etc. certificates because there has been a reorganisation of the company's capital. Thus, for example, the deceased may have certificates for 200 50p shares in XYZ plc — but because of the reorganisation now holds 100 £1 shares. If the value for probate purposes of each share is £5, the deceased's holding will therefore be worth £500, not £1,000!

Shares are usually quoted 'cum div.' — i.e. with the value of any accrued dividend taken into account in the quotation. Where the quotation is 'ex div.', this will not be so and the value of the relevant holding must be adjusted to take this into account. If the deceased has uncashed dividends etc. in respect of investments included in this part of the form, they should be separately accounted for as indicated.

10.4.4.2 National Savings Certificates

In practice, it is usual to obtain from the Director of Savings a letter stating the value of the certificates at the date of death and attach this to the account. If this has not been done, it will be necessary to give full details of the certificates and calculate their value yourself!

10.4.4.3 Debts due to the deceased

Note that business debts should not be included under this heading, but should be entered in Section 3B.

10.4.4.4 Income from settled property

This heading is concerned with income due to the estate of a deceased who had a life interest (or an annuity) under a settlement. It is necessary to give details of the settlement including its date (the date of death if it arose under a will or on intestacy). Separate totals must be entered for any such income which has accrued due but not been received at the date of death, and for income subsequently received but apportioned to the pre-death period. It is important not to include here the value of the settled property itself: this should be entered in Section 5 on Page 8.

10.4.4.5 Life policies

Details are required here of the policy monies due to the deceased's personal representatives as of right — including under a mortgage protection policy in the deceased's sole name. Where the deceased was paying premiums under a policy on the life of someone else, the value is, in effect, the surrender value of the policy.

10.4.4.6 Income tax repayable

Any tax repayment due is part of the deceased's estate and thus prima facie liable to inheritance tax. In practice, it may take some while to finalise the deceased's tax position: it is therefore common, in order not to delay unduly the obtaining of the grant, for the amount of any possible repayment to be estimated. If this is done, once the tax position is finalised any adjustments necessary can be dealt with on a corrective account (see **10.6** below).

10.4.4.7 Household and personal goods

Separate totals are required for those items which have been sold and those which are unsold. If a professional valuation of the latter has been obtained, this should be attached: otherwise an estimate of the market value at the date of death will be needed. The Revenue requires individual values to be included for all items valued at £500 or more.

10.4.4.8 Unadministered estate

Where the deceased had an interest under an estate whose administration has not been completed at the date of death, an estimate of the value of that estate will have to be made. Details of that estate (including the date of the grant) should be given. If appropriate, quick succession relief (**6.3.3.2**) may be claimed (on Page 10).

10.4.4.9 Interest in expectancy

If the deceased had such an interest, it will normally be excluded property (see **6.2.1.1**) and thus not liable to inheritance tax. However, even where this is the case, details of the settlement concerned and the value of such interest at the date of death must be included at the top of Page 5 — because it is part of the estate for succession purposes — but is then deducted as excluded property in Section 6 on Page 9.

10.4.4.10 Liabilities and funeral expenses

The deceased's liabilities at the date of death for which deduction may be claimed (see **6.5.2.6**) should be entered here, as may reasonable funeral expenses (including the family's reasonable mourning expenses and the cost of a tombstone).

Liabilities which should not (normally) feature here include a mortgage secured on land in the deceased's free estate and business debts etc., both of which 'belong' in Section 3B on Page 6. However, should the debts etc. in Section 3B exceed the value of the assets there disclosed, the 'excess' may properly be a deduction in Section 3A.

If the debts etc. in Section 3A exceed the value of the assets in that Section, the excess is deducted (in order) from the value of assets in Section 3B on Page 6, and then from foreign assets in Section 4A or 4B on Page 7. If there is an amount still unabsorbed, it is not carried forward to Page 10, but on that page a 'Nil' entry should be made in Boxes 2, 9, 3 or 10 as appropriate.

10.4.4.11 Totals

The various totals on Page 5 should be carried forward as indicated:

(a) the gross value to Page 11 Box L

INLAND REVENUE ACCOUNTS

      (b) the liabilities to Page 11 Box Q
      (c) the net value to Page 10 Box 2.

10.4.5   PAGE 6 — *SECTION 3B*

This page is still concerned with the deceased's free estate, and requires entries relating to any property in the United Kingdom in respect of which the personal representatives need the grant as evidence of title, where that property has the benefit of the instalment option for inheritance tax purposes. Whether or not the option is to be exercised must be indicated at the bottom of the page.

10.4.5.1 Land

When a general grant is being sought, the value of any land to which the deceased was solely and beneficially entitled, or the value of the deceased's interest as a beneficial tenant in common should be included here. The value of any settled land where the settlement continues after the date of the deceased's death should not be included. However, if the settlement does come to an end on the death of the deceased the value of the formerly settled land should be included — because the deceased's personal representatives need to make title to it.

Form IHT 37 should also be completed.

If the grant relates only to settled land (i.e. where the settlement continues) its value should be shown here, and the value of the rest of the deceased's estate passing under the will or intestacy should be shown in Section 5 on Page 8.

10.4.5.2 Business interests

The net value (i.e. after deducting liabilities) of the value of the deceased's business carried on as a sole trader, or of the deceased's partnership share should be shown. In each case, a balance sheet or a statement of assets and liabilities at the date of death should be attached in support of the valuation.

10.4.5.3 Shares etc.

Shares etc. having the benefit of the instalment option should be included here, with separate totals for controlling and non-controlling holdings so qualifying.

10.4.5.4 Liabilities

Any liabilities (other than business debts which will already have been taken into account — 10.4.5.2 above) which are a charge on any property included in this Section should be included — such as a mortgage charged on land of which the deceased was the sole beneficial owner. Where the deceased was a beneficial tenant in common, the value of the deceased's proportionate share of the liability should be shown.

If the liabilities exceed the value of the assets in this Section, the excess should first be claimed in Section 3A on Page 5. If there is any amount still unabsorbed, it may be deducted from any foreign assets in Section 4A or 4B. Any outstanding amount is not carried to Page 10, but 'Nil' should be entered in Boxes 9, 2, 3 or 10 on that page, as appropriate.

10.4.5.5 Totals

The various totals on Page 6 should be carried forward as indicated:

      (a) the gross value to Page 11 Box M
      (b) the liabilities to Page 11 Box R
      (c) the net value to Page 10 Box 9

10.4.6 PAGE 7 — *SECTION 4*

In this Section, all foreign property in respect of which the personal representatives are liable for inheritance (or would be but for the fact that the value of the deceased's estate is not large enough) should be identified and valued. If they are not liable (e.g. because the property is comprised in a foreign settlement, the trustees of which are liable for any tax) the details should be included in Section 5 on Page 8.

10.4.6.1 *Sections 4A and 4B*

As before, entries relating to such property which does not enjoy the benefit of the instalment option should be included in Part A, and those where the property qualifies for the option in Part B. The question at the bottom of the page as to whether the option is being exercised in the particular case must be answered.

10.4.6.2 Liabilities

These should be entered and deducted from the appropriate part of this Section. If there are insufficient assets in the particular part to absorb the total claimed, the excess should first be claimed against any other foreign property identified on Page 7. If the excess is not then fully absorbed, the 'balance may be claimed against Section 3A or 3B on pages 5 and 6 respectively.

Any outstanding amount is not carried to Page 10, but 'Nil' should be entered in Boxes 3, 10, 2 or 9 on that page as appropriate.

10.4.6.3 Totals

The net totals (i.e. gross values less liabilities) should be carried forward as indicated:

(a) for Section 4A to Page 10 Box 3
(b) for Section 4B to Page 10 Box 10

The gross value totals are not carried forward (to Page 11) because foreign property is not property in respect of which the English grant will issue.

10.4.7 PAGE 8 — *SECTION 5 — SETTLED PROPERTY AND GIFTS WITH RESERVATION*

In this Section, it is necessary to answer the question at the top of the page, and if in the affirmative to account for all other property (including foreign property) in which the deceased had (or was treated as having) a beneficial interest in possession immediately before the death. Such property will include settled property interests in possession, other than in settled land (which should, where a settled land grant is being sought, be included in Section 3B). If under a settlement, the deceased had, and had exercised by will, a general power of appointment over the settled property this must also be included. In addition, there must be entered details of any property caught by the rules relating to gifts with a reservation (**6.2.1.2**) — the gross value of any such property being carried forward to Page 11 Box N; and of any unsettled property over which the deceased had a general power of appointment or disposal at the date of death. All such property must be included, even though the personal representatives are not liable for the tax (if any) — e.g. because the trustees of the settlement or the donee of the gift with a reservation are liable.

10.4.7.1 *Sections 5A and 5B*

Again, distinction must be made between non-instalment option property (Section 5A) and property qualifying for that option (Section 5B). Whether or not the option is being claimed in the particular case must be indicated at the bottom of the page.

INLAND REVENUE ACCOUNTS

10.4.7.2 Totals

There are separate totals in each part of this Section for the net values of property upon which tax is to be paid on the delivery of the account, in which case the totals for Section 5A and 5B are carried forward to Boxes 4 and 11 respectively on Page 10; and for property where this is not the case, when the totals are carried to Boxes 15 and 16 respectively.

10.4.8 PAGE 9 — SECTION 6 — EXEMPTIONS, EXCLUSIONS AND RELIEFS

The purpose of this Section is to identify and quantify any available exemptions and reliefs (including 'excluded property' but not quick succession relief).

10.4.8.1 *Property without the Instalment Option on which tax is being paid on delivery of this Account*

Any property included in Sections 2A, 3A, 4A and 5A for which an exemption or relief is claimed should be identified here.

In the first column, the Section of the account and the property concerned should be itemised. Where the whole or the bulk of the property in a given Section is covered by the same exemption or relief it is not necessary to identify the items individually: it will suffice to say 'The whole' or 'The whole save . . .' as the case may be.

In the second column, the exemption or relief claimed should be specified (e.g. 'Spouse'; 'Charity'; 'Excluded Property').

The net value of the property concerned is inserted into the third column. Thus, where the whole of the property included (e.g.) in Section 3A is covered by the spouse exemption, the figure entered here will be the net total at the very bottom of Page 5. (It is this figure, rather than the gross value of the Section 3A property which is covered by the exemption, since no tax would in any event be payable (i.e. if the exemption was not applicable) on the amount of the deductible liabilities.)

The fourth column should show the amount of the exemption or relief claimed. Where the asset(s) concerned are exempt, this figure will be the same as that in the third column.

The total of the fourth column is then carried to Page 10 Box 6.

10.4.8.2 *Property with the Instalment Option on which tax is being paid on delivery of this Account*

The process is then repeated in respect of property in Sections 2B, 3B, 4B and 5B where the instalment option is not being exercised. The total of all reliefs under this heading is then carried to Page 10 Box 13.

10.4.8.3 *Property on which tax is not being paid on delivery of this Account*

The previous exercise is now repeated in respect of any such property in Sections 2B, 3B, 4B, 5A and 5B qualifying for an exemption or relief. This will include instalment option property where the option is being exercised and also settled property where the trustees are liable for the tax. The total of the reliefs identified in this part is then carried to Page 10 Box 18.

10.4.9 PAGE 9 — SECTION 7

This Section is concerned with the possibility that a deduction for a liability might be disallowed under s. 103, Finance Act 1986 because the consideration for the debt or incumbrance consisted

INLAND REVENUE ACCOUNTS

of property derived from the deceased or someone else who had at some time so derived property (see **6.5.2.6**). The two questions must be answered, and if in the affirmative full particulars given.

10.4.10 PAGES 10 AND 11 — *CALCULATION OF INHERITANCE TAX*

Page 10 will always require completion, even if no tax will be payable in the particular case.

10.4.10.1 *Summary for determining the chargeable estate*

The first part of Page 10 consists of the total of any chargeable lifetime transfers from Page 2 which is entered at [A], and the various net totals brought forward from Sections 2 to 5 of the form as indicated and entered in the first column. In the second column are entered the totals of any exemptions and reliefs identified and claimed on Page 9. In the third column (at Boxes 7, 14 and 19) the various values after reliefs are shown and totalled at [B]. The aggregate of chargeable transfers, lifetime and on death is [A] + [B], and the total is then entered at [C].

10.4.10.2 *Calculation of Tax*

The tax on the figure at [C] is then calculated at the rate(s) applicable at the date of death — currently, on the first £150,000 (or the figure at [C] if smaller) at nil and on any balance at 40%.

The resultant total includes tax on any lifetime transfers: to discover the tax attributable to the transfer on death [B] it is necessary to calculate (in the same way) the tax at the death rate(s) on the total of lifetime transfers [A] and deduct this from the previous figure. If the figure at [B] is within the nil rate band there will of course be nothing to deduct, the whole of the tax being attributable to the transfer on death.

If quick succession relief (see **6.3.3.2**) is available, this is then claimed, giving the figure at [D] — the tax payable on the account.

10.4.10.3 *Apportionment of tax payable on this Account*

It is now necessary to calculate the proportion of the total inheritance tax that is due on the delivery of the account — i.e. the tax (for which the personal representatives are liable) attributable to the property not enjoying the instalment option, plus the tax on any instalment option property for which they are liable where the option is not being exercised. Further, if the option is being exercised, they must also pay on delivery of the account any instalments that have fallen due.

To do this, the appropriate amount of capital is multiplied by $\frac{[D]}{[B]}$. The calculation is first made for the non-instalment option property (the total in Box 7 on Page 10). (The reliefs referred to which may be deducted are most commonly reliefs for any foreign taxation.) The net tax due is entered at [E]. If tax is being paid after the due date, interest must then be calculated and added to give at [F] the total tax and interest on the non-instalment option property.

If tax on the instalment option property is not being paid on the delivery of the account, the remainder of this section can be left blank. Otherwise, the process is then repeated in respect of that part of the total in Box 14 on Page 10 upon which tax is now to be paid in full, or by instalments, and the net tax (after deducting any reliefs for foreign tax as before) entered at [G]. If payment is being made in full and interest is due, it must then be calculated.

If the tax is being paid by instalments and one or more have become due, the amount now due and being paid on the delivery of the account should be entered at [H]. Where an instalment is imminent, it is usually sensible to pay this on the delivery of the account so as to avoid the risk of interest being chargeable. If interest on the instalment(s) is due (see **6.8.2.2**), the appropriate calculation must then be made:

(a) The first calculation is appropriate where the instalment option is 'interest free' provided the instalment is paid on time, and if late is only payable on the late instalment(s).

(b) The second calculation is appropriate where the property qualifies for the instalment option by reason only of being land, in which event interest on the whole of the outstanding tax is payable with each instalment.

The total tax and interest on any instalment property is then entered at [J].

10.4.10.4 *Tax Summary*

The totals at [F] and [J] are then added together to give at [K] the total tax and interest payable now on the delivery of the account. The solicitor acting for the personal representatives should then sign the form — alongside which in due course it will be receipted, a necessary pre-requisite where tax is payable for the obtaining of the grant. There is no need to submit the form to Worthing if no tax is payable.

10.4.10.5 *Probate Summary*

The purpose of this is to identify the figures for the gross and net estate for probate purposes, which are needed to complete the appropriate form of oath (see **Chapter 9**). The total at [P] is the gross estate and that at [S] is the net estate.

10.4.11 PAGE 12— *DECLARATION AND WARNING*

The personal representatives must now indicate the type of grant sought and make the declarations, signing the form in the box(es) alongside the Warning.

10.5 Funding the Payment of Inheritance Tax

As we have seen, in order to obtain the grant the personal representatives will have to pay any inheritance tax due on the delivery of the Inland Revenue account. However, they normally need the grant as evidence of their title — without which those holding the deceased's funds will be unwilling to part with them! How the deceased's personal representatives solve this 'circular' problem is considered at **14.2.6**.

10.6 Corrective Account

If for any reason it transpires that too much or too little tax has been paid, the personal representatives may have to submit a corrective account in Form CAP D-3. However, if the adjustments are only minor the Capital Taxes Office may be prepared to deal with the matter informally.

10.6.1 FORM CAP D-3

This is a four-page form, which must when completed be signed by the personal representatives.

10.6.1.1 Page 1

This deals with essentially formal matters — the identification of the deceased and the personal representatives, plus statements verifying the various adjustments shown in the subsequent pages of the form, whether any further adjustments are necessary and (if appropriate) indicating to whom any overpaid tax should be returned. When the form has been completed, the signatures of the personal representatives should be added at the foot of this page.

10.6.1.2 Page 2

This page deals with any adjustments necessary to the property without the instalment option. The property concerned is identified and its value (if any) previously shown is indicated, with the corrected value shown alongside. The overall increase/decrease is then identified and carried to the summary on Page 4. The same exercise is then undertaken in relation to the debts etc., and the overall increase/decrease in these also carried to Page 4. At the bottom of the page, the reason for the correction(s) should be given — e.g. assets discovered subsequent to the submission of the account.

10.6.1.3 Page 3

On this page, the identical process in respect of the instalment option property is undertaken.

10.6.1.4 Page 4

A summary of the changes to the estate appears at the top of the page, and is followed by details of any necessary changes to claims for exemptions or reliefs.

10.6.2 DELIVERY

The completed CAP D-3 is then submitted to the Capital Taxes Office, which will issue a formal assessment showing the amount of tax payable/repayable as a result of the corrections.

10.7 Form CAP A-5C

This form is appropriate (Form A-5N if in Northern Ireland) where an application is being made for a grant of double probate (**8.5.7.3**), a cessate grant (**8.5.7.4**) or a *de bonis non* grant (**8.5.7.2**). It is not used where a subsequent grant is applied for following the revocation of a previous grant; nor where a full grant is being applied for following a grant pending suit or *ad colligenda bona*: Form IHT 200 (or IHT 201) should be used in all such cases.

In effect, the Form A-5C is an application for a certificate from the Revenue that it has no objection to the issue of the proposed (second) grant. If tax has not already been paid on the unadministered estate this must first be paid on a corrective account. An application for a grant *de bonis non* may now be made direct to the Probate Registry without CAP A-5C having first been submitted to the Capital Taxes Office. In other cases, it should be submitted and the certificate obtained before the papers are lodged to lead the grant.

ELEVEN

AFFIDAVIT EVIDENCE

11.1 Generally

We have already seen (in **Chapter 9**) that all applications for grants of representation are supported by affidavit evidence in the form of the appropriate oath. In the vast majority of cases, no further evidence will be needed. Sometimes, however, the district judge or registrar will require further affidavit evidence to be submitted before issuing a grant. In this chapter we will consider some of the circumstances most frequently encountered in practice where such additional evidence may be called for to facilitate the issue of a grant.

11.1.1 FORM

This is ultimately governed by the Rules of the Supreme Court 1965. An affidavit in a probate matter must bear the heading as described in the context of oaths (**9.1** above). It should be drawn in the first person and commence with details of the deponent(s) name, residential address (business address in the case of a solicitor etc. giving evidence in a professional capacity) and occupation (if none, the description, or in the case of a woman her marital status).

The affidavit should then deal as fully and precisely as possible with the facts and circumstances in issue. In cases of doubt as to what is needed, the advice of the Registry should be sought so that you can try to deliver all the required evidence at the same time. However, remember that the affidavit is evidence being given by the deponent(s) to the court — a point which should also be stressed to the deponent(s).

Where a testamentary document (whether a will, codicil or document to be incorporated by reference) is to be exhibited to an affidavit, it should not be referred to as being 'annexed' (nor should it in fact be annexed). This is because if it is admitted to probate it will have to be detached from the affidavit and thus 'lose' the identification. Rather, the affidavit should refer to the document 'now produced to me/us' and the identification be completed by the endorsement of the title of the matter and the signed and dated certificate of the solicitor administering the oath (or taking the affirmation) that this is the document referred to in the affidavit.

11.1.2 ALTERATIONS

Any alterations, interlineations or erasures in the body of the affidavit or the jurat should be initialled by the solicitor administering the oath or taking the affirmation. No alteration etc. can properly be made to an affidavit after it has been sworn; if any are made, the affidavit must be re-sworn or reaffirmed.

AFFIDAVIT EVIDENCE

11.1.3 SWEARING

The affidavit must be sworn (or affirmed) before an independent solicitor who holds a current practising certificate, or before an independent Justice of the Peace (or if sworn etc. outside England and Wales, before anyone having authority by the laws of the country concerned to administer oaths).

11.2 Due Execution — r. 12, NCPR

We saw in **1.1.4.7** that the inclusion in a will of an attestation clause prima facie showing compliance with the requirements of s. 9, Wills Act 1837 raises a presumption of due execution. If no attestation clause is included, or that included is insufficient, due execution will have to be proved — as it will if there is any reason for possible doubt as to the will's due execution (e.g. where the signature is imperfect or appears in an unusual position). Evidence of due execution may also be required where the deceased was blind, or executed the will with a mark, or where the will was signed by someone on behalf of the testator — though in all these cases the matter is in practice most effectively dealt with by an adjustment to the attestation clause in the will. If this has not been done, an affidavit as to knowledge and approval will also be required: see further **11.3** below.

11.2.1 THE DEPONENT

Rule 12(1) indicates that an affidavit of due execution should ideally come from one or more of the attesting witnesses: in practice, an affidavit from one of them is usually sufficient. If this is not possible, the Registry will accept an affidavit (explaining why one is not being provided by the witnesses) from anyone else present when the will was executed.

If neither of the above is possible, r. 12(2) allows the district judge or registrar to accept affidavit evidence from anyone able to identify the testator's signature (and any other handwritten parts of the will) as being in the deceased's handwriting. Additionally, an affidavit from the applicant for the grant will have to be lodged showing who would be prejudiced by the will being admitted to probate (i.e. those who would otherwise be entitled under the intestacy rules) and that they are all *sui juris* and consent to the will being admitted. (If they are not all *sui juris* or do not all consent, the directions of a district judge or registrar will have to be sought.)

11.2.2 NO SATISFACTORY EVIDENCE

If the district judge or registrar is satisfied that, after considering any affidavit evidence produced, the will was not duly executed it must be marked 'probate refused'.

11.2.3 RULE 12(3), NCPR

A district judge or registrar has a discretion to accept a will without any evidence of the kinds described in **11.2.1** above if satisfied that the distribution of the estate is not affected by doing so — i.e. where the will and the intestacy rules provide for the same distribution of the estate. Thus, for example, in practice if the applicant is the only person entitled on intestacy an affidavit from the applicant stating that fact and as to the deceased's handwriting will normally be acceptable.

11.2.4 RULE 16, NCPR

This effectively provides that any affidavit (for whatever primary purpose it is being provided) by an attesting witness or someone else present at the time of execution of the will must always include a statement as to the due execution of the will — even if this is not, in fact, in issue.

11.3 Knowledge and Approval — r. 13, NCPR

This provides that where a will has been signed by a blind or illiterate person, or by someone else on the testator's behalf, or for any reason (e.g. signs of extreme feebleness in the signature) there is a possible doubt as to whether the testator had the necessary knowledge and approval of the contents of the will (see 1.1.3), a district judge or registrar must be satisfied on these points before the will can be admitted to probate. These matters are (as we have already seen) best dealt with by appropriate adjustments to the attestation clause; if this has not been done, affidavit evidence will be required to support the application for the grant.

11.4 Terms, Condition and Date of Will — r. 14, NCPR

There are various possibilities arising under this Rule.

11.4.1 ALTERATIONS

We discussed the problems connected with alterations in **Chapter 1**, where we saw that (except in the case of the filling in of a blank space) any unexecuted obliteration, interlineation or other alteration is presumed to have been made after execution of the will and thus to be inadmissible. (Any alteration 'authenticated' under s. 21, Wills Act 1837 (e.g. by the initials of the testator and the witnesses) is, of course, effective — and in most cases no further evidence will be required).

11.4.1.1 Rule 14(1)

Where a will contains any such unexecuted alterations etc. it will be necessary — unless the district judge or registrar decides that the alteration is of no practical importance (Rule 14(2)) — for affidavit evidence to be provided as to whether or not each and every such alteration existed at the date of the execution of the will.

11.4.1.2 The deponent

Under r. 16, the district judge or registrar has a discretion to accept an affidavit from anyone. In practice, the best evidence will be that of the witnesses or someone else present at the time of execution. If the alterations were made before execution by the person who wrote out or engrossed the will (perhaps to correct a mistake or on the instructions of the testator) an affidavit from that person will in practice normally be acceptable, without the need to refer to the witnesses etc.

11.4.1.3 'Fiat' copy

A copy of the will, omitting any inadmissible alterations (and showing a blank space where an obliteration has rendered the original wording not apparent) will have to be prepared and lodged with the other papers to lead the grant.

11.4.2 INCORPORATION

Under r. 14(3), where a will refers to another document in such terms as to suggest that it should be incorporated in the will (see 1.1.3), the district judge or registrar will require the document to be produced and may call for further evidence (usually by affidavit) as to (e.g.) the identity of the document concerned.

11.4.3 DATE

By r. 14(4), where there is doubt as to the date upon which a will was executed, affidavit evidence will normally be required to establish the date of its execution.

AFFIDAVIT EVIDENCE

11.4.3.1 The problem

It may be that the will bears no date at all, or an incomplete date (e.g. 26 June 19..). Sometimes a will bears conflicting dates (e.g. one in the body of the will and a different one on the endorsement — though here if the discrepancy is slight affidavit evidence may not be required). Further, if there is one date at the commencement of the will and a later date at its end, the latter may in practice be accepted without the need for affidavit evidence.

11.4.3.2 The deponent

Normally, the affidavit should be provided by an attesting witness or other person present at the execution of the will. If the problem arises because someone has entered in error a date on the endorsement different from that in the body of the will, evidence from the person making the mistake will in practice usually be acceptable without reference to the witnesses etc.

11.4.3.3 The evidence required

The deponent(s) should if possible confirm the exact date of execution — referring in the affidavit to any circumstances that assist in identifying the date (e.g. that it was the testator's birthday and the deponent well recalls the circumstances as the two witnesses and the testator enjoyed a celebratory drink and slice of birthday cake after the will had been executed). If the exact date cannot be stated, evidence as to execution between two definite dates should be given (e.g. 'on a date between 7 and 14 June 1990'). If this is not possible, or the two dates are separated by a substantial period, an affidavit of search will be required — showing that a search has been made and that no will of presumably later date than the one sought to be proved has been found.

11.5 Attempted Revocation — r. 15, NCPR

Where there are circumstances which suggest the possibility of attempted revocation (whether by burning, tearing or otherwise destroying (**1.2.1.6**), or by possible later will or codicil **1.2.1.5**)) the district judge or registrar must (in effect) be satisfied that the will has not been revoked. To this end, an affidavit of 'plight and condition' will often be required. The following are some of the cases where such evidence may be called for.

11.5.1 BURNING, TEARING OR OBLITERATION

Where the will bears scorch marks, or parts of it have been torn, cut out or obliterated, the possibility is that the testator intended to revoke the will. Affidavit evidence may in practice be dispensed with if the 'damage' is slight.

Evidence should ideally be given to show how the will came to be in its present condition by someone having knowledge of the circumstances. If this is not possible, the affidavit should show that the will is in the same condition as when found — and the district judge or registrar may also require affidavits of search for other testamentary documents, and as to the will's condition at the date of execution and its custody from that date until found. An affidavit of plight and condition may also be required where it appears that the will has been written on a piece of paper cut or torn from a larger piece.

11.5.2 SOMETHING ATTACHED?

Never attach anything to a will or other testamentary document — and do your best to persuade your clients not to do so either! If a will shows signs of something once having been attached to it (e.g. pin or staple holes, paper clip indentations) the court will need to be satisfied that whatever was once attached was not a later will or codicil (or perhaps a document which ought to be incorporated).

It will be necessary to try to provide some evidence of what was attached. Where the solicitor dealing with the matter is able to state from his/her personal knowledge what was attached, the solicitor's statement as to this and that the papers concerned were not testamentary will usually in practice be accepted. Otherwise, affidavit evidence from the person who made the attachment should, if possible, be furnished. If this cannot be done, it will be necessary to provide an affidavit that the will is now in the same condition as when found and that search has been made for later testamentary documents.

11.6 Other Cases

Affidavit evidence may be required in support of any application to a district judge or registrar.

11.6.1 MISSING WILLS

If a will has been lost, or accidentally or mistakenly destroyed it has not been revoked (see **1.2.1.6**) yet clearly cannot be submitted for proof. However, application can be made under r. 54, NCPR to a district judge or registrar to allow a draft, copy or reconstruction of the will to be admitted to probate. The district judge or registrar may direct that notice of the application be given to anyone who would be prejudiced if it were to be successful.

In support of such application it will be necessary to lodge:

(a) Evidence of the contents of the missing will — such as a draft or a copy — and as to the accuracy of such draft or copy.
(b) An affidavit of due execution of the original will.
(c) An affidavit as to the circumstances of the disappearance of the will. This should contain evidence sufficient to rebut the presumption of revocation by destruction.

11.6.2 CODICILS

We have seen that codicils must be proved along with the will to which they relate.

11.6.2.1 Missing codicil

It may be possible to prove a copy of any codicil which has been lost, or accidentally or mistakenly destroyed, in the manner described in **11.6.1** above.

11.6.2.2 Revoked codicil

If a codicil is revoked by a later codicil it should nonetheless be preserved since the district judge or registrar may well require it to be lodged on any application for a grant.

If a revoked codicil cannot be produced, affidavit evidence explaining why it cannot be produced and as to its contents will be required. If it has been destroyed, the evidence of the person who destroyed it (or witnessed the destruction) should if possible be obtained; otherwise, an affidavit of search for the revoked codicil will be needed.

11.6.3 RECTIFICATION

Unless a probate action has been commenced (see **12.5**) an application may be made (normally within six months of a grant) to rectify a will under s. 20, Administration of Justice Act 1982. Such an application is possible under the Act (as we saw in **1.4.1.4**) where it is alleged that the will fails to carry out the testator's intentions because of a clerical error or a failure to understand the testator's instructions. The application must be supported by appropriate affidavit evidence.

AFFIDAVIT EVIDENCE

11.6.4   IDENTITY

As we saw in **9.2.2.1**, it may sometimes be necessary to provide an affidavit as to the identity of the executor (unless the matter can be dealt with by the addition of a short statement at the end of the oath). Such evidence might be required, for example, where the will appoints 'Mr Smith of 1 High Street Newtown' or 'John Smith of 1 High Street Newtown' and the applicant's full name is Edward John Smith. In either situation, the affidavit will need to deal with the the circumstances at the date of the will and the possibility that there might be someone else more nearly fitting the description in the will than the applicant. Thus, it should show that there was no one else fitting the description 'Mr Smith' living at 1 High Street at the date of the will; or that the applicant is usually known as and was always referred to by the testator as 'John Smith'.

TWELVE

COURT PROCEEDINGS

12.1 Introduction

The vast majority of probate work is concerned with obtaining grants of representation in unopposed cases. We have seen in **Chapter 8** that such work is classified as non-contentious or 'common form' business and is dealt with by the Family Division of the High Court. The procedure is governed by the Non-Contentious Probate Rules 1987 as amended (NCPR).

There will be occasions where there is a dispute however. This may relate to the documents which should be submitted to probate; as to who is entitled to a grant; or as to whether a grant should be revoked. Such contentious or 'solemn form' business is allotted to the Chancery Division of the High Court, or the county court. The latter has a concurrent jurisdiction if the value of the deceased's estate does not exceed £30,000 (after deduction of debts, liabilities and funeral expenses, and ignoring any property held by the deceased as trustee and not beneficially). Where there has been a dispute determined in contentious proceedings, the matter will however return to the Family Division for the issue of the grant.

The latter part of this chapter deals in outline with solemn form procedure, which must be commenced by the issue of a writ or summons. The issue of a caveat or citation will frequently be a preliminary step to a probate action, but neither of these steps is in itself contentious, and their nature is explained below.

The procedure requesting that a search be made of the index of grants, the standing search, is also explained. This is similarly non-contentious and these three procedures are governed by the NCPR.

12.2 Standing Searches — r. 43, NCPR

12.2.1 DEFINITION AND PURPOSE

This facility was introduced especially to assist persons who wish to make a claim against an estate (for instance, a creditor) or to commence proceedings under the Inheritance (Provision for Family and Dependants) Act 1975 (which was considered in **Chapter 3**) once a grant has been issued. The caveat procedure (below) which prevents the grant being issued without notice to the caveator is, therefore, not appropriate in these circumstances.

A standing search requests that a search be made of the index of grants and that an office copy of the grant relating to a particular estate be sent to the applicant.

COURT PROCEEDINGS

12.2.2 PROCEDURE

The application is made to any Registry or sub-Registry by lodging the prescribed form and fee. The applicant will be sent an office copy of any grant made within 12 months before or six months after the receipt of the application. The application may be renewed at the end of the six months on payment of a further fee.

12.3 Caveats — r. 44, NCPR

12.3.1 DEFINITION AND PURPOSE

A caveat is a notice entered on the records of the court effectively preventing the issue of a grant, except to the caveator (the person entering the caveat) without notice first being given to the caveator. If a person merely wishes to know when a grant is issued, a standing search should instead be issued.

A caveat may be entered (*inter alia*):

(a) to give the caveator time to make enquiries to determine whether there are grounds for opposing the grant;
(b) as a step preliminary to the issue of a citation (see below); or
(c) as a step preliminary to a probate action (see below).

The caveat itself does not institute proceedings.

12.3.2 ENTRY OF CAVEAT

A caveat may be entered by a person having an interest in the estate (or their solicitor) either by attending in person at any Registry and completing the prescribed form, or by sending to the Registry notice in the prescribed form. Entry by post is at the caveator's risk. A fee is payable.

The caveat must contain the name and address of the deceased, the date and place of death and the name and address for service of the caveator. Two or more persons each wishing to enter a caveat must enter separate caveats.

The person entering the caveat is given or sent a receipt: this must be produced if it is subsequently desired to withdraw the caveat.

12.3.3 DATE AND DURATION OF CAVEAT

The caveat is effective from the day following entry and normally ceases to be effective six months thereafter. During the last month of the six-month period (and again in the last month of each successive six-month period) it may be renewed.

The caveat remains in force for a longer period if a citation is issued, or in certain circumstances after a caveat is warned.

12.3.4 WARNING OF CAVEATS

The index of caveats is currently kept at the Leeds District Probate Registry. The index is searched before any grant is issued, and if a caveat has been entered the grant is stopped. The person whose application for a grant is stopped, or any person claiming to have an interest in the estate, may issue a warning to the caveat or start contentious proceedings by issuing a writ or summons (see below). A caveat may be warned only from the Leeds District Probate Registry.

Persons warning the caveat must state in the warning the date of the will or codicil under which they claim, and their interest thereunder (e.g. executor etc.) or, in the case of an intestacy, their

COURT PROCEEDINGS

interest in the deceased's estate. An address for service must be given. The warning requires the caveator to enter an appearance within eight days of service of the warning, or issue within that time a summons for the Registrar's directions. The warning must be served on the caveator.

12.3.5 EFFECT OF WARNING

Once the warning has been served, one of four things will happen:

12.3.5.1 Caveator does nothing

In this case, once the time limit for entering an appearance or summons for directions has expired, the person warning should file an affidavit in the Leeds District Probate Registry showing that the warning was duly served on the caveator. The caveat is thereupon 'warned off', i.e. is no longer effective.

12.3.5.2 Caveator withdraws the caveat

This may be done at any time provided the caveator has not entered an appearance to a warning (see below). If a warning has been issued notice must be given to the person warning. Once a caveat is withdrawn it ceases to have effect and the person warning can proceed with the application for a grant.

The caveat must be withdrawn at the Registry where it was entered, and the original receipt must be produced and left.

12.3.5.3 Caveator enters an appearance

This must be done within eight days of the service of the warning, to avoid the risk of the caveat being 'warned off'. It must be entered personally or by post in the Leeds District Probate Registry. An appearance may only be entered by a person having an interest contrary to that of the person warning (e.g. one claims to be executor under a will whilst the other claims a grant of administration on the grounds that the will is not valid).

After an appearance has been entered, the caveat remains effective until a district judge (or where the parties agree to discontinue the caveat, a registrar) otherwise directs. Frequently the next step will be the commencement of a probate action: in this event, the caveat is no longer necessary since a grant cannot then issue (other than a grant *pendente lite* — see **Chapter 8**) except to the person determined by the court to be entitled.

12.3.5.4 Caveator issues and serves a summons for directions

Again, this must be done within eight days of the service of the warning and notice must be given to the Leeds District Probate Registry. It may be done only by a person having no interest contrary to that of the person warning (e.g. both are entitled to a grant in the same degree, or caveator in a lower degree, but wishes to show cause why the person warning should be passed over). There will subsequently be a hearing before a district judge (or a High Court judge in a difficult case) to decide to whom the grant should be made.

The caveat remains effective until the summons is disposed of unless either a direction is given by a district judge or registrar that it should cease to have effect or it is withdrawn.

12.4 Citations — rr. 46 to 48, NCPR

12.4.1 DEFINITION AND PURPOSE

A citation is a document issued by the Principal or a District Registry whereby the person issuing (the 'citor') calls upon the person cited (the 'citee') to show cause why a certain step should not be

COURT PROCEEDINGS

taken. A citation will be needed where those entitled to a grant delay or decline to apply and refuse to renounce, or where the applicant for a grant knows of the existence of an alleged testamentary document, but wishes to prove on the basis of an earlier will or an intestacy.

Citations are non contentious but may result in a probate action being commenced.

12.4.2 TYPES OF CITATION

The three types of citation are:

12.4.2.1 Citation to take probate (r. 47)

This may be issued at the instance of anyone interested in the estate to require an executor who has intermeddled without proving to show cause why he or she should not be ordered to take a grant. We have noted in **8.10.1** that an executor who has intermeddled cannot renounce probate. The citation may only be issued if at least six months have elapsed since the deceased's death and no proceedings as to the validity of the will are pending.

12.4.2.2 Citation to accept or refuse a grant (r. 47)

This may be issued at the instance of any person who would be entitled to a grant if the citee(s) renounce, at any time after the deceased's death. It is used to force a citee with a superior right to a grant to either take out the grant or to renounce. The citation must cite all persons with a superior right, indicating their entitlement, and the title of the citor.

For instance, where the deceased left a will, the residuary legatee could cite the executor and trustee of the will to accept or renounce probate, and to show cause why letters of administration with the will annexed should not be granted to the citor.

Where power has been reserved to an executor, that person may be cited to accept or refuse a grant by the proving executors or the executor of the sole or last survivor of them.

12.4.2.3 Citation to propound a will (r. 48)

Such a citation is used to force any persons who are interested (whether as executors or beneficiaries) under an alleged will to prove it if they can. It can only be issued at the instance of any person with a contrary interest (in effect entitled under an earlier will or on intestacy) and must be directed to all persons interested under the alleged will.

Such a citation is not appropriate where an executor under a will doubts the validity of a codicil to the will: in such a case the executor should commence a probate action to establish the validity of the will and the invalidity or otherwise of the codicil.

12.4.3 PROCEDURE ON ISSUE (r. 46)

Any person seeking the issue of a citation must first enter a caveat. The citation must be accompanied by an affidavit verifying every statement of fact in the citation. The district judge or registrar must settle the citation before it can be issued. In practice, it is usual to take (or send by post) a draft citation and affidavit in support from the applicant (or one of them) to the Registry where the citation is to be issued. These settled drafts are then lodged with an engrossment of the citation, the sworn affidavit and the receipt issued on entry of the caveat. The only fee payable is that for settling the citation.

Any will or codicil referred to in the citation must be lodged in the Registry before the citation can issue unless the district judge or registrar is satisfied that it is impracticable to require it to be lodged.

The citation sets out what steps will be taken by the court if the citee fails to show cause to the contrary and must normally be served personally on the citee(s).

Appearance may be entered at the Registry from which the citation issued — normally within eight days, or later if no step in default has been taken. A copy must be served on the citor.

12.4.4 SUBSEQUENT PROCEDURE

The procedure will depend upon the type of citation and the action (if any) taken by the citee. In practice, however, an appearance to a citation to propound (12.4.3.3) is likely to lead to a probate action.

12.4.4.1 Citation to take probate

(a) The citee may enter an appearance and seek a grant in favour of the citee.

(b) If the citee has not entered an appearance, or has done so but taken no further steps within a reasonable time, the citor may apply for an order requiring the citee to take a grant within a specified time, or that the citee be passed over and for a grant to be issued to the citor or some other named person.

12.4.4.2 Citation to accept or refuse a grant

(a) The citee may enter an appearance and seek a grant in favour of the citee.

(b) If no appearance is entered, then an application may be made for an order for a grant in favour of the citor. (If the citation was directed to an executor to whom power was reserved, the citor will apply for an order for the grant to be noted with the non-appearance to citation and that the citee's entitlement to a grant has ceased.)

(c) If after service of the citation, the citee renounces, the citor may obtain a grant without the need for an order.

(d) If the citee has appeared, but fails then to take any further steps within a reasonable time, the citor may again apply for an order for a grant, or where power has been reserved to the citee, to strike out the appearance and for the notation of the grant as above.

12.4.4.3 Citation to propound

(a) Where the person cited seeks to propound the will a probate action should be commenced against the citor (see below).

(b) If no appearance is entered, the citor may apply for a grant as stated in the citation as if the will is invalid.

(c) If appearance is entered, but no further steps are taken within a reasonable time, an application should be made for a similar order.

12.5 Solemn Form Procedure

12.5.1 WHEN SOLEMN FORM PROCEEDINGS ARE REQUIRED

As indicated above, contentious (or solemn form) proceedings will be required where there is a dispute as to the validity of an alleged will, as to who is entitled to a grant or as to the revocation of a grant already issued in non contentious proceedings.

The matter may be commenced by writ in the Chancery Division of the High Court or by summons in the county court, if within the county court financial limit. The county court with jurisdiction is the one in whose area the deceased resided at the date of death.

The matter remains contentious until the court determines the issue, but the grant itself will be issued by the Family Division in common form.

COURT PROCEEDINGS

12.5.2 PROCEDURE

The practice in contentious matters is regulated by the Rules of the Supreme Court 1965 — mainly ord. 76, which also applies to probate actions in the county court, save as otherwise provided in the County Court Rules 1981.

12.5.2.1 Issue of writ or summons

A probate action is commenced by the issue of a writ or summons indorsed with a statement of the interest of the plaintiff and the defendant in the deceased's estate.

It may be issued by the executor(s), or a person interested in the will or under any other will whose interest would be adversely affected if the disputed will were admitted to probate, or the persons entitled on intestacy.

Any person interested who is not a plaintiff should be joined as a defendant unless their entitlement will not be affected by the decision: thus, for example, a beneficiary who is entitled to the same specific legacy under the terms of each of two disputed wills need not be joined.

If the proceedings are to be taken in the county court the value of the estate must be established prior to the issue of the summons. Once the summons is issued, notice should be given to the Principal Registry to prevent the issue of a grant other than a grant pending suit (**8.5.5.3**) until the proceedings have been concluded.

12.5.2.2 Pleadings

Where possible, the statement of claim should be indorsed on the writ or summons. Otherwise a separate statement of claim must be served upon every defendant who enters an appearance, within six weeks of their having done so.

Any defence or counterclaim must be served on the plaintiff within 14 days of the expiry of the time limit for entering appearance or of the service of the statement of claim if later. A summons for directions must be taken out once pleadings are closed.

12.5.2.3 Default of appearance or pleadings

In a probate action, it is not possible to obtain judgment in default. If the defendant fails to enter an appearance, the plaintiff may file an affidavit of service and seek an order for trial despite the non-appearance. If one of the parties has failed to serve pleadings the court can order trial of the action on the basis of affidavit evidence.

12.5.2.4 Compromise

A probate action may be compromised provided consent is given by or on behalf of all the beneficiaries who are or might be interested in the estate. Proof of the validity or otherwise of the will is still necessary.

12.5.2.5 Costs

Costs are always at the discretion of the court and usually will follow the event (i.e. the loser will have to pay the winner's costs). However, the costs of the executor will normally come out of the estate independently of any order (since such costs are prima facie a charge on the estate): but an executor who has acted unreasonably may be ordered to bear his or her own costs.

THIRTEEN

POWERS AND DUTIES OF PERSONAL REPRESENTATIVES

In **Chapter 8** we saw that it is generally necessary for personal representatives to obtain a grant of representation to establish title to the deceased's estate. Once the grant has been obtained the personal representatives will need to know what duties and powers they have with regards to the administration of the estate. In the first part of this chapter (**13.1**) we will examine the duties of personal representatives, and (in **13.2**) the administrative powers granted to them by statute or otherwise. We will also see that where the deceased has died testate, the will may extend or alter these implied powers.

The beneficiaries may be concerned to know what rights they have during the administration period. We will consider these rights in **13.3**, and the steps that may be taken by a beneficiary to enforce such rights in **13.4**.

13.1 Duties of Personal Representatives

13.1.1 THE FUNDAMENTAL DUTY OF PERSONAL REPRESENTATIVES

The fundamental duty of a personal representative is to 'collect and get in' the deceased's real and personal estate, and then 'to administer it according to law' (s. 25, Administration of Estates Act 1925, as amended). All the duties of personal representatives must be performed 'with due diligence'.

13.1.1.1 Duty to collect the deceased's assets

Within a reasonable time, taking such steps as may be reasonably necessary, the personal representatives must collect the monies due and other assets belonging to the deceased which vest in them. There is no absolute rule as to what is a 'reasonable' time in this context. Personal representatives will only be liable for loss resulting from their unreasonable conduct.

13.1.1.2 The need to establish title to assets by production of the grant

We have seen (**8.3**) that the deceased's property vests in an executor at death and that, in theory at least, an executor can deal with the deceased's property without obtaining a grant. In the case of an administrator, however, the property only vests when the grant is issued, and the administrator's power to act derives from the grant.

In practice, in both cases it will be necessary for the personal representatives to produce the original (or office copy) **grant** of probate or administration to the persons who hold the deceased's assets,

POWERS AND DUTIES OF PERSONAL REPRESENTATIVES

in order to establish entitlement to deal with such assets. Office copies can be obtained from the Registry on payment of a small fee. Sufficient office copies should therefore be obtained to avoid delay in collecting in the estate assets (see **14.2.8**).

The Administration of Estates (Small Payments) Act 1965 provides that in the case of certain small sums due to the estate production of the grant is not required (**8.4.1**).

13.1.1.3 Property of the deceased which does not vest in the personal representatives

The above duty only relates to the deceased's interests in property which devolve on the personal representatives. The following property passes direct to those entitled on death (see **8.4.2**) and therefore does not vest in the personal representatives:

(a) The deceased's interest in a beneficial joint tenancy.
(b) Nominated property.
(c) *Donationes mortis causa*.
(d) Trust policies.
(e) Pension scheme benefits payable at the discretion of the pension trustees.
(f) The legal title to property held by the deceased as a trustee where there are other trustees at the time of death. In such a case, title vests in the other trustees. If the deceased was a sole trustee at the time of death, however, title devolves on the personal representatives.

13.1.1.4 The duty to administer

Reasonable steps must be taken to preserve the deceased's estate, and within a reasonable time (prima facie within the 'executor's year' — see **13.2.4** below) the personal representatives must realise any investments which is not proper for them to retain (see further **13.1.2** below).

Other duties imposed by s. 25, Administration of Estates Act 1925 relate to the preparation (when required to do so by the court) of an inventory and account, and the delivery up to the court of the grant issued (e.g. so that it can be revoked and a new grant issued) if called upon to do so. You will recall that the various forms of oath (discussed in **Chapter 9**) contain statements (in effect) acknowledging these duties.

Administration of the estate thereafter involves the payment of debts etc. and any legacies, and the distribution of the residue according to the terms of the will and/or the intestacy rules (see further **Chapters 14 and 16**).

13.1.2 LEGAL AND EQUITABLE APPORTIONMENTS

Personal representatives may be under a duty to apportion income by virtue of the Apportionment Act 1870 or under various equitable rules.

13.1.2.1 Apportionment Act 1870

We have already encountered the Apportionment Act 1870 in **4.1.2.2**. If the Act applies, then for distribution purposes the personal representatives have a duty to apportion income of continuing nature (e.g. dividends, rents, interest) on a daily basis to the periods before and after the death of the deceased. A similar duty arises in respect of income arising on the death of a life tenant. Income of a continuing nature will again have to be apportioned to the periods before and after the life tenant's death. As we will see in **18.4.7.7**, the will may exclude the duty to apportion. Whether or not the Act applies will not (as we saw in **4.1.2.2**) affect the income tax position.

13.1.2.2 Equitable apportionments

Various apportionment rules have been developed to achieve fairness between the interests of life tenants and remaindermen. Where the rules apply the personal representatives will be under a duty to sell certain estate assets, and to apportion income pending such sale. When will this be the case?

There is no general duty to convert the property left by the deceased into authorised investments (as to the meaning of which term see further **13.2.9** below). However, such a duty will arise where the trust instrument so directs (e.g. where there is an express trust for sale of the residuary estate in the will); where statute requires (e.g. s. 33, Administration of Estates Act 1925, see **2.1.1**); or under the rule in *Howe* v *Lord Dartmouth* (1802) 7 Ves 137.

The rule in *Howe* v *Lord Dartmouth* applies (in the absence of contrary intention) only where there is a gift in a will of residuary personalty to persons in succession, and there are assets of a wasting, hazardous or reversionary nature or of an unauthorised character.

Where there is a duty to sell (however the duty arises), the income from the asset concerned pending such sale must be dealt with as follows (unless the will otherwise provides):

(a) in the case of land, the life tenant is entitled to the whole of any income produced pending sale.

(b) in any other case, the income must be apportioned. Under the rule in *Howe* v *Lord Dartmouth* the life tenant is entitled to interest at 4% on the capital value of the asset from the date of death until the date of actual conversion. If the actual income exceeds 4%, the balance is added to the capital: if it is less, the life tenant is entitled to have it made up to 4% from future surpluses of income or from the eventual proceeds of sale.

The rule in *Re Earl of Chesterfield's Trust* (1883) 24 ChD 643 applies to reversionary interests (i.e. future interests in trust property) or other non-income producing property. Here, there will be no income which could be apportioned until the interest falls into possession (or the property is sold). When either of these events occurs, an apportionment is made so as to (in effect) treat some of the funds now available as arrears of income due to the life tenant. This is done by identifying (as capital) the sum which, if invested at the testator's death at 4% compound interest (and after deducting income tax at the basic rate), would have produced the sum actually received.

(c) The rule in *Allhusen* v *Whittell* (1867) LR 4 Eq 295 attempts to strike a fair balance between the life tenant and remainderman in respect of the payment of debts and legacies, requiring them (in effect) to be paid out of both capital and income.

In **18.4.7.7** we will see that the rules of equitable apportionment are commonly excluded by contrary provision in a will, it being generally considered that the inconvenience and cost of implementing them outweighs any benefit to the beneficiaries. In any event, the rules are ignored by the Revenue in assessing the income tax position of the estate and life tenant.

13.1.3 LIABILITY OF PERSONAL REPRESENTATIVES

Having accepted office, a personal representative is liable for loss resulting from his own breach of duty. A personal representative will not be liable for loss resulting from breaches of duty by fellow personal representatives, unless he has permitted or negligently allowed such breaches (see also **13.2.6**).

A breach of duty by a personal representative is called a *devastavit*, and may consist of a misappropriation of estate assets, maladministration or negligence. We will see (at **13.4.2** below) that a beneficiary or creditor who has suffered loss as a result of a *devastavit* may bring an action against the personal representative to recover such loss.

POWERS AND DUTIES OF PERSONAL REPRESENTATIVES

13.2 Administrative Powers of Personal Representatives

The Administration of Estates Act 1925 confers upon personal representatives a number of powers in connection with the administration of an estate. In addition, the Trustee Act 1925 and the Trustee Investments Act 1961 give certain powers to trustees — and since the definition of 'trustee' contained in that Act includes a personal representative, personal representatives also have these powers. These statutory powers are implied in all cases whether the deceased died testate or intestate. In most cases they are subject to awkward limitations and thus professionally drawn wills usually give the personal representatives wider powers. This may be by way of a modification to the statutory power or by way of an express clause setting out the particular power conferred on the personal representatives. The statutory powers are set out in outline below, together with an indication, where appropriate, of the type of modification or express clause that will commonly be contained in a will. When drafting a will it is necessary to consider whether the will should grant additional administrative powers to the personal representatives, and this is dealt with in 18.4.7.

13.2.1 POWER TO SELL, MORTGAGE OR LEASE

Section 39, Administration of Estates Act 1925 confers upon personal representatives the same powers in dealing with the deceased's estate (real and personal) as are enjoyed by trustees for sale of land. They may thus sell or exchange any property, raise money by mortgage or charge, and grant or accept surrender of leases.

These wide powers last until the end of the administration period, and are necessary to enable the personal representatives to raise monies to pay a wide range of administration expenses. For instance, the payment of debts, funeral and testamentary expenses, inheritance tax and pecuniary legacies. The personal representatives must decide which assets should be sold, and this is dealt with in 14.3.3.

13.2.2 POWER TO APPROPRIATE

Section 41, Administration of Estates Act 1925 provides that personal representatives may appropriate any part of the estate in or towards satisfaction of any legacy or interest or share in the estate, provided no specific beneficiary is thereby prejudiced. The 'appropriate consents' are necessary: thus, if the beneficiary is absolutely and beneficially entitled, the consent of the beneficiary is required (or of the beneficiary's parent or guardian if a minor). The asset to be appropriated must be valued for this purpose at the date of appropriation rather than at death (*Re Collins* [1975] 1 WLR 309).

13.2.2.1 Example

Tom leaves a pecuniary legacy of £5,000 to Beth and the residue of the estate to Roy. The residue includes shares now worth £3,000 and £2,000 cash. Provided Beth consents, the shares can be appropriated to Beth in partial satisfaction of her legacy, the balance being paid in cash.

13.2.2.2 Stamp duty

An appropriation is (under Stamp Duty (Exempt Instruments) Regulations 1987) exempt from stamp duty provided it is certified as falling within the appropriate category of the schedule to the Regulations. The instrument of appropriation does not have to be presented to the Stamp Office.

13.2.2.3 Provision in will

Although there is now no possibility of substantial stamp duty saving resulting from dispensing with the need for the consents required by s. 41, the will normally continues to so provide for convenience (see 18.4.7.5).

POWERS AND DUTIES OF PERSONAL REPRESENTATIVES

13.2.3 POWER TO APPOINT TRUSTEES OF A MINOR'S PROPERTY

Unless the will provides otherwise, a minor is unable to give a valid receipt for moneys or assets transferred to the minor in satisfaction of a legacy. Neither does statute enable parents or guardians to give a valid receipt to the personal representatives on behalf of a minor, although the will may so provide. In the absence of any such provision in the will, personal representatives will either have to hold the legacy until the minor attains 18, when a valid discharge can be given, or use one of the other methods mentioned in **16.1.5**.

To overcome this difficulty, s. 42, Administration of Estates Act 1925 enables personal representatives to appoint a trust corporation or two to four individuals (one or more of whom could be the personal representatives) to be the trustees of the property for the minor. The personal representatives can then transfer the property to the trustees and a receipt signed by the trustees will be a valid discharge to the personal representatives. This power is only available however where the minor is absolutely entitled to property, and not where the entitlement is merely contingent.

13.2.3.1 Express provision in the will

As indicated above, the will may provide that a parent or guardian may give a valid receipt on behalf of a minor, or that the minor may personally give a receipt having reached a specified age, commonly 16 — see **18.4.7.6**).

13.2.4 POWER TO POSTPONE DISTRIBUTION

Section 44, Administration of Estates Act 1925 provides that personal representatives are not bound to distribute the estate of the deceased before the expiration of one year from the death (the 'executor's year'), so that a beneficiary cannot insist on earlier payment. As to the entitlement of beneficiaries to interest on pecuniary and general legacies see **13.3.2.3** and **13.3.2.4** below.

13.2.5 Section 15, Trustee Act 1925

This section gives personal representatives (and trustees) wide powers to settle claims made by or against the estate. This very useful power enables personal representatives to make a reasonable compromise instead of having to litigate in order to protect themselves against claims for breach of duty.

13.2.6 POWER TO INSURE

By s. 19, Trustee Act 1925, personal representatives may insure against loss or damage by fire (only) for up to three-quarters of the value of the property (the premiums to be payable from income).

The statutory power does not extend to property which the personal representatives are bound to convey forthwith to a beneficiary absolutely entitled. A personal representative is not generally bound to convey property until it is indicated, by means of an assent (see **16.4**), that the property is not required for the payment of debts. This limitation is therefore not relevant until the personal representatives have assented.

Insurance moneys received under a policy of insurance are held as capital. They may be used to reinstate the property lost or damaged providing that the consent of any person whose consent is required to investment is obtained (s. 20, Trustee Act 1925).

13.2.6.1 Express provision in the will

Because of the above limitations it is common for a will to provide that the property may be insured to full value, or reinstatement value, and against all risks. It may also provide that the property may be reinstated at the discretion of the personal representatives or trustees (**18.4.7.4**).

POWERS AND DUTIES OF PERSONAL REPRESENTATIVES

13.2.7 POWER TO DELEGATE

13.2.7.1 Section 23(1), Trustee Act 1925

By this section, instead of acting personally, personal representatives may employ and pay an agent (solicitor, banker, stockbroker, etc.) to act on their behalf in connection with the administration, though not to exercise any discretion or execute any duty.

Personal representatives are not liable for the default of such agent if employed in good faith. However, personal representatives may be liable for their own breach of duty if they fail to take reasonable care in the choice of agent or fail to exercise proper supervision.

13.2.7.2 Section 30, Trustee Act 1925

This section provides that personal representatives are only liable for money etc. actually received by them (even if they have signed a receipt for the sake of conformity) and for their own defaults and not for those of any co-executor or co-administrator, or any other person with whom the estate's property is deposited, nor for any loss unless the same happens through the personal representative's 'wilful default' ('a consciousness of negligence or breach of duty or a recklessness in the performance of such a duty' — per Romer J in *Re City Equitable Fire Insurance Company Limited* [1925] 1 Ch 407).

13.2.7.3 Section 25, Trustee Act 1925 (as amended by s. 9, Powers of Attorney Act 1971)

This allows personal representatives to delegate by power of attorney for a period not exceeding 12 months any of the duties, powers and discretion vested in them. In this case, however, the personal representative remains fully liable for the acts of the delegate.

13.2.8 IMPLIED INDEMNITY

Section 30(2), Trustee Act 1925 authorises trustees and personal representatives to reimburse themselves for all expenses incurred in the execution of their powers and duties. This does not include a power to charge for work done in the administration, and if this is required specific provision will have to be made in the will.

13.2.9 POWER TO RUN THE DECEASED'S BUSINESS

As a first step, it must be ascertained whether the deceased was a sole trader or ran the business through the medium of a partnership or limited company.

13.2.9.1 Where the deceased was a sole trader

The general rule is that personal representatives have no authority to carry on the deceased's business. As an exception to this rule, however, they may do so with a view to the proper realisation of the deceased's estate, for example, to enable it to be sold as a going concern. This would not enable them, normally, to carry on the business for more than the executor's year.

If there is a trust for sale and conversion imposed upon property including the business (e.g. as part of residue) and power to postpone such sale etc. is also conferred, it appears that there is an implied power to carry on the business during the period of such postponement (*Re Crowther* [1985] 2 Ch 56 where it was carried on for the benefit of the life tenant).

In exercising such implied powers it seems that personal representatives will only have authority to utilise assets used in the business at the date of death and will not be entitled to have resort to any other part of the estate.

Personal representatives are personally liable for debts incurred in running the deceased's business after his death, though they are entitled to an indemnity from the estate. If they are carrying on the business for the purpose of realisation only, this right of indemnity takes priority over the rights of creditors and beneficiaries. If the business is being carried on under a power in the will, the right of indemnity has priority over the rights of beneficiaries but not creditors of the deceased unless they have expressly assented to the carrying on of the business.

13.2.9.2 Express provision in the will

Ideally a testator will have considered the succession to his business in his lifetime. Where the testator insists on remaining a sole proprietor until death, careful consideration must be given as to whether the business is to be handed on as a going concern, or whether it is to be wound up. In either case, wider powers will probably be contained in the will — for instance, enabling the personal representatives to use a wider range of estate assets in running the business.

13.2.9.3 Where the deceased traded as a partner

The personal representatives will usually have no power to intervene in the business. The partnership agreement must be consulted as it will usually contain provisions relating to the succession of a deceased partner's share, which will therefore pass outside the terms of the will.

13.2.9.4 Where the deceased was a shareholder in a limited company

In such a case the company will, of course, continue despite the death of a shareholder. The articles of association should be consulted, as these may give other shareholders rights to purchase the deceased shareholder's shares.

13.2.10 POWER TO INVEST

The Trustee Investments Act 1961 gives personal representatives the same power as trustees to invest in the investments specified in the first schedule to the Act, Parts I, II and III. The Act prescribes a somewhat cumbersome regime and the major provisions are set out below.

13.2.10.1 The three categories of authorised investments

These are:

(a) Part I, Narrower Range not requiring expert advice before investment. These are fixed interest investments whose capital value does not fluctuate. For example, National Savings Certificates, National Savings Bank deposits.

(b) Part II, Narrower Range requiring advice. Although these are 'safe' investments their value may fluctuate. The list includes government and local authority stocks, building society deposit accounts, debentures of certain companies (see **13.2.10.2**), mortgages of freeholds or leaseholds with at least 60 years to run. In this last case, s. 8, Trustee Act 1925 contains further provisions as to the obtaining of advice and as to the amount of the loan.

(c) Part III, Wider Range requiring advice. For example, building society share accounts, authorised unit trusts, stocks and shares in certain companies (**13.2.10.2**). Before investing in Part III investments, the fund must be divided (**13.2.10.3**).

13.2.10.2 Investment in company securities

Investment in debentures (Part II) and stocks and shares (Part III) is only possible if certain conditions are met. These include:

(a) The securities must be issued in the United Kingdom by a United Kingdom incorporated company.

POWERS AND DUTIES OF PERSONAL REPRESENTATIVES

    (b) They must be quoted on a recognised stock exchange.

    (c) The company must have total issued and paid up capital of at least £1 million, and have the requisite dividend record.

13.2.10.3 The requirement to divide the fund before investing in Wider Range investments

Investment may always be made in the Narrower Range Parts I and II, but before investment is made in Wider Range investments the fund must be divided into two equal parts (Narrower and Wider Range). Funds in the Narrower Range part can only be invested in Narrower Range investments. Funds in the Wider Range part may be invested in Narrower or Wider Range investments as the personal representatives think fit.

13.2.10.4 Transferring funds between the Narrower and Wider Range

Funds may not be transferred between the Narrower and Wider Range parts unless a compensating transfer is made.

13.2.10.5 Accruals to the trust fund

Property subsequently accruing must prima facie be dealt with so as to increase both parts of the fund equally. However, if the accrual is due to ownership of property in a particular part of the fund (e.g. a bonus issue of shares), the accrual is exclusively to that part of the fund.

13.2.10.6 Withdrawals

Withdrawal for the purposes of the administration (e.g. to pay debts etc. or to advance a beneficiary) may be made from either part of the fund without any need for compensating transfers.

13.2.10.7 Requirement to consider diversification

In all cases, including where the will contains an express power of investment, regard must be had to the need for diversification of investments and the suitability (generally and particularly) of the investments contemplated (s. 6(1), Trustee Investments Act 1961).

13.2.10.8 Requirement to take advice

Before investing in Part II or III investments, proper written advice on the suitability of the investment must be obtained and considered (though not necessarily followed). Further, such advice should be obtained and considered periodically during the retention of such investments (s. 6, Trustee Investments Act 1961).

13.2.10.9 Special range property

The will may extend the statutory power (see further **13.2.10.11** below) in which event investments so authorised form a special range and the provisions of the Act apply to the balance of the fund not covered by the express power.

13.2.10.10 Purchase of land

The purchase of land is not authorised by the Trustee Investments Act 1961, though other statutory provisions may apply.

Section 73, Settled Land Act 1925 provides that capital money arising under a strict settlement may be used to purchase freehold land or leasehold land with at least 60 years to run.

Section 28, Law of Property Act 1925 confers the same power upon trustees for sale of land. However, in *Re Wakeman* [1945] Ch 177, it was held that where trustees for sale of land have sold all the land which they held on trust for sale, they have no authority to purchase further land.

13.2.10.11 Express provision in the will

To avoid the complex limitations of the 1961 Act many wills confer upon personal representatives an unfettered discretion to choose investments. Even a widely drafted investment clause will not, however, enable the personal representatives to purchase non-income yielding assets: a power may also be given to apply money in the purchase of such assets, for example, a house as a residence for a beneficiary (see further **18.4.7.3**).

13.2.11 POWER TO MAINTAIN A MINOR

Section 31, Trustee Act 1925 provides that where property is held for an minor beneficiary and the gift carries the right to the intermediate income (see further **13.3.2** below), the trustees or personal representatives may apply the income for the maintenance education or benefit of the minor, and must accumulate the income not so applied. The following points should be noted:

(a) It does not matter whether the minor's interest is vested or contingent.

(b) In exercising their discretion, the personal representatives must consider the age and requirements of the minor and the circumstances of the case, generally including what other income is applicable for the same purpose.

(c) Once the beneficiary attains the age of 18, accumulated income is normally added to capital and devolves with it (s. 31(2)).

(d) If, although the minor has attained 18, the interest remains contingent, the discretion to use income for maintenance etc. ceases, and henceforth the income *must* be paid to the beneficiary until such time as the contingency is fulfilled or the interest fails (s. 31(1)). Remember that for inheritance tax purposes the beneficiary will then have an interest in possession (see **7.3.2**).

(e) The statutory power is only available to permit maintenance where the gift carries the intermediate income: most testamentary gifts will (in the absence of contrary provision in the will) carry such income. However, contingent pecuniary legacies generally do not (see further **13.3.2** below), in which event s. 31 will not apply: the intermediate income belongs in this case to the residuary beneficiaries.

(f) As to the income tax liability of the trustees and the beneficiary, see **7.1**.

13.2.11.1 Example

In her will Tessa leaves £100,000 to her niece, Penny, contingently upon her attaining the age of 18, and the residue of her estate upon trust for her son, Rex, contingently upon his attaining the age of 25.

Both Penny and Rex are minors when Tessa dies.

The gift to Penny is a contingent pecuniary legacy, and unless it is one of the exceptional cases, or there is specific provision in the will, the statutory power to maintain is not available. The income will form part of the residue.

So far as Rex is concerned the statutory power is available, and the trustees may choose to pay the income yielded by the residue for Rex's maintenance. Any income not so paid over must be accumulated.

When Rex reaches the age of 18 the power to maintain ceases, and the trustee must pay the current income to Rex until he reaches 25, or dies without having satisfied the contingency. If Rex attains the age of 25, he is then entitled to capital and accumulations.

POWERS AND DUTIES OF PERSONAL REPRESENTATIVES

13.2.11.2 Express provision in the will varying s. 31

The statutory power may be considered to be adequate. The will may however make the following modifications (see **18.4.7.1**):

(a) Conferring an absolute discretion on the trustees as to the amount of income available.
(b) Where the gift is contingent on the beneficiary attaining an age greater than 18, removing the right to receive income at 18.

13.2.12 POWER TO ADVANCE CAPITAL

Section 32, Trustee Act 1925 gives trustees and personal representatives a discretion to apply capital for the advancement or benefit of a beneficiary (whether or not a minor) who has a vested or contingent interest in capital. The following points should be noted:

(a) This discretion is not available in respect of land or capital money under a Settled Land Act settlement: but it is available in relation to the proceeds of sale of land held on trust for sale.
(b) Up to one half of the beneficiary's vested or presumptive share may be advanced.
(c) Any person with a prior interest (e.g. a life tenant) must consent in writing to the advance.
(d) Any advance made must be brought into account when the beneficiary becomes absolutely entitled.
(e) If a beneficiary contingently entitled receives an advance but fails to fulfil the contingency (e.g. the beneficiary dies before attaining the age specified for vesting) the amount advanced is not recoverable from the beneficiary's estate.
(f) An advancement is a substantial payment made with a view to setting the recipient up in life: the term 'benefit' has been construed extremely widely. It may include (e.g.) a saving of tax: *Pilkington* v *IRC* [1964] AC 612.

13.2.12.1 Express provision in the will

The will may amend the statutory power (see **18.4.7.2**) by removing the limitations referred to in **13.2.12** (b), (c), or (d) above. The statutory power does not of course enable advancements to be made to a life tenant, but this power may be granted by the will.

13.2.13 EXERCISE OF PERSONAL REPRSENTATIVES' POWERS

A sole personal representative (whether originally so appointed or by survivorship) has the same powers as two or more personal representatives. A sole personal representative may thus give a valid receipt for the proceeds of sale of land (s. 27, Law of Property Act 1925). Joint personal representatives generally have joint and several authority, so that the act of one binds the others and the estate.

There are statutory exceptions in relation to the conveyance of land and the transfer of shares. In these cases, the conveyance or transfer will normally require all living personal representatives (i.e. to whom a grant has been issued) to join in.

Personal representatives' powers are in nature fiduciary and, therefore, must be exercised in good faith in the interest of the estate as a whole.

13.3 Beneficiaries' Rights during Administration

The beneficiaries will want to know that the estate is being efficiently administered by the personal representatives, and will be concerned to receive their entitlements under the will or intestacy as quickly as possible. In this section we will consider the nature of the beneficiaries' rights, and in **13.4** how they may be enforced.

POWERS AND DUTIES OF PERSONAL REPRESENTATIVES

13.3.1 THE BENEFICIARIES' RIGHT TO COMPEL DUE ADMINISTRATION

The deceased's assets vest in the personal representatives 'in full ownership without distinction between legal and equitable interests' (*Commissioner of Stamp Duties (Queensland)* v *Livingston* [1965] AC 694).

Thus, until the administration is complete the beneficiary (whether under the will or intestacy rules) has neither a legal nor equitable interest in the deceased's assets. It is only at this point that the personal representatives will know which of the deceased's assets have had to be sold to pay debts and administration expenses, and which are available for distribution to beneficiaries.

The beneficiary does, however, have a chose in action, the right to have the deceased's estate properly administered. It seems likely that this is true even of specific beneficiaries (*Re Hayes' Will Trusts* [1971] 1 WLR 758).

13.3.2 DATE FOR PAYMENT OF ENTITLEMENT UNDER WILL OR INTESTACY

We have seen that personal representatives cannot be compelled to distribute the estate before the end of the executor's year (**13.2.4** above). Beneficiaries will want to know whether they are entitled to income or interest between the date of death and the date of distribution.

Whether the beneficiary is entitled to income from, or interest on, the value of the asset(s) during this period will depend on the provisions of any will, on the nature of the asset (i.e. whether or not it is income producing) and on the nature of the gift.

13.3.2.1 Specific gifts

Where the entitlement of the beneficiary is immediate, such gifts carry the right to any income accruing between the date of death and the vesting of the property in the beneficiary. The assent by the personal representatives vesting the property in the beneficiary operates retrospectively to give the beneficiary the right to such income (see **16.4.2.3**). If the beneficiary has a contingent or future (deferred) entitlement, again such gifts carry the intermediate income which will be added to capital (and devolve with it) for so long as the rules against indefinite accumulation permit. (Thereafter, the income either falls into residue or passes under the intestacy rules.)

13.3.2.2 Residuary gifts

Whether the beneficiary's entitlement is immediate or contingent, and whether of personalty or realty, such gifts carry the intermediate income. Where the beneficiary has a future (deferred) interest, devises (i.e. gifts of realty) probably carry the intermediate income: bequests (i.e. gifts of personalty) do not carry such right and the income passes under the intestacy rules.

13.3.2.3 Contingent pecuniary legacies

Where the will contains such a legacy, so that the sum involved has to be invested pending the fulfilment of the contingency, the gift does not normally carry the intermediate income; the income from the investment therefore belongs to the residuary beneficiaries. There are exceptions to this rule where the gift is to the child or person to whom the testator stands *in loco parentis*, and the contingency is attaining an age not greater than 18 (or earlier marriage); or where the gift is to any child made with the intention of providing for that child's maintenance.

All the rules stated above apply in the absence of provision to the contrary in the will.

13.3.2.4 Pecuniary legacies

As a general rule, a pecuniary legatee, general legatee, or demonstrative legatee (if the designated fund is exhausted) is entitled to interest at 6% only from the date upon which such legacy is payable. In the absence of any direction to the contrary in the will, such a legacy is payable at the end of the executor's year. Any interest payable is regarded as an administration expense, payable therefore normally from residue.

Exceptionally, however, interest on such legacies is payable from the date of death, unless the will otherwise provides. This is so where:

(a) the legacy is in satisfaction of a debt;
(b) the legacy is charged on realty;
(c) the legacy is to testator's infant child or to an infant to whom he stands *in loco parentis*;
(d) the legacy is to any infant with the intention to provide for that child's maintenance.

13.4 Remedies Available to Beneficiaries

Where difficulties arise during the administration of an estate, there are a number of formal remedies available to a beneficiary. Essentially, they fall into two categories. First, there are 'administration proceedings' (**13.4.1**), designed to ensure that the administration of the estate is properly conducted. Such actions may be general, or for specific relief, and need not necessarily be 'contentious', in that the personal representatives are equally entitled to seek the court's assistance in this way. Second, there are actions to 'recover loss' suffered (see **13.4.2**).

13.4.1 GENERAL ADMINISTRATION ACTIONS

13.4.1.1 The reason for commencing administration proceedings

An application may be made to the court wherever difficulties are encountered in the administration of an estate. It may be that the personal representatives need the court's assistance to resolve a particular problem that has arisen. Such actions are for specific relief and are dealt with in **Chapter 14** when considering practical considerations in the administration of the estate (see **14.3.7.7**).

There may however be a more general problem concerning the administration: perhaps the beneficiaries are alleging that the personal representatives have committed a *devastavit* by misappropriating estate assets. In such a case the action will be one for the general administration of the whole or part of the estate by the court. If the court makes such an order, the personal representatives cannot exercise their powers of sale or distribute the assets without the court's consent.

13.4.1.2 Jurisdiction

Such an action may be commenced by originating summons or writ. A writ should be used if there are likely to be substantial disputes of fact, and must be used where there is an allegation of fraud or a claim for damages for breach of duty. The action may be commenced in:

(a) The Chancery Division of the High Court.
(b) The county court where the estate does not exceed £30,000 in value (or, if greater, the parties agree).
(c) The bankruptcy court if the estate is insolvent.

As an alternative to commencing an administration action, the Public Trustee can be required to administer a solvent estate, where the gross capital value of the estate is less than £1,000 and those beneficially entitled are of small means.

13.4.1.3 Parties to proceedings

Proceedings may be brought by any personal representative, beneficiary (whether under the will or intestacy) or creditor. All the personal representatives must be parties; as plaintiffs if they consent, otherwise as defendants (RSC ord. 85, r. 3(1)).

13.4.1.4 The order for administration

The court is not bound to make an order for administration unless it is satisfied that the questions at issue between the parties cannot otherwise be properly determined.

If the whole estate is to be administered under the court's direction, accounts and inquiries will be taken and made as to the whole conduct of the administration, and when satisfied the court will order distribution. Alternatively, the court may order specific accounts and inquiries to be taken and made to deal with any particular problems.

13.4.1.5 Costs

The costs of the personal representatives will normally be payable from the estate, unless they have acted unreasonably. Costs of other parties are in the court's discretion.

13.4.1.6 Appointing a judicial trustee

Where it is sought to avoid the expense of an administration action and the administration by the personal representatives 'out of court' has for some reason broken down, they or the beneficiaries may apply to the Chancery Division for the appointment of a judicial trustee to complete the administration. Such appointment may be to act alone or jointly with others, or (if sufficient cause is shown) in place of the existing personal representatives. As an officer of the court, such a trustee, once appointed, does not require the court's consent before exercising his powers.

13.4.1.7 Removal of a personal representative

As noted at **8.7.6** above, s. 50, Administration of Justice Act 1985 enables the High Court to remove an existing personal representative and to appoint a substitute. An application can be made by a beneficiary or a personal representative.

13.4.2 OTHER REMEDIES AVAILABLE TO BENEFICIARIES

13.4.2.1 Personal action against the personal representatives

Instead of commencing administration proceedings a personal action may be brought against the personal representatives. As we have seen at **13.1.3**, a failure by a personal representative to carry out the duties of the office is a *devastavit*, for which the personal representative is personally liable to the beneficiaries or creditors, unless they have acquiesced in or encouraged the breach.

Personal representatives may, however, be relieved from liability:

(a) By provisions in the will relieving personal representatives from liability — (e.g.) where mistakes are made in good faith.
(b) By s. 61, Trustee Act 1925 the court may wholly or partly relieve the personal representative from personal liability where it is satisfied that the personal representative acted 'honestly, reasonably and ought fairly to be excused'.
(c) By agreement with the beneficiaries, being *sui juris* and fully aware of the breach, the personal representatives may be released from liability.

POWERS AND DUTIES OF PERSONAL REPRESENTATIVES

13.4.2.2 Tracing

A beneficiary (whether under a will or the intestacy rules) or a creditor may have the right to trace and recover property of the estate (or property representing such property) from the personal representatives or any other recipient of it, other than a bona fide purchaser for value or person deriving title from such purchaser. The right to trace is also lost if the property has been dissipated, or where to allow tracing would be inequitable. This remedy may be sought whether or not a personal action has been brought against the personal representative, though in so far as such action has been 'successful' the right to trace is clearly not also going to be available.

13.4.2.3 Personal action against recipients of estate assets

Where all other remedies of a beneficiary (whether under the will or intestacy rules) or creditor have been exhausted, a personal action may be brought against a person who has wrongly received the assets of the estate (*Ministry of Health* v *Simpson* [1951] AC 251).

FOURTEEN

ADMINISTERING THE ESTATE — SOME PRACTICAL CONSIDERATIONS

In **Chapter 8**, we explored the legal background to the role of personal representatives and the various grants of representation to which they may (in differing circumstances) be entitled. In the last chapter, we considered the legal basis of the powers and duties of the personal representatives and the position of the beneficiaries. In this and the two following chapters we are going to look at the practical context within which those roles, powers and duties will be exercised and some of the problems which may be encountered.

In this chapter, we will concentrate upon the earlier stages of the administration. **Chapter 15** will look at certain changes in the deceased's dispositions which may be effected after the death, while **Chapter 16** will examine the concluding stages of the winding up of the estate.

This chapter will begin by looking at some general matters (**14.1**). We will then consider the steps to be taken in the early (pre-grant) stages of the administration (**14.2**), and then look at the practice following the issue of the grant (**14.3**). The chapter will conclude (**14.4**) with a consideration of the financial services aspects relevant to these stages of the administration of the estate.

14.1 General Matters

As we have seen it is the duty of the personal representatives to ascertain the extent and value of the deceased's assets and liabilities, obtain the appropriate grant of representation, collect in and (if necessary) realise the various assets, pay the debts and legacies and then distribute the residue of the estate to those entitled under the terms of the will or under the intestacy rules. In this chapter we will be concentrating upon all these activities other than the payment of the legacies and the distribution of the residue (as to which see **Chapter 16**).

In general terms, the duties of the solicitor acting for the personal representatives are to advise them upon all aspects of the administration and to take all appropriate action on their behalf which may be needed to bring the matter efficiently to its proper conclusion. Proper consultation with the clients is essential and they should be kept regularly and fully informed as to the progress of the matter.

Be careful to remember who your clients are! Where you are instructed by the personal representatives, they are your clients — not the members of the deceased's family or the beneficiaries. If you (or your firm) are the executor(s) then (effectively) the family and beneficiaries become your 'clients'.

ADMINISTERING THE ESTATE — SOME PRACTICAL CONSIDERATIONS

14.2 The Early Stages

We have already considered in some detail much of the practice involved in the early stages of the administration of an estate — in the chapters concerned with oaths, Inland Revenue accounts and affidavit evidence (**Chapters 9, 10** and **11** respectively). Here we will endeavour to put those matters in context and consider other practical issues which may arise in the pre-grant period of the matter.

14.2.1 INSTRUCTIONS

The personal representatives may (and frequently do) instruct a solicitor to act for them in the conduct of the administration. You may yourself be appointed an executor, or be a partner in a firm which has been appointed to act. In all of these cases you will have to obtain the information you need to begin the task from the personal representatives or family members who may — especially initially — be in a distressed state. Whilst it is, of course, important that you perform your role efficiently, it is equally important that you conduct matters with sensitivity and with a proper concern for those who may not only be very upset but perhaps in temporary difficult financial circumstances resulting from the death.

14.2.1.1 What do you need to know?

Much of the information required to enable you to complete the first stage of the administration of the estate (obtaining the grant) will be apparent from the discussions in **Chapters 9, 10** and **11**. In addition, you will also need to establish how and to whom the estate is to be distributed, and whether any problems are likely to be encountered in this connection. There may, for example, be missing beneficiaries (see **14.3.6** below) or the possibility of a claim under Inheritance (Provision for Family and Dependants) Act 1975 (see **Chapters 3** and **15.3**).

14.2.1.2 Checklists

The best way to ensure the efficient collection of the information you need from the personal representatives or family members is to use a suitable checklist. Most firms will have their own version of such a checklist, which should prompt you to discover the details appropriate to any given case relating to the following matters:

(a) Full personal details relating to the deceased, the immediate family and any dependants.
(b) Full personal details relating to the proposed personal representative(s), and to those entitled to share in the estate. In both cases, as we have seen, who these people are will very much depend upon whether or not there is a will (see further **14.2.2** below).
(c) Details of the various assets:

(i) in the deceased's succession estate (i.e. passing under the will or the intestacy rules);
(ii) not in the succession estate but in the taxable estate (i.e. including details of any property passing outside of the will; any settled property of which the deceased had been a tenant for life);
(iii) not forming part of the estate for either succession or taxation purposes (such as s. 11, Married Women's Property Act 1882 and other trust policies; certain lump sum pension scheme benefits).

(d) Details of the various liabilities due from the estate or charged upon any of the assets listed in (c).
(e) Details of any lifetime gifts within the seven years prior to the death (or at any time if a benefit was reserved).
(f) Details of those entitled to share in the estate, whether under the will or the intestacy rules.

ADMINISTERING THE ESTATE — SOME PRACTICAL CONSIDERATIONS

14.2.2 WHAT ELSE WILL YOU NEED?

In addition to the information identified above, you will need (as appropriate) the following:

(a) The death certificate — ideally several copies to enable you more speedily to register the death (see **14.2.4** below).

(b) The original will and any codicil(s). Your firm may already be holding these, or perhaps they have been lodged for safe keeping with the deceased's bank. Once obtained, it will be necessary to consider any issues of validity which may arise (see **1.1**) and whether affidavit evidence may be required to support the application (see **Chapter 11**).

(c) Any 'paperwork' associated with the various assets and liabilities. Thus, for example, you will need the title deeds relating to any land (or at least to discover their whereabouts). Similarly, such things as share certificates, insurance policies, bank and building society account details, outstanding bills, etc. should be obtained.

(d) Details of any insurances (e.g. house and contents cover) effected by the deceased. Arrangements should be made, as soon as possible, either to have the interest of the personal representatives noted on any such policies, or for fresh cover in their name to be taken out. In the case of motor insurance, ensure (if needed) that appropriate cover is (or has been) arranged to enable family members to continue to use the vehicle.

14.2.3 FINANCIAL DIFFICULTIES?

Always check at the first interview whether the deceased's family have any immediate financial needs as a result of the death. It will be some weeks (perhaps months) before significant funds will become available from the estate: do any surviving spouse and children have access to adequate funds in the meantime?

What sources of funds might there be to assist here? Where the deceased had a joint bank or building society account with the surviving spouse, or the survivor has adequate funds of their own the problem may not be acute. Where there are funds which could be released without a grant (particularly, any s. 11, Married Women's Property Act 1882 or other trust policies; certain pension fund lump sum benefits payable at the discretion of the trustees of the scheme) try to take the necessary steps to enable payment to be made as quickly as possible. Similarly, where a state or employment related 'pension' may be payable, deal with this as a matter of priority.

14.2.4 REGISTERING THE DEATH

The first task upon receipt of instructions is to register the death with the various banks, building societies, insurance companies, etc. in which the deceased had investments and to establish the amounts due to the estate as at the date of death.

This is done by sending a copy death certificate (not a photocopy) to the various institutions with a request to inform you of the amount due — and to return the copy death certificate to you: however, where a special certificate has been issued by the registrar (e.g. for National Savings or social security purposes) that certificate will be retained by the appropriate agency.

In the case of shareholdings, you should register the death with the various companies and ask them to confirm the extent of the deceased's holding: it may be that the personal representatives have not in fact located all the share certificates. You may then wish to instruct a stockbroker to prepare a valuation for you. Where the deceased owned land, the assistance of a surveyor may be required: it will be helpful in such a case if the surveyor can also give a valuation of the household and personal effects. Expert assistance in valuing the deceased's assets will also be necessary where, for example, the deceased was 'in business' — whether as a sole trader or partner, or the business was conducted through the medium of a company.

ADMINISTERING THE ESTATE — SOME PRACTICAL CONSIDERATIONS

The deceased's Inspector of Taxes should also be notified of the death: you will then usually receive a tax return to be completed in due course in respect of the pre-death period of the tax year in question and another relating to the post-death period: if the administration period stretches beyond the end of that tax year, further returns for the later years will be required.

At an early stage, you should also notify the various creditors of the death and that the estate is now responsible for the debts due to them. This will hopefully stop the family being further distressed by demands for payment.

If there is a will and there are beneficiaries other than those instructing you, you should inform them of their 'interest' under the will, and that — subject to the will being admitted to probate and the needs of the administration — you will be contacting them again as soon as you are able to deal with their legacies. It will be helpful if you give them an estimate of the timescale involved, being as realistic as possible in this. It is important to be cautious in what you say because the will might prove not to be admissible and/or there might not be sufficient funds to enable payment in full of all the legacies after the various liabilities have been discharged.

14.2.5 PREPARING THE PAPERS TO LEAD THE GRANT

As confirmation of the amounts due to the estate is received, the appropriate oath and Inland Revenue account forms can be drafted, along with any other supporting evidence (such as affidavits and copy testamentary documents) which may be required in the particular case.

Fair copies will have to be prepared for swearing or signature (as appropriate) before being lodged at the selected Registry.

14.2.6 PAYMENT OF INHERITANCE TAX

As we have seen, in order to obtain the grant the personal representatives will have to pay any inheritance tax due on the delivery of the Inland Revenue account. In cases where tax is payable, the grant cannot normally be issued unless a receipted account is lodged with the papers. However, they normally need the grant as evidence of their title — without which those holding the deceased's funds will be unwilling to part with them! How can the deceased's personal representatives solve this 'circular' problem?

We saw in **8.4.1** that it is possible to obtain amounts due to the estate without production of a grant under the Administration of Estates (Small Payments) Act 1965 and any such funds could be used to help pay the tax bill. However, it is likely in many cases that much more will be needed than can be raised in this way. In the following paragraphs we consider other sources of funding which may be available to the personal representatives.

14.2.6.1 Bank loan

Either the deceased's or the personal representatives' bank will normally be happy to lend whatever is needed to pay the inheritance tax. The bank will usually insist upon an undertaking from the personal representatives to account to it from the first proceeds of the realisation of the estate assets once the grant has been obtained. An undertaking may also be required from the solicitor acting for the personal representatives — in which event the solicitors should first obtain an irrevocable authority from the personal representatives.

The bank will of course charge interest, so that, irrespective of the terms of any undertaking, the loan should be discharged as soon as possible.

Provided the arrangement with the bank takes the form of a loan (rather than an overdraft facility) the personal representatives may be entitled to income tax relief for the interest payable. Such relief is available to the extent that the loan has been used to pay the inheritance tax on the personalty to which the deceased was beneficially entitled immediately before the death and which vests in the personal representatives (or would do so if it were situated in the United Kingdom). The relief is only available for interest paid in respect of a period of 12 months from the commencement of the loan.

14.2.6.2 Loan from beneficiary

A beneficiary may well be prepared (in order to mitigate or avoid the cost of bank borrowing) to lend money to help pay the inheritance tax — either interest free or at a rate less than the commercial rate charged by the bank. (If interest is paid, it will also qualify for income tax relief in the manner described in **14.2.6.1** above.)

This approach will only work, of course, if the beneficiaries have money readily available — either from existing resources, or from monies passing to them on the death but outside of the will or the intestacy rules (such as the proceeds of a s. 11, Married Women's Property Act 1882 or other trust policy; jointly-held property accruing by survivorship; nominated property; lump sum benefits under a superannuation scheme payable at the discretion of the trustees of the scheme).

14.2.6.3 Sale of assets

We saw in **8.3** that an executor's authority derives from the will, the grant merely confirming this: administrators, on the other hand, actually have their authority conferred by the grant. In principle, therefore, it is possible for an executor (but not an administrator) to sell estate assets prior to the issue of the grant: in practice, however, purchasers may well wish to see confirmation of the vendor's title before parting with their money! In particular, although it is possible to enter into a contract to sell land 'subject to probate', the grant will be needed to make the executor's title before the sale can be completed.

However, it may be possible for an executor to sell some assets before grant. A grant is not needed to pass title to chattels; this is achieved by delivery coupled with the necessary intention.

Further, under Stock Exchange rules an executor can sell quoted shares before the grant is issued, subject to an undertaking for its production being given.

14.2.6.4 Direct payment to the Revenue

Where the deceased's assets include monies held in a building society account or policies of life assurance whose proceeds are payable to the personal representatives, the building society or insurance company may be prepared to release some/all the monies due to the estate direct to the Revenue in payment of inheritance tax.

14.2.7 SWEARING OR AFFIRMING THE OATH

Remember that this must be done before an independent solicitor (or Justice of the Peace), and will be a necessary formality for any other affidavit evidence required. The fees payable are currently £3.50 per deponent for each oath or other affidavit, plus £1.00 per deponent for marking each will, codicil or exhibit to any other affidavit.

14.2.8 LODGING THE PAPERS

When all is ready, it is necessary to lodge (by post or in person) at the selected Registry:

    (a) the appropriate oath;
    (b) the appropriate Inland Revenue account (where required) duly receipted where tax is payable;

ADMINISTERING THE ESTATE — SOME PRACTICAL CONSIDERATIONS

(c) any further supporting documents, such as further affidavits, copy testamentary documents and renunciations;

(d) a cheque for the probate fees. Where the net estate does not exceed £10,000, no fee is payable. Thereafter, the fees are currently:

Net estate not exceeding	Court fee
£25,000	£40
£40,000	£80
£70,000	£150
£100,000	£215
£200,000	£300

Where the net estate exceeds £200,000, the fees payable on the excess above that figure are £50 for every additional £100,000 or part thereof.

Normally, the issue of one or more office copies of the grant should be requested on lodging the application. This will (*inter alia*) help to speed-up the process of registering the grant: the fee payable for each such copy is 25p.

14.3 On Receipt of the Grant

Once the grant has been received from the issuing Registry, various issues will need to be considered.

14.3.1 ADVERTISEMENTS UNDER s. 27, TRUSTEE ACT 1925

Even though they were not aware of the claims of a beneficiary or creditor at the time of distribution, the personal representatives remain personally liable to any unpaid beneficiary or creditor — *Knatchbull* v *Fearnhead* (1837) 3 M & C 122. By complying with the requirements of s. 27 the personal representatives can protect themselves against such liability. It is important, however, to appreciate that s. 27 only affords protection to the personal representatives as such. Any disappointed beneficiary or creditor may recover from the person(s) to whom the personal representatives have distributed — including themselves if also beneficiaries.

In the case of an executor, whose authority derives from the will, advertisements under this section can (and to save time should) be made even before the grant is issued. Where the personal representatives are administrators they cannot properly do this, since they are authorised to act only by the grant itself. Once this has been issued, however, the placing of the required advertisements should be a matter of priority.

14.3.1.1 The advertisements

These are usually made by the solicitor acting for the personal representatives and on their behalf, requiring any person interested (as beneficiary or creditor) to send particulars to the personal representatives' solicitor within a stated time — which must not be less than two months from the date upon which the advertisement appears — after which time the estate will be distributed on the basis of claims of which the personal representatives then have notice (whether from a response to the advertisements or otherwise).

Such advertisements must be placed in:

(a) the London Gazette; and
(b) a newspaper circulating in the district in which any land forming part of the estate is situated (in practice, this will often be a local newspaper); and

(c) (in effect) any other newspaper etc. (whether in this country or abroad) as might be appropriate to the particular case (i.e. in which a court from which directions were being sought in an administration action might order advertisement). Thus, for example, where the deceased had been in business it might be appropriate to advertise in a relevant trade journal. If the personal representatives are in doubt they should apply to the court for directions.

14.3.1.2 Searches

The personal representatives should also make such searches as a purchaser of land would make — s. 27(2). Searches should therefore be made in the Land Registry or Land Charges Registry; in the Local Land Charges Register; and a bankruptcy search against the deceased and the beneficiaries.

14.3.2 REGISTERING THE GRANT

The personal representatives now have their evidence of title and should proceed apace to register the grant with the various institutions (banks, building societies, insurance companies, etc.) holding the deceased's assets and obtain from them the sums due to the estate.

Office copies of the grant, bearing the seal of the Registry, should be used rather than the original: photocopies are not acceptable evidence! The original is an important document of title and therefore should so far as possible be protected from the risk of loss and be kept in the file. However, the Inland Revenue certainly like to see the original.

Hopefully, you will have obtained enough office copies of the grant to enable this process to be completed swiftly. The absolute priority should be the release of sufficient funds to discharge any loan to pay the inheritance tax (**14.2.6** above). After this has been done, normally you should aim to discharge interest-bearing liabilities first so as to minimise the 'cost' to the estate.

As we have seen (**13.1.1**), the personal representatives' duty is to 'collect and get in' all the deceased's real and personal estate (and then administer it according to law). This must be done with 'reasonable diligence'.

Unsecured debts due to the deceased should be collected as soon as practicable — the personal representatives taking proceedings for their recovery if necessary. There is no need to call in or realise loans secured on mortgages of land which are authorised investments, unless the money is needed to discharge the funeral, testamentary and administration expenses, debts and pecuniary legacies.

Where the estate's assets include a reversionary (i.e. future) interest under a trust, this should not be sold unless there is some special reason for doing so (e.g. that there are no other funds available for the payment of the various expenses and debts of the estate).

Generally, causes of action vested in the deceased at the date of death survive for the benefit of the estate (as do those subsisting against the deceased against the estate) — s. 1(1), Law Reform (Miscellaneous Provisions) Act 1934. The main exceptions relate to contracts for the provision of personal services and the tort of defamation.

The personal representatives may also have an action to recover damages on behalf of certain dependants where the deceased's death has been caused by a wrongful act in respect of which the deceased could have sued if still alive — Fatal Accidents Act 1976. Any damages recovered under this Act do not form part of the deceased's estate for any purpose, but 'belong' to the dependants concerned.

The personal representatives (as we saw in **13.2.5**) have wide powers of settling claims made by or against the estate, so that they are not obliged to litigate every possible point or risk being held liable for not doing so.

ADMINISTERING THE ESTATE — SOME PRACTICAL CONSIDERATIONS

14.3.3 SALES OF ASSETS

In order to be able to pay taxes and other liabilities, the personal representatives may have to sell assets in the estate. In principle, they are at liberty to use any assets coming into their hands for this purpose (see further **14.3.4** below). However, in practice there are a number of 'constraints' which they should bear in mind.

14.3.3.1 The will

The terms of any will should very much influence their decision. Thus, if the will makes specific gifts the property so given should not be sold unless other assets have been exhausted. Further, beneficiaries may have indicated a wish to receive particular assets in partial or total satisfaction of (as the case may be) a pecuniary legacy or share of residue. The personal representatives should endeavour to respect those wishes and avoid selling the assets concerned, if possible to do so.

14.3.3.2 Tax implications

We have already encountered (in **6.5.2.7**) the so-called 'loss on sale' reliefs for land and quoted securities sold within the prescribed statutory periods for less than their probate values. Where there are assets which might qualify for such relief, the personal representatives should consider whether to sell such assets and thus be able to reclaim any inheritance tax paid on the 'difference'. (If this relief is claimed, we have seen that no loss relief is available for capital gains tax purposes).

Where personal representatives sell any assets during the course of the administration, there will prima facie be a charge to capital gains tax on gains accruing since the date of death (see **5.2.2**). Such gains may be relieved from charge by the annual exempt slice — as we have seen, personal representatives have the same exemption as an individual (currently £5,800) for gains made on disposals in the tax year in which the death occurs and in the following two tax years. Thus, for example, if in March they are contemplating selling shares which show a gain of £10,000 since the date of death, they would be well advised to consider selling immediately sufficient to utilise the current year's exemption and the rest after 6 April.

Where personal representatives realise an allowable loss on a sale of estate assets, it may be set against their gains of that year and any amount not thereby absorbed is carried forward to be set against their gains in future tax years. Their loss cannot be passed on to the beneficiaries, so if it is possible that the personal representatives will not have sufficient gains to absorb any loss an alternative strategy should be considered. If the asset concerned, instead of being sold, is vested in a beneficiary (as we saw in **5.2.3** this is not a chargeable event and the beneficiary acquires at the value at the date of death) the beneficiary can sell realising a loss to be set against any chargeable gains of the beneficiary.

14.3.4 PAYMENT OF DEBTS (SOLVENT ESTATE)

A solvent estate is one where the assets are sufficient to cover in full the funeral, testamentary and administration expenses, debts and other liabilities. It is immaterial whether or not legacies can also be paid in full.

So far as the creditors (including secured creditors) are concerned, they are entitled to be paid what is due to them from any part of the estate available for the payment of debts. As long as they are paid, it does not matter to them upon what part of the estate the burden of the payment falls. However, this is a matter of considerable importance from the viewpoint of the beneficiaries. Thus, to take a simple example, if the will leaves Blackacre to Beatrice and the residue of the estate to Rosalind, it will matter very much to them who has to bear the burden of the debts — particularly if Blackacre is subject to a mortgage at the date of the testator's death. It is with the resolution of such problems that this section is concerned: as we shall see, the answer will depend upon whether (and what) provision is made in any will.

ADMINISTERING THE ESTATE — SOME PRACTICAL CONSIDERATIONS

14.3.4.1 Secured creditors

We are here concerned with the situation where a debt has been charged on the deceased's property during the deceased's lifetime — for example, a mortgage on Blackacre. A charge may also arise by operation of law — for example, on the property of a judgment debtor or an Inland Revenue charge for unpaid tax.

Subject to the testator showing contrary intention (see **14.3.4.5** below), by s. 35, Administration of Estates Act 1925 the property so charged is liable for the payment of that debt. So, in the example above, Beatrice will prima facie take Blackacre subject to the mortgage debt. If the value of Blackacre is insufficient to cover the mortgage debt, the 'deficit' would have to be met by the residuary estate, so that Rosalind's entitlement would be correspondingly reduced.

Where several properties are each charged with separate debts, any deficit in relation to one property will normally have to be met out of the residuary estate (rather than being born by the beneficiaries taking the other charged properties). If, however, several properties are charged as security for the same debt, and they are given to different beneficiaries, each bears a proportionate part of the burden (i.e. according to the respective values at the date of death).

14.3.4.2 Other debts — the statutory order

So far as unsecured creditors are concerned — again, subject to any express provision in the will (see **14.3.4.5** below) — the order in which the estate's assets should be used is laid down by s. 34(3) and Part II of the First Schedule, Administration of Estates Act 1925. These provisions draw no distinction between realty and personalty.

The order is as follows — if there is nothing in a given 'category', or what there is proves insufficient, you move on down the list:

(a) Property undisposed of by the will (subject to the setting aside of a fund from which to pay any pecuniary legacies). Thus, where a partial intestacy arises (because the deceased's will contains no residuary gift, or where such residuary gift has totally or partially failed) the property not disposed of by the effective provisions of the will is primarily liable for the payment of the unsecured debts of the deceased. However, it is only so much of such undisposed property as is not set aside to pay any pecuniary legacies (see **16.1.2**) that is so liable.
(b) Residue (again, subject to the setting aside of a fund from which to pay any pecuniary legacies — i.e to the extent that these are not fully covered by the retention made under (a) above).
(c) Property specifically given for the payment of debts. Property is within this category if the will contains a direction that the identified property (e.g. Greenacre) is to be used to fund the payment of debts, but nothing is said as to what is to happen to any surplus.
(d) Property specifically charged with the payment of debts. Property falls within this category where the will contains a direction as in (c) above, but goes on to provide what is to happen to any surplus.

You may be pardoned for thinking that where the deceased has taken the trouble to identify specific property in the estate to fund the payment of debts, this would place such property firmly at the head of the list! Faced with the problem of reconciling logic with the statutory order, the courts have concluded that such a provision can only make the specifically given or charged property primarily liable where the will shows an intention to exonerate any property falling within categories (a) and (b) above — see further **14.3.4.5** below.

(e) The pecuniary legacy fund (retained under (a) and/or (b) above). At this point, any such fund will be used to help pay the debts. Unless the testator has indicated that any such legacies are to be paid in priority, they will abate proportionately — so that each legatee bears a share of the burden of the payment.

(f) Property specifically devised or bequeathed, rateably according to the property's value (i.e. to the deceased) at the date of death. Thus, if Whiteacre (the subject of a specific gift in the will) is worth £100,000 and is subject to an outstanding mortgage of £25,000, its value for the purposes of this exercise will be £75,000.

(g) Property appointed under a general power of appointment (again, rateably according to value). This category comprises only property subject to such a power which the deceased has expressly exercised in the will. It will not include property over which the deceased had such a power but which (though the power is not expressly exercised in the will) is deemed to pass under a general gift in the will by virtue of s. 27, Wills Act 1837. Thus, if the testator has a power of appointment over Pinkacre — which is not expressly exercised in the will, nor is Pinkacre the subject of a specific gift — Pinkacre will pass as part of the residuary gift, and thus be available for the payment of debts under category (b) above.

14.3.4.3 Property not included in the statutory order

Certain other categories of property may also be available for the payment of debts, but only after all other categories have been exhausted. It is not certain in what order *inter se* such property should be used. The categories include:

(a) *donationes mortis causa*
(b) nominated property
(c) property in respect of which an option to purchase has been given by the will — *Re Eve* [1956] Ch 479.

14.3.4.4 Marshalling

Where (as they are entitled to do) the personal representatives discharge a debt out of property within a category which is not — as between the beneficiaries — liable to bear the burden of that debt, the equitable doctrine of marshalling can be invoked by the disappointed beneficiary so as to ensure that the debt is (at the end of the day) borne by the appropriate property. Thus, if the will makes a specific gift of some shares to Peter and these are in fact sold to pay the debts (although the residuary estate is sufficient to cover them), Peter will be entitled to 'compensation' from the residue.

14.3.4.5 Contrary provision

The above rules only apply in the absence of contrary provision in the will. What constitutes such provision?

(a) Secured creditors. The effect of s. 35, Administration of Estates Act 1925 can be avoided in several ways. Thus, the gift of Blackacre in our earlier example (in **14.3.4.1**) might have been expressed to be 'free of mortgage', in which event the mortgage would be repayable out of the residue. Alternatively, the will might have contained a direction to pay debts 'including any mortgage charged on Blackacre' out of residue.

It is important to appreciate, however, that a simple direction to pay 'debts' from residue without specifically mentioning the charge on Blackacre would not oust s. 35. On the other hand, where the testator has identified a particular fund other than residue for the payment of 'debts', this is prima facie sufficient to cover all debts including the mortgage on Blackacre. However, Blackacre would remain charged with the payment of any deficit if the particular fund proved insufficient to discharge the debt completely.

(b) Unsecured creditors. There are three formulae commonly met in practice for varying the statutory order. They are:

(i) gift of residue on trust for sale with a direction for payment of debts out of the proceeds (before division amongst the beneficiaries).

(ii) gift of residue 'subject to' or 'after' payment of debts.

In both of these cases, the effect will be to make the residue as a whole — including the property undisposed of by the will in the case of a partial intestacy — primarily liable for the payment of the debts.

(iii) property 'given for' or 'charged with' payment of debts with intention to exonerate residue.

As we saw in **14.3.4.2** above, without some evidence of intention to exonerate residue such property remains in the third and fourth categories in the statutory order. However, provided this intention is clear, the property given or charged will become primarily liable.

14.3.5 PAYMENT OF DEBTS (INSOLVENT ESTATE)

An estate is insolvent if the assets are insufficient to pay in full all the funeral, testamentary and administration expenses, debts and liabilities. Clearly, in such a case, the beneficiaries can receive nothing, and the creditors will not be paid in full. In what order are the creditors entitled to be paid?

This is a question of crucial importance for the personal representatives because if they pay 'out of order' they will prima facie incur personal liability for debts in a higher category that have not been paid (see further **14.3.5.3** below). As a result, if there is any risk that the estate may prove to be insolvent it is necessary to be extremely careful strictly to observe the prescribed order for payment.

14.3.5.1 Secured creditors

Such creditors will in practice have a choice.

(a) They may simply rely on their security. Thus, for example, the mortgagee will rely on the (eventual) proceeds of sale of the mortgaged property to obtain repayment of the loan.
(b) They may realise their security (i.e. sell the property) and to the extent that this proves inadequate join the 'queue' of unsecured creditors (see further **14.3.5.2** below).
(c) They may (without selling) place a value on their security and seek payment of any deficit as unsecured creditors.

There is, in principle, a fourth choice — unlikely (for what will hopefully become fairly obvious reasons) to be often adopted: they could surrender their security and simply be treated as unsecured creditors!

To the extent that secured creditors rely upon their security to obtain repayment, they enjoy priority over the unsecured creditors.

14.3.5.2 Unsecured creditors

The order of priority — which cannot be varied by the testator — is governed by Administration of Insolvent Estates of Deceased Persons Order 1986.

This order applies whatever the circumstances in which the insolvent estate is being administered. In the majority of cases, the personal representatives will be administering the estate 'out of court' — i.e. they will be acting in the ordinary way, but happen to be dealing with an insolvent estate. They may, however, be acting under the court's direction — under an administration action, or in bankruptcy (because bankruptcy proceedings had been commenced before the deceased's death, or since the death an insolvency administration order has been made: in the latter case, the deceased's estate vests in the trustee in bankruptcy who administers the estate in bankruptcy).

The order is:

(a) Reasonable funeral, testamentary and administration expenses. By tradition, reasonable funeral expenses take precedence.
(b) The bankruptcy order.

Within each of these categories debts rank equally. Personal representatives have no right to 'prefer' one creditor above the others in the same category, so that if there is insufficient to pay all the creditors in the given category in full, those debts abate proportionately, so that everyone receives (e.g.) 50p in the pound (see further 14.3.5.3 below).

Under the bankruptcy order, debts rank as follows:

(a) Preferred debts. These include:

(i) Amounts due to the Inland Revenue in respect of PAYE deductions which the deceased was liable to make from wages or salaries of employees paid during the 12 months prior to the death.
(ii) Certain social security contributions which became due in the like period.
(iii) VAT referable to the period of six months prior to the death and certain excise duties due in the 12 months prior to death.
(iv) Wages and salaries of the deceased's employees in the period of four months prior to the death, up to a maximum in the case of each employee of (currently) £800.

(b) Ordinary debts. These are all other debts (except deferred debts) including the balance of any claim that does not rank as a preferred debt. Thus, for example, an employee who was owed wages of £1,000 could (subject to meeting the conditions above) claim £800 as a preferred creditor and the balance as an ordinary creditor.
(c) Interest on preferred and ordinary debts. The rate of interest will be the greater of the rate specified in s. 17, Judgments Act 1838 at the date of death (currently 8%) or the contractual rate applicable to the particular debt. Interest is payable from the date of death until payment, and the two categories rank equally for this purpose.
(d) Deferred debts. These are loans from the deceased's spouse — i.e. spouse at the date of death (the position at the date of the loan is irrelevant).

14.3.5.3 Protection of the personal representatives

If personal representatives pay (say) an ordinary debt having knowledge that there are preferred debts, the payment is an implied 'warranty' that there are sufficient assets to meet all the preferred debts of which they have notice (whether as a result of s. 27, Trustee Act 1925 advertisements or otherwise). If there are not sufficient funds to do this, the personal representatives are personally liable.

However, it has long been settled that they will not be personally liable where, without undue haste, they have paid an inferior debt without notice of a debt in a higher category — *Harman* v *Harman* (1686) 2 Show 492.

We have seen that personal representatives must not 'prefer' one creditor in a given category above any other in the same category. By s. 10(2), Administration of Estates Act 1925, personal representatives are protected from liability to creditors of the same class where payment to others in that class has been made in full should the estate subsequently prove to be insolvent, provided that at the time of the payment the personal representatives were acting in good faith and had no reason to believe that the estate was insolvent. This protection is available even where a personal representative has paid a debt due to himself, unless the grant was taken as a creditor.

14.3.6 MISSING BENEFICIARIES OR CREDITORS

We saw in **14.3.1** above that personal representatives can protect themselves against the claims of unknown beneficiaries or creditors by complying with the requirements of s. 27, Trustee Act 1925. No protection, however, is afforded to them by s. 27 where they are aware of the existence of claimants who simply cannot be found. In practice, the personal representatives should still make s. 27 advertisements: some further steps will be necessary to safeguard their position.

14.3.6.1 Payment into court

The personal representatives could pay the amount due to the missing beneficiary or creditor into court and distribute the rest of the estate in the normal way. The personal representatives will thereby achieve total protection, but from the viewpoint of the beneficiaries this is far from an ideal solution!

14.3.6.2 Indemnity

The personal representatives could distribute the whole of the available estate against an agreement by the beneficiaries to indemnify them in the event of the missing beneficiary or creditor subsequently appearing to claim his entitlement. This will certainly be more attractive to the beneficiaries, but is obviously risky from the standpoint of the personal representatives!

14.3.6.3 Benjamin order

This is an order of the court giving the personal representatives leave to distribute the estate on the basis of an assumption set out in the order: in the case from which the order takes its name — *Re Benjamin* [1902] 1 Ch 723 — the assumption was that a missing beneficiary had predeceased.

Before an application for such an order can be made, it will be necessary to make full enquiries for the missing claimant. In addition to the s. 27 advertisements, the personal representatives should advertise for information in a newspaper circulating in the locality where the missing beneficiary was last heard of. The court may direct further enquiries and advertisements if it considers them to be necessary.

If the assumption in the order subsequently turns out to be wrong, the personal representatives are fully protected. The (no longer) missing beneficiary will have to seek his remedies against those to whom the estate has been distributed.

14.3.6.4 Insurance

As an alternative to a Benjamin order, the personal representatives could seek cover against the risk of the missing beneficiary or creditor subsequently appearing. The insurance company will almost certainly require the same sort of enquiries etc. as the court might require before making a Benjamin order. However, where the risk is not great (e.g. because the sum involved is not large or the chances of a claim being made are remote) this may be a cheaper and quicker solution than an application to the court.

14.3.7 OTHER PROTECTION FOR THE PERSONAL REPRESENTATIVES

There are a number of other situations where the personal representatives need protection against possible claims from potential beneficiaries, creditors or other claimants. These include:

14.3.7.1 Future and contingent liabilities

Where personal representatives distribute with knowledge of such liabilities, they receive no protection under s. 27, Trustee Act 1925. Where, therefore, there is a known future liability a fund should be set aside by the personal representatives to meet it.

ADMINISTERING THE ESTATE — SOME PRACTICAL CONSIDERATIONS

A contingent liability might arise, for example, where the deceased had acted as a guarantor for the repayment of a loan, or there is a threat of legal proceedings against the estate. There are several possible courses open to the personal representatives to deal with such a problem. First, they could estimate the amount of the possible liability and set aside an appropriate amount — distributing the rest of the estate. This is really unsatisfactory on two counts: an accurate estimate may be difficult (even impossible) to make and the beneficiaries will have to wait for payment of the full amount due to them until the danger of the liability arising has passed. The personal representatives could, of course, distribute the whole estate subject to an agreement from the beneficiaries to indemnify them should the liability actually materialise. This (again) is not a course which should appeal to the personal representatives for fairly obvious reasons! If they wish to be able to distribute the whole estate (which is certainly what the beneficiaries would want) they could safely do so if they can arrange suitable (i.e. not too expensive) insurance cover. Failing this, the only other approach is an application to the court for directions.

14.3.7.2 Inheritance tax

We saw, in **6.6.2**, that the personal representatives can become liable for the inheritance tax on former PETs (and for the supplementary charge in respect of LCTs) where the transferor dies within seven years, and the transferee has not paid the tax concerned within 12 months after the end of the month in which the transferor dies. A similar liability can also arise in respect of gifts with a reservation.

This potential liability is obviously something of which the personal representatives must take account. The trouble is, however, that (e.g.) the existence of a PET might not come to light until after they have distributed the estate (there is no obligation to report PETs in the transferor's lifetime). Further, the tax position on death may have been calculated on the assumption that there were no lifetime transfers: the discovery of the former PET may mean that the tax liability of the personal representatives in respect of the estate deemed to be transferred on death will also be increased.

The position of the personal representatives in such circumstances has been clarified by the Revenue (see statement in *The Law Society's Gazette*, 13 March 1991). Broadly, it seems that the Capital Taxes Office will not normally pursue the personal representatives for any further inheritance tax where they have made 'the fullest enquiries that are reasonably practicable in the circumstances' to discover lifetime transfers, and have obtained a certificate of discharge (see further **16.2.2.4**) and distributed the estate before the former PET comes to light.

Where the personal representative is a practising solicitor, some protection may be afforded by the Solicitors' Indemnity Fund — see *The Law Society's Gazette*, 7 March 1990.

14.3.7.3 Adopted and illegitimate beneficiaries

Personal representatives are protected where they distribute an estate in ignorance of an adoption of which they do not have notice — s. 45, Adoption Act 1975. This does not prevent the disappointed beneficiary from claiming from the other beneficiaries to whom the estate has been distributed.

The Family Law Reform Act 1987 has effectively abolished the concept of illegitimacy for most purposes of succession to property. No special protection is offered to personal representatives who distribute in ignorance of beneficiaries who may as a result be entitled under the terms of the deceased's will or under the intestacy rules — though in the case of the latter, there is a rebuttable presumption that a child (whether of the deceased or any other relative) whose mother and father were not married to each other at the time of the child's birth is not survived by the father or anyone claiming through him (s. 18(2), Family Law Reform Act 1987). The personal representatives must clearly make tactful enquiries about the possibility of the existence of such persons, and presumably can rely upon the protection afforded by compliance with s. 27, Trustee Act 1925.

14.3.7.4 Leaseholds

Such interests held by the deceased at the date of death devolve upon the personal representatives as part of the estate vesting in them (except a statutory tenancy under the Rent Acts). This happens automatically and it does not matter whether or not they enter into possession. However, the extent of their liability for rent and breaches of covenant will depend upon whether their liability is (a) representative (deriving from their office) or (b) personal (arising from an actual or constructive (e.g. by accepting rent from a sub-tenant) entry into possession).

(a) *Representative liability.* The personal representatives are liable for rent due and any breaches of covenant committed prior to the death. They will also be liable for the rent and any breaches of covenant after the date of death. This liability is to the extent of the deceased's assets only and continues until the expiry (or surrender) of the lease, although if the deceased was an assignee of the lease the personal representatives can terminate their liability by assigning the lease.

Where the deceased was the original lessee (and so liable under privity of contract) an assignment of the lease does not bring the personal representatives' liability to an end. They can, however, be protected from further liability in such circumstances under s. 26, Trustee Act 1925. Under this section, the personal representatives can distribute the estate without the need to make provision for the possibility of any future liability under the lease and without the risk of personal liability for any future claims, provided they do three things:

(i) satisfy all existing claims arising under the lease;
(ii) set aside a fund to meet any future claims in respect of any fixed and ascertained sum which the deceased lessee had agreed to lay out on the property (although the time for doing this has not yet arrived);
(iii) assign the lease to a purchaser or beneficiary entitled.

This protection afforded to the personal representatives does not prevent the lessor from pursuing any future claim against the beneficiaries — s. 26(2).

(b) *Personal liability.* Where the personal representatives enter into possession, they become personally liable as assignees of the deceased's interest. This liability will continue until assignment, surrender or expiry of the lease.

There are different limits upon this personal liability of the personal representatives. For rent, the limit is the rent actually received (or which might have been received had they acted with reasonable diligence) — *Rendall* v *Andreae* (1892) 61 LJQB 630. For breaches of other covenants, the liability is unlimited.

No protection against personal liability is afforded by s. 26 (above). The personal representatives can either seek an indemnity from the beneficiaries (not very satisfactory from the viewpoint of the personal representatives), or create an indemnity fund — this can be distributed once the risk of further liability has ended — which is unlikely to be popular with the beneficiaries. The best solution in practice is to seek insurance cover.

14.3.7.5 Claims under Inheritance (Provision for Family and Dependants) Act 1975

We saw in **3.2.3.2** that personal representatives are protected (should the court allow an 'out of time' application) if they have refrained from distributing the estate for six months after the grant of representation. This does not, however, protect the beneficiaries to whom the assets may have been distributed.

14.3.7.6 Rectification

The personal representatives (but, again, not the beneficiaries) are given similar protection against out of time applications for rectification under s. 20, Administration of Justice Act 1982 (see **1.4.1.4**).

14.3.7.7 Applications to the court for specific relief

The personal representatives (or for that matter any beneficiary or creditor) can bring an administration action for specific relief — such as the resolution of a specific problem or difficulty which has arisen in the course of the administration. Like general administration actions (**13.4.1**), these applications are made to the Chancery Division, or county court where the net estate does not exceed the county court limit (currently £30,000). The personal representatives will in practice usually be the plaintiffs seeking the guidance of the court, but they must always be parties to such an action. The personal representatives acting in accordance with the court's directions will be fully protected.

Normally, in an action for specific relief, the costs of all parties are payable from the estate — provided the court is satisfied that there was in fact a problem justifying the application.

14.3.7.8 Section 48, Administration of Justice Act 1985

This provision allows a relatively speedy resolution of problems of construction — provided there is no dispute. The section allows the High Court, without hearing any argument, to authorise the personal representatives to act on the basis of an opinion of a barrister of at least ten years' standing; the personal representatives acting in reliance upon that opinion are protected from the possibility of an action for breach of their duty.

14.4 Financial Services

It is not intended here to examine in any detail the basic framework of the Financial Services Act 1986 (FSA) and the compliance requirements of that Act and the Solicitors' Investment Business Rules 1990 (SIBR). You will already have encountered these matters elsewhere. Our purpose here is to consider their impact upon the personal representatives and the solicitors acting for and advising them.

14.4.1 PERSONAL REPRESENTATIVES

Although personal representatives (and trustees) who buy and sell investments in their own name are not 'dealing' (FSA, sch. 1, para. 17), they will almost certainly be involved in other investment activities — such as 'managing assets belonging to another' (FSA, sch. 1, para. 14). However, by sch. 1, para. 22, personal representatives (and trustees) are not carrying on investment business in the shape of 'arranging deals in investments', 'managing investments' or 'investment advice' (within the meaning of FSA, sch. 1, paras 13, 14 and 15) unless remunerated for such matters in addition to any remuneration received for acting as personal representative (or trustee). Whilst these exclusions clearly operate in favour of lay personal representatives (or trustees), it will be very unlikely that a solicitor who is a personal representative (or trustee) could rely on them — see further **14.4.2** below.

14.4.2 SOLICITORS

In practice, it is highly unlikely that any firm of solicitors engaging in probate and administration work could avoid carrying on investment business as defined by the FSA. Thus, whether partners or employees of the firm are themselves the personal representatives or are simply acting for the personal representatives, it is virtually impossible for them not to be 'managing investments on behalf of another' — unless the particular estate comprised only assets which are not 'investments' for the purposes of the FSA (e.g. land, bank deposits, building society shares or deposits). Again, in whatever capacity partners or employees of the firm are involved, it is more likely than not that at some stage they may be called upon to give 'investment advice' (e.g. as to whether to sell certain investments) or to 'arrange deals in investments' (e.g. by arranging for the sale of shares by a stockbroker).

ADMINISTERING THE ESTATE — SOME PRACTICAL CONSIDERATIONS

The question then arises (for those solicitors authorised by The Law Society) whether such investment business is, for the purposes of SIBR, 'discrete' or 'non-discrete'. In practice, most investment business within the context of the administration of an estate is capable of being non-discrete investment business — with, therefore, limited compliance requirements in relation to the Conduct of Business Rules in SIBR, the most onerous of which are the record-keeping requirements of r. 12(5), relating to dealing and arranging deals.

Broadly (as you will have discovered elsewhere), solicitors avoid investment business being 'discrete' in one of two ways:

(a) by showing that the investment business is incidental to other services being provided by the firm which do not themselves constitute discrete investment business; or
(b) by using a 'permitted third party' (e.g. a stockbroker) on a fully disclosed basis.

14.4.2.1 Non-discrete investment business

Where partners or employees of the firm are themselves personal representatives, no investment business carried out by such partners or employees in their capacity as personal representatives can be discrete investment business (r. 2(3), SIBR). However, even where the firm is merely acting for the personal representatives, any investment business is likely to classified as 'non-discrete' as being incidental to the administration of the estate — r. 2(2), SIBR. However, it is important to appreciate that this 'exception' to discrete business does not apply once the personal representatives have become trustees (see **16.6**).

14.4.2.2 Discrete investment business

Investment business (as we saw in **14.4.2.1**) cannot be classified as 'discrete' where it is being carried out by members of the firm who are themselves personal representatives and in that capacity. Where the firm is merely acting for the personal representatives, investment business will, in practice, only be likely to be so classified where advice is being given to beneficiaries (see **16.5**) or where the firm has a specialist financial services department. In this latter case, it is effectively holding itself out as capable of supplying mainstream financial services — so that it is unlikely that the provision of those investment business services (even as part of the administration of the estate) could be 'incidental'.

Where investment business is 'discrete', full compliance with the Conduct of Business Rules in SIBR is required.

FIFTEEN

POST MORTEM CHANGES

In **Chapters 1** and **2** we saw that the devolution of a person's estate will largely depend on whether that person has died testate or not. It may be however that when that person dies the dispositions effected by the will or intestacy, or otherwise, are unsuitable in some way. This may be for a number of reasons: for example, they may fail to make adequate provision for the surviving spouse another relative or dependant of the deceased; or it may be that the beneficiaries do not want the property to which they are entitled. Another possibility is that tax-saving opportunities will be wasted if the estate is distributed in accordance with the will or intestacy.

In this chapter we will consider the methods whereby alterations can be made to the dispositions of a deceased person's property after that person's death, and the effect of these alterations on succession to property and taxation. The methods are:

(a) Disclaimers (**15.1**)
(b) Variations (**15.2**)
(c) Orders under the Inheritance (Provision for Family and Dependants) Act 1975 (**15.3**)
(d) 'Flexible' wills (**15.4**).

Where a surviving spouse is given a life interest in the residue under the intestacy rules, an election may be made to capitalise that interest. Whilst this is not strictly an alteration but rather the exercise of a right given by the intestacy rules, it is convenient to consider here the taxation effect of such election (**15.5**).

15.1 Disclaimers

15.1.1 THE SUCCESSION EFFECTS OF A DISCLAIMER

15.1.1.1 What is a disclaimer?

In the much quoted words of Abbot CJ 'the law is not so absurd as to force a man to take an estate against his will' (*Townson* v *Tickell* [1819] B & Ald 31). A beneficiary under a will or intestacy can disclaim an interest that is not wanted and otherwise would be taken. All that is necessary for a disclaimer to be effective is for disclaiming beneficiaries to indicate their intention to refuse the gift either orally or in writing to the deceased's personal representatives. We will see that if the disclaimer is to be effective for inheritance tax or capital gains tax purposes, however, it must be in writing.

15.1.1.2 Restrictions on the right to disclaim

As a disclaimer operates by way of refusal, the right to disclaim is lost once any benefit has been accepted by the beneficiary. Acceptance includes taking income or any other benefit from the property, or permitting it to be vested in the beneficiary's name.

Similarly, unless the will otherwise provides, it is not possible for a beneficiary to disclaim part only of a single gift, although one of several gifts may be disclaimed.

15.1.1.3 Legal effect of a disclaimer

The effect of a disclaimer is that the property will pass as if the disclaiming beneficiary had predeceased the testator or intestate.

In the case of a specific or pecuniary gift in a will, on disclaimer this will normally fall into residue. In the case of a residuary gift, the subject matter will pass under the intestacy rules (except in the case of a class gift or gift to joint tenants, when it will accrue to the other class members/joint tenants as appropriate). In both cases this is subject to contrary intention in the will.

A disclaimer of a gift under a will does not operate so as to prevent the person disclaiming receiving the property under the intestacy rules. Thus if residue is left by Tom, a widower, to his two children Ann and Ben in equal shares and Ann disclaims her share under the will, one half of the residue will pass on Tom's intestacy. Ann's disclaimer of her entitlement under the will does not operate to prevent her taking under the intestacy, however, and if this is desired she will have to do so expressly.

Where all members of a class disclaim on intestacy, the property will pass to the next category of relatives entitled. If only one member of a class disclaims the succession effect is not entirely clear, at least in the case where the property is held for the class on statutory trusts (see **2.1.3**). Thus if one of two daughters, the intestate's only children, disclaims her entitlement under the intestacy rules there are three alternatives. Either her share passes to the other members of the same class (her sister), or it passes to her issue (if any) on the statutory trusts, or to the persons next entitled on intestacy (the intestate's parents, if alive).

The disadvantage of a disclaimer is then that the original beneficiary has no control over the ultimate destination of the gift. This may be satisfactory if the beneficiary merely wishes to give up entitlement to certain property — for instance, if the property is subject to onerous conditions — but not if the intention is to benefit someone other than the person next entitled under the will or intestacy rules. In such a case a 'variation' (see **15.2** below) will be more appropriate.

15.1.2 THE TAXATION CONSEQUENCES OF A DISCLAIMER

15.1.2.1 Inheritance tax

For inheritance tax purposes, prima facie a disclaimer constitutes a transfer of value by the disclaiming beneficiary. The relevant parts of ss. 17(a) and 142, Inheritance Tax Act 1984, however, provide that if certain conditions are complied with then the disclaimer itself will not be a transfer of value. Inheritance tax will instead be chargeable as if the deceased had left the property to the person entitled once the disclaimer takes effect. The conditions are:

(a) The disclaimer must be made within two years of the death.
(b) The disclaimer must be in writing.
(c) The disclaimer must not be made for any consideration in money or money's worth other than consideration consisting of the making of another disclaimer or variation to which s. 142 applies.

If these three conditions are met then the above-mentioned inheritance tax relief is given automatically.

This inheritance tax relief relates to disclaimers of property comprised within the deceased's estate immediately before death 'whether passing by will, intestacy or otherwise', so that a joint tenancy interest and nominated property are within the scope of the s. 142 rules (s. 142(1), Inheritance Tax Act 1984).

15.1.2.2 Example of inheritance tax relief on disclaimer

Horace has died leaving shares worth £200,000 to his son, Samson, and the residue of his estate to his wife, Delilah. Unfortunately, Horace has left substantial debts which have depleted the value of the residue to such an extent that it is inadequate to support Delilah. If within two years of Horace's death, Samson disclaims the gift of the shares in writing, they will form part of the residue and will pass to Delilah. The disclaimer is not a PET by Samson but Horace is treated as having given the shares to Delilah direct by his will, which will thus pass tax free because of the spouse exemption. If inheritance tax has already been paid in respect of the estate, the personal representatives will have to submit a corrective account to the Inland Revenue and reclaim the tax (see **10.6**).

15.1.2.3 Capital gains tax

Prima facie, a disclaimer is a disposal for capital gains tax purposes. However s. 62(6), Taxation of Chargeable Gains Act 1992 provides that if certain conditions are met a disclaimer will not be treated as a disposal. Instead the effect will be as if the deceased had made on death the gift which will now take effect. As death is not a disposal no capital gains tax will be payable. The conditions are identical to those required for inheritance tax relief set out at **15.1.2.1**.

Thus in the example given at **15.1.2.2**, Samson would not be treated as making a disposal when he disclaims the legacy of the shares. Instead, Delilah will take the shares as if Horace had left them to her. Her acquisition cost for capital gains tax purposes will be the market value of the shares at the date of Horace's death.

15.1.2.4 Income tax

There are no specific income tax provisions to deal with disclaimers so the normal rules apply. The effect of a disclaimer depends on the type of benefit disclaimed, although as noted above (**15.1.1.2**) if a beneficiary in fact receives income this will amount to acceptance of the gift and a disclaimer will no longer be possible.

So far as income arising before the disclaimer is concerned, normally a beneficiary entitled to a general or pecuniary legacy is not entitled to interest (see **16.13.3.2**). Where, exceptionally, interest is payable but is disclaimed, the beneficiary will not normally be liable to income tax on it. With regards to specific and residuary gifts, the position is probably the same as for variations (below at **15.2.2.5**). The disclaiming beneficiary will be assessed to income tax up to the date of disclaimer (although no income has been received). In respect of income arising after a disclaimer, this belongs to the new beneficiary who will be liable to income tax on it.

15.1.2.5 Stamp duty

No stamp duty liability arises, nor does the instrument have to be presented to the Stamp Office.

15.2 Variations

15.2.1 SUCCESSION EFFECTS OF A VARIATION

15.2.1.1 What is a variation?

A variation is a direction by the original beneficiary to the personal representatives to transfer property that would otherwise be taken by the beneficiary to someone else. The original beneficiary must be capable of giving consent, and thus a variation can only be made in respect of persons who are not minors, or otherwise incapable of giving consent: in these cases the asistance of the court will be needed to consent on their behalf. This is usually under the Variation of Trusts Act 1958,

POST MORTEM CHANGES

but the procedure can be lengthy and expensive. The tax saving must therefore be substantial to make this worthwhile, and there can be problems with the two-year time limit (see below).

Normally a variation will be in writing, and commonly by deed (see **15.2.2.1**).

15.2.1.2 Differences between a disclaimer and a variation

Unlike a disclaimer:

(a) A variation is possible even though the original beneficiary has accepted a benefit. A variation can even be made when the relevant property has been vested in the beneficiary and the administration of the deceased's estate is complete.

(b) A partial variation of a gift is possible.

(c) The original beneficiary can control the destination of the property following the variation. Those taking under the variation do not have to be other beneficiaries or members of the deceased's family.

We will also see below that in the case of a written variation an election must be made to obtain the benefit of the inheritance tax and capital gains tax reliefs. In the case of a disclaimer the reliefs apply automatically.

15.2.2 THE TAXATION CONSEQUENCES OF A VARIATION

15.2.2.1 Inheritance tax

Prima facie a variation is a lifetime gift and constitutes a transfer of value, normally a PET. However if the conditions set out in s. 142, Inheritance Tax Act 1984 are complied with then the variation itself is not a transfer of value (s. 17(a), Inheritance Tax Act 1984) but inheritance tax will be payable as if the deceased had left the property to the substituted beneficiary (or beneficiaries). The conditions are identical to those set out in **15.1.2.1** above, relating to disclaimers, but there are two further conditions which do not apply to disclaimers. These are:

(a) For the disposition to be treated as if it were made by the deceased the person(s) making the variation must so elect in writing to the Revenue within six months of the variation (s. 142(2), Inheritance Tax Act 1984). This notice is quite distinct from that required to obtain the capital gains tax relief (**15.2.2.2**).

(b) If the variation results in more tax being payable, the personal representatives must join in the election. Personal representatives can only refuse to join in an election if no, or insufficient, assets are held by them to discharge such additional tax.

There is no specific form for the written instrument of variation or for the notice of election. So far as the written variation is concerned, the Revenue have stated that it must clearly indicate the dispositions that are the subject of it, and vary their destination as laid down by the deceased's will, or intestacy or otherwise (see *The Law Society Gazette*, 22 May 1985). A variation will usually be by deed, since very often the dispositions thereby effected will not be for consideration, not even the consideration permitted by s. 142. The notice of election will commonly form part of such deed.

As is the case with disclaimers (**15.1.2.1**), a variation within s. 142 can be made in respect of property passing by will, under the intestacy rules, 'or otherwise'.

In *Russell* v *IRC* [1988] STC 195, it was held that there could be no s. 142 relief in respect of a variation where there had already been an earlier variation in respect of the same property (even though the second variation took place within the two-year time limit).

15.2.2.2 Example of whether to take advantage of the s. 142 relief

A beneficiary could, of course, instead of varying the disposition of the deceased's estate and claiming the relief simply give the property in question to the donee by way of *inter vivos* gift, or make a written variation but not make the election under s. 142(2). The inheritance tax consequences will have to be considered in each case to decide whether the relief should be claimed. For example:

In her will Doreen left shares worth £140,000 to her husband, Eric, and the residue of her estate to charity. No inheritance tax will be payable on her death estate because of the availability of the spouse and charity exemptions. Eric, who is 45 and in good health, has no need of the shares and wishes to give them to Pamela, his adult daughter by a previous marriage. He can either do this by way of written variation complying with s. 142, making a s. 142(2) election (note that a disclaimer would not achieve the desired objective), or simply give the shares to Pamela by way of *inter vivos* gift (or not make an election). The choice between these two methods will largely depend on whether the nil rate band of tax is available to benefit the death estate.

If the nil rate band is available, then a written variation accompanied by an election will be preferable. This will avoid Doreen's nil rate band being 'wasted' and no additional inheritance tax will be payable on her estate.

On the other hand, if in the seven years prior to her death Doreen had made chargeable transfers in excess of the nil rate band, then it will be preferable for Eric to give the shares to Pamela by way of *inter vivos* gift (or not make an election). Eric will be treated as having made a PET of £140,000, if that is their value at the time of the PET (less any available annual reliefs). This is within Eric's nil rate band of tax, and will fall out of account if he survives for seven years from the date of the gift. If he entered into a written variation claiming the 'benefit' of s. 142, then Doreen's estate would be liable to inheritance tax in respect of the shares, thus reducing the value of the residue passing to charity.

15.2.2.3 Capital gains tax

Prima facie, a variation is a disposal for capital gains tax purposes. However, s. 62(2), Taxation of Chargeable Gains Act 1992 provides that if certain conditions are complied with a variation will not be treated as a disposal, but will instead be treated as if the deceased had left the property to the substituted beneficiary (or beneficiaries). The substituted beneficiary will be treated as acquiring the property direct from the deceased's personal representatives at market value at the date of death.

The conditions are identical to those for inheritance tax set out in **15.2.2.1**, save that a separate written election to the Revenue must be made within six months of the variation to claim the capital gains tax relief. Again this may be incorporated into the written variation.

Commonly an election will be made in respect of both inheritance tax and capital gains tax, but each tax should be considered separately. It may be that it is beneficial to make an election in respect of one tax but not the other.

15.2.2.4 Whether to claim the s. 62 relief

Just as with inheritance tax, a decision must be made as to whether it is more beneficial to enter into a written variation and make an election to claim the benefit of the s. 62 relief, or whether it is preferable to transfer the property to the donee by way of *inter vivos* gift (or fail to make an election). In the latter case the original beneficiary will be treated as making a disposal.

If the property has fallen in value since the date of death and the original beneficiary wants to set the loss against his own gains, then an *inter vivos* gift (or not making an election) may be preferable.

If however the disposal is to a connected person, as will frequently be the case, the loss can only be set against gains on subsequent disposals to the same person, and it may be better for the disposition to be made by way of written variation, making the election to claim the relief, thus enabling the recipient to take over any unrealised loss.

What is the position if the shares in the example given at **15.2.2.2** above have increased in value by (say) £5,000 since the date of Doreen's death? If the election is made, Eric will not be treated as having made a disposal and Pamela will be treated as having acquired the shares at the value at the date of death (£140,000). If however Eric transfers the shares to Pamela by way of *inter vivos* gift (or does not make an election), then Eric will be treated as having made a gain of £5,000 (less any indexation allowance) — but (assuming no other chargeable gains in the year in question) as this is within his exempt slice for capital gains tax no tax will in fact be payable. Pamela will have the benefit of an increased acquisition value (£145,000).

15.2.2.5 Income tax

Just as we saw in connection with disclaimers, there are no statutory provisions giving variations retrospective effect for income tax purposes. Once there has been an assent to a specific legatee, that person is liable to income tax on all income arising from the date of death until the date of the assent (*IRC* v *Hawley* [1928] 1 KB 578). Where there is a variation (whether before or after an assent), it seems that the effect of the assent will be to make the original beneficiary (and not the 'new' beneficiary) liable for tax on income from the date of death to the date of the variation.

In the case of a residuary gift, the Revenue practice is to tax the original beneficiary on income arising up to the date of the variation, whether or not paid over to that person.

In both cases, income arising after the date of the variation is taxed as income of the 'new' beneficiary.

15.2.2.6 Stamp duty

No stamp duty liability arises provided the instrument is certified as falling within the schedule to the Stamp Duty (Exempt Instruments) Regulations 1987. Variations will either fall into category L or M of the schedule. Instruments falling within the Regulations do not have to be presented to the Stamp Office.

15.3 Orders under the Inheritance (Provision for Family and Dependants) Act 1975

We have seen, in **Chapter 3**, that an application can be made to the court under s. 1 of the 1975 Act by a range of applicants on the basis that the deceased's will or intestacy fails to make reasonable financial provision for them. Application must generally be made within six months of the first effective grant of representation (see **3.2.1**) and a standing search can be entered (**12.2**) to search the index of grants. If the applicant's case is proved, the court can order reasonable financial provision out of the deceased's 'net estate' (s. 2), thus altering the devolution of the estate (see **3.7**). An outline of the procedure is set out below. The personal representatives, and others affected by the order, will need to know the tax effect of such an order.

15.3.1 AN OUTLINE OF PROCEDURE

15.3.1.1 High Court or county court?

We saw (at **3.2.2**) that the High Court and county court have concurrent jurisdiction to hear a claim. The general jurisdiction provisions (High Court and County Courts Jurisdiction Order 1991, art. 7) allocates cases to courts by reference to the 'value' of the action. If it is less than £25,000 it prima facie should be tried in the county court; if more than £50,000 it ought to be tried in the High Court. Other factors such as general importance, complexity, etc. are pertinent in deciding upon the relevant forum (art. 7(5)). The 'value of the action' appears to relate to the value of the applicant's claim in the case of an application under the 1975 Act, but this may be difficult to quantify. Unless an applicant can say with certainty that provision less than a certain sum is sought, the only factor the court will have to go on is the size of the 'net estate'. Thus, except in cases where these values are clearly within the above limits, application will probably be made to the High Court.

Where the application is made to the High Court, this may be made either to the Family Division or to the Chancery Division. Certain applications may be more appropriate to one division rather than the other. If the application is by a spouse or cohabitee, and there are no complexities relating to the interpretation of the will (if any), then it should be commenced in the Family Division; otherwise, the application will probably be to the Chancery Division.

15.3.1.2 Procedure in the High Court

The practice in the High Court is regulated by RSC ord. 99 and references within this section are to that order unless otherwise stated. As mentioned above, cases may be assigned to the Family Division or the Chancery Division. The procedure is the same in both Divisions and the action is commenced by originating summons in the prescribed form, which may be issued out of Chancery Chambers, the Principal Registry of the Family Division or any District Registry of the High Court (r. 3(1)). Thus the applicant can choose, at least initially, the Division and the venue.

An affidavit by the applicant in support of the summons must be lodged with the court, exhibiting an official copy both of the grant of representation to the deceased's estate and of any will admitted to probate.

The personal representatives (unless they are applicants) and any persons whose beneficial interests may be affected will be defendants. A copy of the applicant's affidavit must be served on each defendant together with the summons (r. 3(3)).

A defendant who is a personal representative must file and serve an affidavit in reply within 21 days of the service of the summons, and any other defendant may do so. Rule 5(2) specifies that the affidavit filed by a personal representative must contain certain information as to the value of the deceased's net estate; as to those beneficially entitled; whether any beneficiaries are minors; and as to any other information which might affect the exercise of the court's powers under the Act.

The hearing may be in chambers or in open court, before a master, district judge, or judge. A case will be referred to a judge if it is likely to involve a long or complex issue of fact or law.

The personal representatives must deposit the grant of representation to the deceased's estate with the court (r. 7). Every final order will contain a direction that a memorandum thereof shall be endorsed on the grant, and a copy of the order must be sent to the Principal Registry of the Family Division together with the relevant grant for endorsement to comply with s. 19(3) of the 1975 Act (see **8.6.1.4**).

15.3.1.3 Procedure in the county court

Applications in the county court are regulated by ord. 48 of the County Court Rules 1981 and references in this section are to that order unless otherwise stated.

The procedure mirrors that in the High Court, but the application is commenced by originating application, which must contain the information specified in r. 2. For instance, the application must state the name of the deceased and date of death; the relationship of the applicant to the deceased or other qualification of the applicant for making the application; the names and addresses of the personal representatives; and to the best of the applicant's knowledge the persons entitled to the estate.

The originating application will generally be filed in the court for the district in which the deceased resided at the date of death (r. 3(1)). It must be accompanied by as many copies as there are respondents (CCR, ord. 3, r. 4(3)(a)), and, just as in the High Court, official copies of the grant of representation and any will admitted to probate (r. 3(2)). The return day is the day fixed for the pre-trial review, unless the court otherwise directs (r. 3(3)).

The respondents to the action will be the persons who would be defendants if the matter were commenced in the High Court, and r. 5 provides that every respondent must file an answer within 21 days of the service of the originating application upon that respondent. If the respondent is a personal representative the answer must contain the same information as in the High Court (see above). A copy of the answer will be sent to every other party by the court (CCR, ord. 9, r. 18(4)).

The application may be heard and dealt with by the district judge and may, if the court thinks fit, be dealt with in chambers (r. 7). The court may order that the matter be transferred to the High Court (r. 9).

Rule 8 provides that the personal representative shall produce the grant of representation to the court on the hearing of the application, and if an order is made under the Act, the proper officer will send a copy thereof, together with the grant, to the Principal Registry of the Family Division for a memorandum of the order to be endorsed on the grant, in accordance with s. 19(3) of the 1975 Act (see **8.6.1.4**).

15.3.1.4 Costs

There is no general provision in the Act or the rules of court that costs should follow the event, but a useful deterrent to the making of vexatious applications is the power of the judge to order dismissal of an application with costs. Note particularly the warning given by Ormorod LJ in *Re Fullard* [1981] 2 All ER 796, that judges should look very closely at the merits of each application before ordering that the estate pays the applicant's costs if the application is unsuccessful (see also **3.5.1.3**). If the applicant is however a 'man of straw' the personal representatives' costs will have to come out of the deceased's estate.

Many claims under the Act are compromised and it has become the practice for the defendant's solicitors to write to the plaintiffs solicitors a '*Calderbank*' letter, written without prejudice to the issue as to quantum but reserving the right of the defendants to refer to it as to costs: see *Calderbank v Calderbank* [1976] Fam 93. A plaintiff who pursues a claim after the receipt of such a letter does so at the risk of liability for costs from that date, if less is ultimately recovered than the amount offered by way of settlement.

15.3.2 TAX EFFECT OF AN ORDER UNDER THE 1975 ACT

An order for provision out of the deceased's net estate made under s. 2 of the 1975 Act (see **3.7**) is treated for all tax purposes as if it were a disposition by the deceased (s. 19(1), Inheritance (Provision for Family and Dependants) Act 1975 and s. 146(1), Inheritance Tax Act 1984). The effect of the order may, therefore, vary the amount of inheritance tax that would otherwise be payable in respect of the death, for example, where an order in favour of the surviving spouse is made.

Section 19(1) of the 1975 Act does not apply to orders under s. 10 of the Act, setting aside a lifetime gift by the deceased (see **3.8.1**), but s. 146(2), Inheritance Tax Act 1984 provides for the (unlikely) situation where the gift was a chargeable transfer. There are no special Capital Gains or income tax provisions relating to orders under s. 10 of the 1975 Act.

15.4 'Flexible' Wills

We shall see in **Chapter 17** that a will can be drafted with an element of flexibility built into it. This may be appropriate where the testator is undecided as to who should inherit the whole or part of the estate on death, possibly because the testator wishes to benefit the most 'needy' of a range of potential beneficiaries, and this cannot be known with certainty until the date of death. The personal representatives can then look at the circumstances existing at that time, and make an appropriate distribution, taking into account the deceased's wishes. The testator may well leave a letter of intent, explaining who is to benefit.

At **17.4.3** we will consider some of the possible methods of achieving such flexibility. We will look in particular at creating a 'mini-discretionary trust', a two-year discretionary trust and a precatory 'trust'. The taxation consequences of each of these is considered at that stage.

15.5 Capitalisation of a Life Interest on Intestacy

Where a surviving spouse exercises the right to capitalise the life interest received under the intestacy rules (see **2.2.4.1**) there will not be a transfer of value and the inheritance tax on the death of the intestate will be calculated on the basis that the surviving spouse had been entitled to the capital sum on death (ss. 17(c) and 145, Inheritance Tax Act 1984). Increased inheritance tax may however be payable as the spouse exemption will no longer apply to that part of the capital in which the spouse no longer has an interest.

There are no special capital gains tax or income tax rules enabling the capitalisation to be 'read back' to the date of the intestate's death, so the normal rules apply.

SIXTEEN

DISTRIBUTING THE ESTATE

In **Chapter 14**, we examined various practical issues surrounding the early and 'middle' stages of the administration — to the point where the various debts and liabilities were discharged — and how personal representatives might protect themselves against claims for breach of their duty. In **Chapter 15**, we looked at how changes might be effected to the deceased's dispositions otherwise taking effect on death.

In this chapter we will consider the 'endgame' — the distribution of the estate to those entitled under the terms of the will or the operation of the intestacy rules.

Although we have arbitrarily divided up our consideration in this way, it is of course an artificial division: the process of winding up an estate is a continuum with no 'natural breaks' or (necessarily) clearly definable stages (except, perhaps, 'pre-grant' and 'post-grant').

We will first look at some practical issues concerning the payment of the various legacies in any will (**16.1**). We will then consider how the residue (to which the residuary beneficiaries are entitled) is ascertained (**16.2**). Next, we will discuss estate accounts (**16.3**) and assents (**16.4**). Finally we will consider whether and when personal representatives may become trustees (**16.5**).

16.1 Payment of Legacies

Once the personal representatives are satisfied that assets are not needed for administration purposes (i.e. to pay the debts etc.), they can give effect to the various specific, general and pecuniary gifts made by the will. An indication by them that a particular asset is not needed for the purposes of the administration is technically 'an assent' (see further **16.4** below).

16.1.1 SPECIFIC LEGACIES AND DEVISES

The property which has been specifically given by the will is vested in the beneficiaries entitled by the method appropriate to the assets concerned. Thus, for example, chattels will be transferred by delivery, and company shares by the completion of the appropriate stock transfer form — which with the share certificate(s) is lodged with the company's registrar for registration of the change of ownership and the issue of a new share certificate. In the case of land, an assent in writing will be needed (see further **16.4.2** below).

Unless the will otherwise provides, beneficiaries entitled to specific gifts will have to bear the costs of the transfer of the gifted property, and also the cost of its preservation and upkeep between the date of death and assent or actual transfer — *Re Rooke* [1933] Ch 970; *Re Pearce* [1909] 1 Ch 819.

DISTRIBUTING THE ESTATE

However, specific beneficiaries are entitled to the income (if any) produced by the asset since the date of death. Thus, for example, on a specific gift of shares or land, the assent retrospectively passes to the beneficiary concerned any dividends or rent arising since the date of death.

16.1.2 PECUNIARY LEGACIES

In s. 55(1)(ix), Administration of Estates Act 1925 the term 'pecuniary legacy' is defined so as to include general legacies; demonstrative legacies in so far as they cannot be paid from the designated fund; and any general direction for the payment of money (such as the inheritance tax on a specific gift which is to be free of tax). In this section we will use the term 'pecuniary legacy' as so defined.

The problem for the personal representatives in all these cases is essentially the same: from what part of the estate should they take the money to pay the beneficiary, or to purchase the subject matter of the general legacy, or to pay the inheritance tax? We have seen that there is a similar problem for the personal representatives in relation to the payment of the various debts and liabilities of the estate (see **14.3.4** above).

Unfortunately, the general law regarding the incidence of pecuniary legacies is sometimes far from clear! The problems centre upon the extent to which s. 33, Administration of Estates Act 1925 has displaced the pre-1926 rules.

16.1.2.1 Provision in the will

The will may (and when you have grappled with the following paragraphs you will probably (rightly) conclude should!) contain express provision as to the property to be used to fund the payment of pecuniary legacies. In practice, the formulae usually adopted for dealing with the payment of debts (**14.3.4** above) are simply adapted to include legacies as well. So, if residue is to be the chosen source, the trust for sale of the residuary estate will direct the payment out of the proceeds of 'debts and legacies' before division. Alternatively, the residue may be given 'subject to' or 'after payment of' the 'debts and legacies'. Any of these provisions will make the residue as a whole (including any lapsed share) primarily liable. Where a specific fund is identified, it can similarly be made liable for the payment of the legacies in addition to the debts.

16.1.2.2 No provision in the will and no partial intestacy

Where the deceased's will effectively disposes of the whole of the estate, the pre-1926 rules apply (as they will on a partial intestacy to the extent that the property undisposed of by the will is insufficient — see **16.1.2.3** below).

Under the pre-1926 rules, pecuniary legacies were (in the absence of contrary intention shown in the will) payable from 'general personalty' (i.e. any personalty not the subject of a specific gift) including any undisposed of by the will — for example, because a gift of a share of residuary personalty had lapsed. Realty was not generally available, so that if the general personalty was insufficient the pecuniary legacies would abate. However, realty would be available where the will disclosed a contrary intention:

(a) where realty was specifically charged with the payment of pecuniary legacies.
(b) under the rule in *Roberts* v *Walker* (1830) 1 R & My 752. If the testator directed that pecuniary legacies be paid from a mixed fund of realty and personalty they were payable proportionally from both parts of the mixture.
(c) under the rule in *Greville* v *Brown* (1859) 7 HLC 689. Where the testator left the residue (both realty and personalty) in one mass the realty would be available to support the payment of the pecuniary legacies if (and to the extent that) the personalty proved insufficient.

DISTRIBUTING THE ESTATE

16.1.2.3 Partial intestacy and no express trust for sale of the residue in the will

In such a case, a statutory trust for sale is imposed upon the property undisposed of by the will (s. 33(1), Administration of Estates Act 1925) and (in effect) the pecuniary legacies in the will are payable primarily out of the proceeds of sale — s. 33(2).

16.1.2.4 Partial intestacy but express trust for sale of the residue in the will (though no direction for the payment of legacies as in 16.1.2.1 above)

This is the really problematical situation! Where the will contains an express trust for sale this 'supplants' the statutory trust for sale — s. 33(7). Where this happens, s. 33(2) cannot apply, because it only applies where the statutory trust for sale arises under s. 33(1). So what rules determine the incidence of the pecuniary legacies in such a case?

The better view seems to be that the pre-1926 rules apply. The contrary argument (that the property undisposed of by the will is still primarily liable) is based upon a construction of the rules regarding the payment of debts (14.3.4 above) which, as we saw, talk of the retention out of any property undisposed of by the will of a pecuniary legacy fund. The argument that this imposed an obligation upon the personal representatives to use such a fund to pay the legacies was rejected (in favour of the pre-1926 rules) in *Re Beaumont's Will Trusts* [1950] Ch 462 and in *Re Taylor's Estate* [1969] 2 Ch 245. It was, however, accepted in *Re Midgley* [1955] Ch 576.

16.1.3 ABATEMENT

If the property identified under the rules discussed in **16.1.2** above is insufficient to meet the pecuniary legacies in full, they will abate proportionately.

16.1.4 APPROPRIATION

If a beneficiary wishes to have a particular asset from the estate in total or partial satisfaction of a pecuniary legacy given by the will, the personal representatives will normally be able to accede to the request by exercising the power of appropriation in s. 41, Administration of Estates Act 1925, or that conferred by the will (see **13.2.2** above).

16.1.5 RECEIPTS

The personal representatives are entitled to a discharge from the beneficiaries, which normally is obtained by getting them to sign a receipt.

Beneficiaries who are under 18 cannot (unless the will otherwise provides) give a good receipt — nor can their parent, guardian or spouse do so for them. In such cases, it will be necessary for the personal representatives to adopt one of the following solutions:

(a) Hold the gifted property until the infant attains the age of 18 — in the case of a pecuniary legacy in the meantime investing in an authorised investment.
(b) Use the power of appropriation (in s. 41, Administration of Estates Act 1925 or the will), with the infant's parent, guardian or (if none) the court giving any necessary consent.
(c) Use the power in s. 42, Administration of Estates Act 1925 to appoint trustees to receive and hold the property for the infant until 18 (see **13.2.3** above).
(d) Obtain their discharge by payment of the legacy into court under s. 63, Trustee Act 1925.

16.2 Ascertainment of Residue

Once the various legacies have been paid, the personal representatives can direct their attention to establishing the amount available for distribution to the residuary beneficiaries. In order to do this, they will have to finalise the tax position and deal with the expenses of the administration.

DISTRIBUTING THE ESTATE

16.2.1 INCOME TAX AND CAPITAL GAINS TAX

The personal representatives will need to have dealt with two matters here.

16.2.1.1 The deceased's tax affairs

The deceased's income tax and capital gains tax liability must be finalised — with any further tax payable being paid, or any repayment due being recovered (see **4.1** and **5.1**). In either event, there will be adjustments to be made to the inheritance tax liability of the estate on a corrective account (see **16.2.2.3** below).

16.2.1.2 The administration period

The personal representatives must make tax returns for each of the tax years which the administration spans and discharge any assessments (see again **4.2** and **5.2**).

16.2.2 Inheritance tax

Various issues concerning this tax will also need to be resolved.

16.2.2.1 The deceased's liability

Where the deceased at the date of death had an outstanding liability to inheritance tax, this will need to be discharged — and if met by the estate (as we saw in **6.5.2.6**) is an allowable deduction in arriving at the taxable estate on the death.

16.2.2.2 Recovery of tax

As we saw in **6.6** and **6.7**, the personal representatives may be liable to pay tax on property where the burden of the tax is in fact to be borne by the beneficiary to whom the property passes on the death. This may happen, for example, because the will expressly makes the beneficiary responsible for the tax attributable to the value of the gifted property. It may also happen where the property passes outside of the will (for example, where the deceased's interest as a beneficial joint tenant accrues by right of survivorship to the surviving joint tenant(s) — though this is not a problem, of course, where it accrues to a surviving spouse!). How can the personal representatives ensure that they recover for the benefit of the residuary estate the tax ultimately to be borne by others?

Where a pecuniary legacy is given 'subject to tax' the problem is easily resolved: the personal representatives simply withhold the appropriate amount and pay the net legacy to the beneficiary. That solution is clearly not appropriate where there has been a specific legacy of, for example, Blackacre or a diamond necklace. In such cases, the personal representatives should not vest the asset in the beneficiary concerned until the tax has been paid or satisfactory arrangements have been made for their reimbursement.

If the property has passed by survivorship, the personal representatives may have a ready solution if other assets are due to the beneficiary concerned under the will or the intestacy rules: before they part with any such assets, they should ensure that they are paid — e.g. by deducting the amount due. Where there are no other amounts due to the beneficiary concerned, they may ultimately have to sue to recover the amount due.

16.2.2.3 Corrective accounts

As we saw in **10.6**, any variations in the value or content of the estate will need to be reported on Form D-3 (or by letter if the adjustments are minor). Any further inheritance tax then due will have to be paid — or any repayment due claimed.

16.2.2.4 Certificates of discharge

When the inheritance tax position has been finalised, the personal representatives should seek a discharge from any further liability to inheritance tax on Form 30. This requests the issue of a certificate of discharge of the property in the estate and all persons liable from any further claims to inheritance tax. When given, the certificate is an effective discharge except in the case of fraud, failure to disclose material facts, the subsequent discovery of further assets, or changes in the 'tax bill' arising as a result of any variations etc. discussed in **Chapter 15**. It also extinguishes any Inland Revenue charge on the property for the payment of that tax. Such a charge attaches on death to property (other than United Kingdom personalty) beneficially owned by the deceased before death which vests in the personal representatives.

If the personal representatives have paid all the tax other than that attributable to instalment option property, a limited form of certificate may be issued — expressed to be a complete discharge except for the outstanding tax on the instalment option property. In such cases, the personal representatives will need to ensure that there are appropriate arrangements to protect them against claims for future instalments.

If property is to be sold, it is possible to obtain a limited form of certificate which is sufficient to discharge the Inland Revenue charge on the property (thus satisfying the purchaser) but which does not discharge any accountable party. This is not necessary, as we have just noted, in the case of United Kingdom personalty passing to the personal representatives (since no Inland Revenue charge attaches to such property. It will, in practice, only rarely be required where the personal representatives are selling land, because the purchaser will take free of any such charge unless it is registered as a Land Charge — Class D(i) — or (in the case of registered land) is protected by notice on the register.

No certificate of discharge is necessary (nor should it be sought) where the estate is an 'excepted estate' (see **10.2**) so that no Inland Revenue account was required to be submitted. In such cases, there is, as we saw, normally an automatic discharge 35 days after the issue of the grant — unless the Revenue call for an account or it is subsequently discovered that the estate is not, after all, an excepted estate.

16.2.3 ADMINISTRATION EXPENSES

The expenses of the administration — i.e. in addition to reasonable funeral expenses, the properly incurred expenses of the personal representatives themselves in the carrying out of their duties — will have to be ascertained and met.

16.2.3.1 Reasonable funeral expenses

The personal representatives may be liable to the undertaker in contract or quasi-contract, or to any other person who has ordered and paid for the funeral. However, the estate is only liable for 'reasonable funeral expenses': any excess will be the personal responsibility of the person incurring the expenses. What is reasonable is a question of fact: matters to be taken into account would include the deceased's position in life, religious beliefs and expressed wishes as to funeral arrangements.

16.2.3.2 Legal costs

The personal representatives are, as we have seen, at liberty to instruct solicitors to act for them in the administration of the estate. The costs (including disbursements) of such solicitors are part of the expenses of the administration.

Solicitors' charges in non-contentious probate matters are governed by the Rules of the Supreme Court (Non-Contentious Probate Costs) 1956. Under these Rules, a solicitor is entitled to charge and be paid 'such sum as may be fair and reasonable' having regard to all the circumstances of the case, and in particular to:

(a) the complexity of the matter or the difficulty or novelty of questions raised;
(b) the skill, labour, specialised knowledge and responsibility involved on the part of the solicitor;
(c) the number and importance of the documents prepared or perused, without regard to length;
(d) the place where and circumstances in which the business or any part of it is transacted;
(e) the time expended by the solicitor;
(f) the nature and value of the property involved;
(g) the importance of the matter to the client.

16.2.3.3 Fees of other professionals

Where, for example, stockbrokers or surveyors are employed to assist with valuations of the deceased's assets their fees are also part of the expenses of the administration. Where such professionals have been instructed by the solicitors acting for the personal representatives, the solicitors will — as a matter of professional conduct — incur liability to meet their proper fees, which will then feature as disbursements in the solicitors' bill of costs.

16.2.4 REMUNERATION

Personal representatives, like trustees, are not entitled to remuneration for their services unless in some way this is authorised.

16.2.4.1 Legacy to proving executors

There is a presumption that any specific or general legacy (but not a gift of residue) given to someone appointed as executor is intended to be conditional upon that person accepting the office — *Re Appleton* (1885) 29 ChD 893. The presumption is rebuttable (e.g. by the testator indicating some other motive for the legacy — such as 'in recognition of a lifetime's friendship', or making it clear that the legacy should be payable whether or not the beneficiary proves the will).

16.2.4.2 Charging clause in the will

In practice, this will be the usual means by which authority to charge for their services will be conferred upon the personal representatives. Such clauses are routinely included where professionals (such as solicitors and accountants) or institutions (such as banks) are appointed.

What exactly is authorised by such a clause is a matter of construction: the courts tend to a 'strict interpretation' — per Harman J in *Re Gee* [1948] Ch 284, 292; *Re Orwell's Will Trusts* [1982] 3 All ER 177, 179.

A charging clause is a legacy, which will abate as a pecuniary legacy — i.e. rateably with the other pecuniary legacies unless there is specific provision in the will giving the executor priority over other pecuniary legatees. It will also be important that neither the executor nor the executor's spouse witnesses the will — otherwise that executor will be unable to charge (s. 15, Wills Act 1837).

In the absence of a charging clause, solicitors who are executors are not entitled to 'get round the problem' by employing their own firm (of which they are salaried or equity partners) to do the work — even though the other partners do all the work, or the executor partners agree that they will not share the profit costs. It is, however, possible for a partner of the solicitor/executor (as opposed to the firm) to be so employed and be paid — provided there is express agreement that the solicitor/executor shall not derive any benefit from the costs charged. Another firm of solicitors could, of course, be employed and charge for their services!

16.2.4.3 Agreement with beneficiaries

Remuneration can be paid to the personal representatives as a result of an agreement with the beneficiaries (being *sui juris*) out of assets to which they are entitled. There must, of course, be no hint of undue influence.

16.2.4.4 The court

The court, as part of its inherent jurisdiction, has power to authorise remuneration for the personal representatives — whether for past, present or future services. There are also various statutory provisions which enable the court to authorise a personal representative to charge — e.g. s. 42, Trustee Act 1925 (trustees to hold infant's legacy); s. 50, Administration of Justice Act 1985 (substituted personal representative).

16.2.4.5 Rule in *Cradock* v *Piper* (1850) 1 Mac & G 664

This rule applies where a solicitor (being one of two or more personal representatives) acts in connection with litigation on behalf of all the personal representatives. Such a solicitor (or his firm) may charge for such work provided the bill is not 'inflated' by virtue of the solicitor being one of the parties.

16.2.4.6 Foreign remuneration

Where the law of a foreign jurisdiction entitles the personal representatives to remuneration, they will it seems be entitled to receive it — *Re Northcote's Will Trusts* [1949] 1 All ER 442.

16.3 Estate Accounts

If beneficiaries are left, for example, 'Blackacre' or '£1,000' by the will, they are clearly able to identify their entitlement. Unlike pecuniary or specific beneficiaries, the residuary beneficiaries have no ready means of knowing what they are entitled to receive. The estate accounts are, in effect, the means whereby the personal representatives identify the property available for distribution to the residuary beneficiaries, and they will also show how that entitlement is to be met.

16.3.1 FORM

There are no particular rules, save that the accounts should be clear and easy to follow.

16.3.1.1 The accounts

Three accounts will, in practice, be needed — an income account (**16.3.2**), a capital account (**16.3.3**) and a distribution account (**16.3.4**). In the case of small estates, the income and capital accounts will often be combined — indeed, sometimes all three are combined in a single account: this is perfectly acceptable as long as the end result is clear and easy to follow.

16.3.1.2 Apportionments

Separate income and capital accounts will certainly be needed where there is (under the will or the intestacy rules) a life interest in the residue. Unless excluded by the terms of the will, the Apportionment Act 1870 (**13.1.2.1**) will require the apportionment of income received after death which relates partly to a period before and partly to a period after the death: the former will be shown in the capital account and the latter in the income account.

The equitable apportionment rules (**13.1.2.2**) will — unless excluded — also affect the entries to be made in the income and capital accounts.

DISTRIBUTING THE ESTATE

16.3.1.3 Commentary

The accounts are, in practice, often accompanied by a commentary to explain the various entries, so as to assist the beneficiaries to understand how their entitlement has been arrived at. Thus, for example, the commentary will identify the gross and net values of the estate; indicate its disposition (whether under the terms of the will or under the intestacy rules); and deal with any other relevant matters — such as interim distributions and distributions *in specie* (e.g. as a result of the personal representatives exercising a power of appropriation).

16.3.2 INCOME ACCOUNT

This should essentially do three things:

(a) Give details of income receipts, itemising receipts from different sources (e.g. building society interest, bank interest, dividends, rent, etc.).
(b) Itemise details of expenditure from income (e.g. income tax, interest paid on legacies, legal costs properly attributable to income — such as the cost of preparing income tax returns).
(c) Show the net amount available for distribution.

16.3.3 CAPITAL ACCOUNT

This will, in practice, need to do four things:

(a) Itemise all the assets of the estate at their probate values: it may be more convenient to give the details required in a schedule or schedules to the account, simply bringing in the total(s).
(b) Show realisations by the personal representatives during the course of the administration. The proceeds of sale may well differ from the probate valuation of the asset(s) concerned and any such variations have to be taken on board when accounting to the residuary beneficiaries.
(c) Give details of all the liabilities discharged, pecuniary and specific legacies and expenses paid — including inheritance tax, capital gains tax and income tax; and legal costs properly attributable to capital.
(d) Show the balance available for distribution.

16.3.4 DISTRIBUTION ACCOUNT

This should show how the beneficiary's entitlement (whether this be to income or capital) is to be met. It should show details of any interim distribution(s) and indicate how the balance is to be paid (perhaps partly *in specie* and partly in cash).

16.3.5 DISCHARGE

The estate accounts are the personal representatives' accounts and where you or your firm are not yourselves the personal representatives they should, therefore, first be presented to them for their approval. The personal representatives' acceptance of the accounts is usually signified by an endorsement to that effect signed by them.

The approved accounts are then presented (usually in duplicate) to the residuary beneficiaries, from whom the personal representatives are entitled to a discharge. Again, this is achieved by requesting the beneficiaries to return one of the copies of the accounts sent to them with an appropriate endorsement, such as 'I . . . . . . agree to accept the amount due to me as shown by the within written accounts', duly signed. The endorsement will usually also contain a formal discharge of the personal representatives and an agreement to indemnify them against all claims and demands.

If a beneficiary refuses to approve the accounts, there are, in practice, ultimately only two possible solutions. An administration action for the examination of the accounts by the court may be

DISTRIBUTING THE ESTATE

commenced, or the personal representatives may pay the beneficiary's share into court under s. 63, Trustee Act 1925.

It may not be possible for acceptance to be signified because the beneficiary is an infant or suffering from some other disability (e.g. mental incapacity).

In the case of an infant beneficiary, the solution may be the appointment of trustees under s. 42, Trustee Act 1925 (**13.2.3** above). If this section cannot be used (because the beneficiary's interest is contingent only) the personal representatives will in practice have to continue to hold the assets until the beneficiary concerned attains the age of 18 — unless one of the other solutions outlined in **16.1.5** is adopted.

If the beneficiary is suffering from mental disability, the personal representatives should inform any receiver appointed by the Court of Protection to manage the beneficiary's affairs of the entitlement, and then proceed in accordance with the court's directions. If no receiver has been appointed, ideally application should be made for this to be done (usually this is done by a close relative of the person concerned). If not, the personal representatives may be forced to consider payment into court to obtain their discharge.

If approval cannot be obtained because a beneficiary is missing, we saw (**14.3.6**) that the personal representatives should — at an earlier stage of the administration — have taken steps to overcome this difficulty. In practice, this will have probably involved either obtaining a 'Benjamin order' or some insurance cover — so that the full amount of the residue can be distributed to the other beneficiaries.

16.3.6 TRANSFER OF ASSETS

Once the personal representatives have obtained their discharge, they can arrange for the transfer of the assets to the beneficiaries entitled. As we saw in **16.1** above, the method of doing this will depend upon the nature of the assets concerned — see also **16.4** below.

16.4 Assents

As we noted in **16.1**, an assent occurs when the personal representatives acknowledge that they do not require an asset for the purposes of the administration. Prior to this, the beneficiaries do not generally have any legal or equitable proprietary interest in the asset, but merely the right to have the deceased's estate duly administered (see **13.3.1**).

16.4.1 PURE PERSONALTY

At common law, an assent may be in writing, made orally or implied from conduct. Although the equitable title passes by virtue of such assent, if there are particular formalities needed to transfer the legal title, these must also be complied with — the personal representatives holding in the meantime as trustees for the beneficiary concerned.

16.4.2 LAND

Here, the position is governed by s. 36, Administration of Estates Act 1925.

16.4.2.1 The power to assent

By this section, personal representatives are enabled to vest any interest in freehold or leasehold land in any person entitled to it — whether beneficially, as trustee, as personal representative of a beneficiary who has died before the assent can be made, or otherwise (such as a purchaser under a contract made by the deceased: *GHR Co. Ltd.* v *IRC* [1943] KB 303). An assent should not, in

DISTRIBUTING THE ESTATE

practice, be used where the personal representative is selling, or is asked to give effect to a contract for sale entered into by a beneficiary.

16.4.2.2 Form

By s. 36(4), an assent must be in writing, signed by the personal representative(s) and naming the person(s) in whose favour it is given. Although technically a form of conveyance, an assent does not bear *ad valorem* stamp duty (except where being used to give effect to a contract).

Sometimes, a deed will in practice be needed — e.g. because indemnity covenants are required from the beneficiary.

It has been held that an assent complying with the requirements of s. 36(4) is needed even where the personal representative is the person in whose favour the assent is being made — whether as beneficiary, trustee or as personal representative of a deceased beneficiary: *Re King's Will Trusts* [1964] Ch 542.

16.4.2.3 Effect

By s. 36(2), unless there is evidence of a contrary intention, an assent relates back to the date of the deceased's death. Thus, the beneficiary will now be entitled to rents or profits produced by the land since the date of the deceased's death.

16.4.2.4 Protection of beneficiaries

Anyone in whose favour an assent is made is entitled to require (at the expense of the estate) a memorandum of the assent to be endorsed upon the (original) grant of representation — and to call for the production of the grant to prove that this has been done: s. 36(5).

16.4.2.5 Protection of purchasers

There are two provisions affording protection to purchasers from personal representatives:

(a) Section 36(6). If a purchaser takes in good faith a conveyance from personal representatives containing a statement that the personal representatives have not previously made any assent or conveyance relating to the legal estate, the purchaser will take priority over any beneficiary in whose favour a prior assent or conveyance had been made unless notice of the earlier transaction had been endorsed upon the (original) grant. It is essential, therefore, that the purchaser ensures that the conveyance contains such a statement and that the grant is inspected to check for previous memoranda. Further, an endorsement on the grant relating to the conveyance to the purchaser should also be insisted upon.

(b) Section 36(7). The protection here is, again, afforded to the purchaser in the absence of any memorandum relating to a previous assent or conveyance endorsed on the grant. Subject to this, an assent or conveyance by a personal representative is sufficient evidence that the person in whose favour it is given or made is the person entitled to the legal estate. Thus the purchaser is not concerned, for example, to see the terms of the will to check that the recipient of the property was indeed entitled to it. However, the section does not provide that the assent or conveyance is 'conclusive' evidence — so that a purchaser in possession of information which indicates that the assent or conveyance was given or made to the wrong person will not be protected: *Re Duce and Boots Cash Chemists (Southern) Limited's Contract* [1937] Ch 642.

16.4.2.6 Protection of personal representatives

By s. 36(10), personal representatives may — as a condition of giving an assent or conveyance — require security for the discharge of any debts or liabilities to which the property is subject (such as a mortgage or liability to instalments of inheritance tax). However, personal representatives cannot refuse to give an assent once 'reasonable arrangements' have been made.

16.5 Financial Services

We have seen (in **14.4** above) that, in the context of probate and administration, most investment business will, in practice, be 'non-discrete' business. However, where solicitors advise beneficiaries as to, for example, the investment of their inheritance, such advice will be prima facie discrete investment business. Avoiding this consequence will normally involve taking the advice of a permitted third party (such as a stockbroker) and making arrangements through such a person.

16.6 Personal Representatives as Trustees

Frequently, the personal representatives are also expressly appointed by the will to be trustees: or it may be that property has been left in the will on trust, but no appointment of trustees has been made. Perhaps the will leaves property directly (i.e. without creating any trust) to a beneficiary who is an infant.

A trust may also arise under the intestacy rules — e.g. because a life interest arises in favour of a surviving spouse or property has to be held for beneficiaries as yet only contingently entitled under the statutory trusts.

In any of these situations, it may be important to know if and when a change of status (from personal representative to trustee) has occurred. As will be seen, the position is far from certain — and in practice is best rendered so by an express assent.

16.6.1 PERSONAL REPRESENTATIVE ALSO TRUSTEE UNDER THE WILL

We are here concerned with the situation where the personal representatives are also trustees under the will — either by virtue of an express appointment or in default of anyone else being appointed.

Clearly, there is little difficulty in establishing the change of status and its timing where there is an assent by the personal representatives to themselves as trustees. Will the change in the capacity in which they hold the property occur, however, without such assent? There are conflicting authorities. In *Re Cockburn's Will Trusts* [1957] Ch 438, it was held that the change automatically occurs as soon as liabilities have been discharged and the residue ascertained. On the other hand, in *Attenborough* v *Solomon* [1913] AC 76, there are dicta to suggest that an assent is required to effect the change.

16.6.2 PERSONAL REPRESENTATIVE NOT TRUSTEE UNDER THE WILL

What happens where the will makes direct gifts without creating any trust? There is authority for the proposition that, in the case of a specific gift, once the personal representatives have assented they hold the subject matter of the gift on trust for the specific beneficiary: *Re Grosvenor* [1916] 2 Ch 375.

In the case of a general or residuary gift, however, it seems that the personal representatives do not in similar circumstances become trustees, but remain personal representatives: *Re Richardson* [1920] 1 Ch 423. This appears to be so even where the beneficiary concerned is an infant — *Harvell* v *Foster* [1954] 2 QB 367.

16.6.3 INTESTACY

Where a trust arises on an intestacy, it is not entirely clear whether the administrators do in fact become 'full blown' trustees unless they assent to themselves in that capacity — or (failing any such assent) continue to hold the property as personal representatives.

DISTRIBUTING THE ESTATE

In *Re Yerburgh* [1928] WN 208, Romer J indicated that when the administrators became trustees they 'ought' to assent to the vesting of the property in themselves as trustees. Unfortunately, it is not clear whether he meant by this that an assent was necessary to effect the change in their status, or merely desirable as evidence of a change which had automatically occurred.

SEVENTEEN

TAX AND ESTATE PLANNING

We have seen in **Chapter 6** that, subject to exemptions and reliefs, inheritance tax is payable where there is a transfer of wealth to a non-exempt recipient. Although there can be cases where inheritance tax is payable in respect of lifetime transfers (see **6.1.2**) the liability to pay inheritance tax mainly arises when a person dies. At this point inheritance tax will be payable, in broad terms, on the deceased's estate, and in respect of transfers made within the seven years prior to death.

The purpose of this chapter is to consider by what methods the liability to pay inheritance tax can be mitigated by taking appropriate steps in a testator's lifetime and by careful planning of the will (it being assumed that an intestacy is not 'planned'). Although we are mainly concerned here with the consequences of inheritance tax, a lifetime transfer for inheritance tax purposes may well constitute a disposal for capital gains tax purposes and there may also be income tax implications.

Before proceeding further, two points should be noted. First, in the vast majority of cases inheritance tax planning is either not relevant, or if it is, it may not be a realistic option. Only about 4% of death estates exceed the inheritance tax nil rate band, although undoubtedly inheritance tax will be a relevant consideration in a much larger percentage of cases where a solicitor is consulted about drawing up a will. We will mainly be concerned here, as are most practitioners, with testators whose main consideration will be providing for their immediate families. In these cases the tax planning potential may be very limited, particularly where the testator wishes to ensure that the surviving spouse will be financially secure, the estate is only marginally above the inheritance tax nil rate band and/or the majority of the wealth is tied up in the family home. The solicitor's first responsibility is to give effect to the client's wishes in making the best possible provision for the beneficiaries. Tax planning will in many cases be a relevant consideration, but rarely will it be the dominant factor.

Second, the inheritance tax legislation contains complex anti-avoidance legislation, particularly relating to associated operations — s. 268, Inheritance Tax Act 1984. When considering tax planning these provisions should be taken into account, and wherever possible it is preferable to use available exemptions and reliefs in as straightforward a manner as possible, rather than to devise sophisticated schemes that will be challenged by the Revenue.

This chapter is set out as follows:

(a) A summary of the main inheritance tax exemptions and reliefs relevant to tax and estate planning (**17.1**).
(b) A brief reminder of some capital gains tax provisions which should be taken into account when considering tax planning (**17.2**).
(c) Lifetime tax planning undertaken with the primary objective of eliminating or mitigating inheritance tax liability on death, and consequent capital gains tax implications (**17.3**).
(d) A consideration of the different ways of planning a will, with the same objective in mind (**17.4**).

17.1 Inheritance Tax: The Nil Rate Band, Exemptions, Reliefs and Excluded Property

The cornerstone of effective tax and estate planning is the effective use of the available inheritance tax exemptions and reliefs. These have already been encountered in **Chapter 6**, but for convenience the most commonly used exemptions and reliefs (in alphabetical order) are set out in Tables I and II below, together with the relevant statutory reference and the reference to the paragraph in **Chapter 6** of this book where you will find further details of each of them. Some of these are only available in lifetime and some are available both in lifetime and on death. This is also indicated in the tables.

Table I Main IHT exemptions

Type/Transaction	Book paragraph reference	IHTA 1984 reference	Availability Lifetime only = L Death only = D Lifetime and death = L + D
1. Annual exclusion (£3,000 per tax year cumulative for one year)	6.3.1.1	s. 19	L
2. Charities, gifts to	6.3.2.2	s. 23	L + D
3. Family maintenance, dispositions for	6.3	s. 11	L
4. Marriage gifts (£5,000, £2,500 or £1,000)	6.3.1.4	s. 22	L
5. National purposes, e.g. gifts for museums, art galleries	6.3.2.2	s. 25(1), sch. 1	L + D
6. Normal expenditure out of income	6.3.1.3	s. 21	L
7. PETs made seven years before transferor's death (note PETs can be made into certain settlements)	6.1.1	s. 3A	L + D
8. Small gifts (up to £250 per donee per tax year)	6.3.1.2	s. 20	L
9. Spouses, transfers between	6.3.2.1	s. 18	L + D

TAX AND ESTATE PLANNING

Table II Main IHT reliefs

Type/Transaction	Book paragraph reference	IHTA 1984 reference	Availability Lifetime only = L Death only = D Lifetime and death = L+D
1. Agricultural property (relief reduces value of agricultural property by either 100% (vacant possession) or 50% (tenanted))	6.3.2.5	ss. 115–124B	L+D
2. Business property (relief reduces value of business property by either 100% or 50% depending on the type of property)	6.3.2.4	ss. 103–114	L+D
3. Quick succession relief (here considered only in relation to free assets on gift or death)	6.3.3.2	s. 141	D
4. Taper relief (in respect of former PETs or lifetime chargeable transfers made within seven years of death)	6.4.2.4	s. 7(4)	D
5. Woodlands	6.3.3.1	ss. 125–130	D

17.1.1 EXEMPTIONS

The significance of the exemptions is of course that an exempt transfer has no inheritance tax consequences. An exempt transfer does not 'eat into' the nil rate band of tax, since only chargeable transfers enter into a transferor's cumulative total. The main exemptions are set out in Table I.

No reference is made in Table I to potentially exempt transfers (**6.1.1**). You will recall that the potentially 'exempt' status of such a gift is only confirmed if the transferor survives the gift by seven years.

17.1.2 RELIEFS

In general, reliefs will reduce the value of the property or the rate of tax payable, depending on which relief is claimed.

The main reliefs are set out in Table II. Note that the table does not make reference to the availability of the instalment option (see **6.8.2.2**) which, subject to conditions, is available both for lifetime transfers and on death in respect of certain property. Claiming the benefit, where available, of the instalment option can mitigate the possible harsh effect of inheritance tax, as it may avoid the need to sell the property transferred to pay the tax thereon.

17.1.3 EXCLUDED PROPERTY

Transfers of excluded property (see **6.2.1.1**) will again have no inheritance tax consequences, whether the transfer be in lifetime or on death.

TAX AND ESTATE PLANNING

The main categories of excluded property are:

(a) reversionary interests not acquired for money or money's worth or to which the settlor or settlor's spouse is not or has not been entitled
(b) certain property owned or settled by a person domiciled outside the United Kingdom.

17.1.4 THE NIL RATE BAND

The other matter that must be considered is the use of the nil rate band of inheritance tax, which is of course neither an exemption nor a relief, but a rate of tax. Nevertheless as tax will only be paid on the amount by which the chargeable transfer, whether in lifetime or on death, exceeds the nil rate band of tax, this is also a valuable tool which can be used to mitigate inheritance tax liability. For the tax year 1993/94 the nil rate applies to the first £150,000 of a chargeable transfer, the balance being taxed at 40%, or half that rate in respect of lifetime chargeable transfers.

17.2 Taking Account of Capital Gains Tax

You have studied capital gains tax elsewhere. It is not the purpose of this section therefore to set out the relevant capital gains tax provisions in any detail, but merely to highlight some aspects of the capital gains tax legislation which are relevant when advising clients who are contemplating making lifetime gifts of property, in order to reduce their estates for inheritance tax purposes.

All statutory references in **17.2** are to the Taxation of Chargeable Gains Act 1992, unless otherwise stated.

17.2.1 CONFLICT BETWEEN INHERITANCE TAX PLANNING AND CAPITAL GAINS TAX PLANNING

In a sense there is an inherent conflict between inheritance tax planning and capital gains tax planning. Leaving aside practical considerations for a moment, clients who wish to mitigate inheritance tax should be advised to give away the bulk of their estates to family members in their lifetime, ensuring that their net death estate falls within the nil rate band of inheritance tax. If such clients survive for seven years from the date of the last of these gifts, then there will be no inheritance tax to pay. The lifetime gifts will have fallen out of account, and there is no tax to pay on the death estate.

From a capital gains tax point of view, however, such a strategy could be extremely expensive. Save for a few exceptions, all assets are chargeable assets for capital gains tax, and if a lifetime disposal (e.g., a gift) gives rise to a chargeable gain, then subject to exemptions and reliefs, capital gains tax will be payable. On the other hand, the death of a tax payer is not a chargeable event for capital gains tax purposes (see **5.2.1**). The personal representatives, however, acquire the deceased's assets at their market value at the date of death, thus obtaining the benefit of a 'tax-free' uplift of the estate assets, which is then passed on to the beneficiaries (see **5.2.3** and **5.3**). In effect then, death 'wipes out' capital gains tax liability. In broad terms therefore, for capital gains tax purposes it is cheaper to retain assets until death, rather than dispose of them in lifetime. If lifetime gifts are contemplated however, the best possible use of the available exemptions and reliefs should be made. Some of these are outlined in the following section; for a detailed consideration of these (and the other provisions referred to below) you should consult your taxation book.

17.2.2 CAPITAL GAINS TAX PROVISIONS RELEVANT TO LIFETIME TAX PLANNING

When contemplating lifetime tax planning, consideration should be given to (inter alia) the following capital gains tax provisions.

TAX AND ESTATE PLANNING

17.2.2.1 Disposals to relatives

Clients will probably primarily wish to benefit family members when making lifetime gifts. Relatives (and their spouses) are 'connected persons' (s. 286) and the consideration for such disposal will be the market value of the asset at the time of transfer. For disposals between spouses living together however, the disposal is deemed to be of such sum that neither gain nor loss results (s. 58). Gifts to charities are treated in a similar way (s. 257).

17.2.2.2 Capital gains tax exemptions

Gains on certain disposals will not be chargeable because of the availability of exemptions. For instance:

(a) Gains within the annual exempt slice (currently £5,800) are not subject to charge. Married couples are taxed independently, and each has their own annual exemption.

(b) Gains on the disposal of certain assets are exempt. Your specialist tax book should be consulted for details of these but you will recall that, for example, the gain made on the disposal of the taxpayers's principal private residence (ss. 222–226) is exempt. So too is the gain made on the disposal of a life policy by the original beneficial owner (s. 210).

17.2.2.3 The indexation allowance

The indexation allowance should ensure that purely inflationary gains are not subject to charge (ss. 53–57).

17.2.2.4 Holding over the gain (CGT)

In some cases the gain can be 'held over', the donee then being deemed to acquire the asset at the donor's acquisition cost. We have noted at **17.2.2.1** above, that where there is a transfer between spouses the gain is automatically held over. In certain other cases an election can be made to hold over the gain. The election is usually made jointly by the donor and the donee (although in the case of a transfer into a settlement the election is made by the transferor alone). Although tax on the held over gain will be payable if the donee makes a disposal of the gifted property in lifetime, the gain will be 'wiped out' if the donee still owns the property at death.

Remember that if an election is made to hold over the gain, the donor's exempt slice will be wasted. Where the gain is within, or marginally above the donor's exempt slice, then no election should be made.

An election to hold over a gain can be made (inter alia) in the following cases:

(a) Where there is a gift of 'business assets' (s. 165). For example, if Fred transfers his holding of shares in the family trading company to his daughter, Diane, they may jointly elect that the gain be held over.

(b) Where the gift is an LCT (see **6.1.2**) for inheritance tax purposes (s. 260). The gain may be held over even if the transfer falls within the donor's annual exclusion or nil rate band of inheritance tax (s. 260(2)(a)).

The most common example of a lifetime chargeable transfer is the creation or termination of a discretionary trust (see **7.3.3**). Thus, assuming no prior lifetime chargeable transfers have been made, Sarah could transfer chargeable assets worth £150,000 into a discretionary trust for the benefit of her family. As inheritance tax is technically payable, even though at nil per cent, Sarah can elect that the gain be held over. Relief under s. 260 is not available where the gift is a PET (e.g., a gift to an individual or into an accumulation and maintenance settlement) even if the gift becomes chargeable because of the donor's death within seven years thereof.

TAX AND ESTATE PLANNING

17.3 Lifetime Tax Planning

17.3.1 CONSIDERING THE CLIENT'S OBJECTIVES

This part of the chapter is of course closely linked with **17.4** dealing with estate planning. When a client comes in to make a will it is necessary, as a preliminary step, to consider the client's priorities as between his family and other beneficiaries, and to take account of the nature and extent of the client's estate. This presents an ideal opportunity to consider the wider aspects of tax planning in general.

The instructions sheet or checklist containing information about the client's assets that you will have prepared and completed to assist in drafting an appropriate will for the client (see **18.3**) is also an essential source of information when considering whether lifetime tax planning is a realistic possibility. In many cases the client's own needs or those of the family will mean that it is impractical for the client to dispose of any income yielding assets prior to death.

In what follows in this chapter, it will be assumed that the client's objective, after having provided for the needs of the surviving spouse (if any) is to transfer wealth to the next generation as efficiently as possible. This will mean that a balance will have to be struck between the need to ensure that the family as a whole can live in a reasonable degree of comfort both now and after the testator's death, and the need to avoid or minimise inheritance tax liability.

Where there is sufficient available wealth to satisfy immediate needs the following lifetime tax planning steps can be considered.

17.3.2 LIFETIME GIFTS

The objective here is to reduce the value of the testator's death estate.

17.3.2.1 Using exemptions

This is clearly a first step, as a lifetime transfer of excluded or exempt property will have no adverse effect on liability for inheritance tax. In some cases there will be no capital gains tax liability either because the exempt slice can be used or the gift is of income. As noted in Table I above, certain exemptions are only available in lifetime. The following points should be noted.

(a) The exemptions, save for those relating to small gifts, are cumulative and therefore a transferor whose child is about to be married could give the child £11,000 (rolling forward an annual exemption for one year and using the marriage exemption) in that tax year without using any part of the nil rate band of tax. The transferor's spouse could make a similar transfer in the same tax year without incurring any inheritance tax liability.

(b) The exemption for normal gifts out of income can be used to fund a life assurance policy written in trust for family member(s) (see **17.3.3** below).

(c) Advantage can be taken of the provisions relating to excluded property where the transferor has a reversionary interest. For example: Anastasia, aged 70, is the life tenant under a settlement, and Boris, her son aged 50, is entitled in remainder. A double charge to inheritance tax will arise; once on the death of Anastasia and again on the death of Boris. Boris is currently deriving no benefit from his interest, and as this is excluded property (**17.1.3**) he could assign the benefit of his reversionary interest to his child, Camilla, without incurring any inheritance tax liability, thus avoiding the second charge to inheritance tax.

(d) The surviving spouse exemption is dealt with separately at **17.3.2.6**.

17.3.2.2 Making PETs

A number of points should be noted:

(a) If the transferor is in good health (such that it appears that the transferor may survive the gift by seven years) and can afford to do so, then such gifts or settlements should be considered. If the transferor does survive for the seven-year period, the gift will not form part of the cumulative total on death, and the transferee will not be liable for inheritance tax.

(b) Consideration should also be given to making PETs of interests in possession in settled property if the income is not required by the life tenant. In the example given at **17.3.2.1**(c), on the death of Anastasia not only will the settled property be subject to the payment of inheritance tax, but this will also affect the rate of tax payable on Anastasia's free estate, as the settled fund will form part of her cumulative total. Once Boris has assigned his interest to Camilla then Anastasia could surrender her life interest to Camilla. This would be a PET, but a charge on Anastasia's death will be avoided if she survives for the seven-year period.

(c) In deciding what, if any, assets should be transferred, capital gains tax liability must also be borne in mind — especially as capital gains may only be held over in limited cases (see **17.2.2.4**). If chargeable assets are transferred the benefit of the capital gains tax, tax free uplift on death is lost, and the consequences of this will be particularly unfortunate if it turns out that the transferor dies shortly after making the transfer. There will also have been no benefit from an inheritance tax standpoint.

(d) If the transferor does not survive for the full seven years there may still be some inheritance tax benefits of the 'failed' PET:

(i) The value of the gift is 'frozen' at the date it was made (unless it has fallen in value). Thus it is most tax efficient to transfer an appreciating asset, such as the landlord's reversion where the lease is a wasting asset.

(ii) Taper relief will reduce the amount of tax paid by the transferee (but will not affect the deceased's cumulative total) once the transferor survives the gift by three years.

If the PET does become subject to charge because of the donor's death within the seven year period, then as we have seen at **6.6.2** the donee will become primarily liable for such tax. In some cases the instalment option (**6.8.2.2**) may be available, depending on the nature of the property transferred. The donee has an insurable interest in the donor's life, and can take out a seven year term life policy on the life of the donor, in order to ensure that cash will be available should inheritance tax become payable.

We have also seen at **6.6.2** that the personal representatives have a secondary liablity in respect of such tax, if it is unpaid 12 months after the end of the month in which the death occurs. As pointed out at **14.3.7.2**, this potential liability can cause considerable problems for the personal representatives when dealing with the administration of the estate, especially as statute gives them no right of recovery against the donee if they do pay such tax. The donor should address this problem at the time when the gift is made. It could be made a condition of such gift that the donee gives an indemnity for the benefit of the donor's estate in respect of such potential inheritance tax liability.

Similar considerations apply to the supplementary charge in respect of LCTs, and gifts with a reservation, save that s. 211(3), Inheritance Tax Act 1984 affords the personal representatives a right of recovery against the donee in the latter case.

17.3.2.3 Using the nil rate band

Because of the seven-year cumulation period, assets to the value of the nil rate band (currently £150,000) can be given away every seven years. Most gifts and transfers into settlements will be PETs, but if the transferor wants to make a lifetime chargeable transfer the ability to use the nil rate band will be crucial.

Thus a transferor could use the nil rate band to set up a discretionary trust for the benefit of his family (the settlor should not be one of the beneficiaries or a benefit would be reserved for inheritance tax purposes — see **17.3.2.5**). There would be no tax liability in respect of the transfer when made, or on the transferor's death. Once a further seven years had elapsed from the date of the transfer it would fall out of account, leaving the nil rate band of tax available to make further chargeable transfers or for the benefit of the transferor's death estate.

As the transfer is chargeable for inheritance tax when made, capital gains tax holdover relief would be available.

17.3.2.4 In what order should gifts be made?

As inheritance tax is a cumulative tax, if PETs are made and it transpires that the donor does not survive for the full seven years, the PETs will 'eat into' the nil rate band in the order in which they are made. Thus as a general rule the earliest gifts should be made to those the transferor wishes to benefit the most.

If however the transferor is contemplating making a nil rate band transfer into a discretionary trust (as in **17.3.2.3**) and also contemplating PETs, the chargeable transfer should be made first, to ensure that the periodic and other charges are kept to the minimum.

17.3.2.5 Gifts with a reservation

These have been considered at **6.2.1.2**. The main practical restriction on the use of PETs is that the transferor will usually still have need of the asset in his lifetime. This is particularly the case with the family home, as noted at **17.3.2.7**. The rules currently under consideration prevent the transferor continuing to have the use or benefit of the gifted property and at the same time claiming the inheritance tax advantages of a PET. Such use or benefit will constitute a reservation and will mean that the gifted property will still form part of the transferor's estate on death for inheritance tax purposes.

There are exceptions to this general position when the gift with reservation rules do not apply (see **6.2.1.2**) but the conditions are onerous. Schemes may be devised whereby an interest is 'carved out' before the property is gifted, and thus no interest reserved. All such schemes should be treated with caution until they are tested, however, and the risks should be made clear to the client.

17.3.2.6 Transfers between spouses

Using the spouse exemption on transfers between spouses is one of the most useful tools in inheritance tax planning. Such disposals will not give rise to a chargeable gain for capital gains tax (see **17.2.2.1** above) and in addition there may well be income tax benefits in transferring income bearing assets from the wealthier spouse, X, to the poorer spouse, Y. From an inheritance tax viewpoint the following should be noted:

(a) Sufficient wealth should be transferred to Y to enable Y to use the nil rate band of tax, say by leaving a nil rate legacy to the children by will (see **17.4.2.1**). If X retains all the wealth then a tax saving, at current rates, of £60,000 (£150,000 x 40%) will have been sacrificed.

(b) Sufficient wealth should be transferred to the spouse with the greater life expectancy to enable that spouse to make PETs to the children.

Provided that the transfer is not subject to a condition that PETs are immediately made, such transfers should not fall foul of the associated operations rule (s. 268, Inheritance Tax Act 1984) referred to in the introduction to this chapter.

Neither the inheritance tax spouse exemption nor the 'no gain no loss' capital gains tax provisions are available to cohabitees, who are thus at a significant disadvantage so far as tax planning is concerned.

17.3.2.7 The family home

It will frequently be the case that the bulk of a testator's wealth will be tied up in the family home. If the family home is solely owned by one spouse, say H, then on death this asset may well comprise the bulk of his estate, without which there may be little or no inheritance tax liability. If the house is left by will to his spouse W, and she survives him, the spouse exemption will ensure that there is no inheritance tax liability on his death, but on her death the same problem will arise. Can this prospective liability be avoided by dividing the beneficial ownership in some way between H and W and their adult child C?

Whilst this is certainly possible, there is no easy solution. This is because a house is not, in practice, primarily a tax asset but a home for H and W, and will continue to be required as such for the survivor of them. The following can be considered:

(a) H could transfer the property into the joint names of H and W, each spouse becoming a beneficial joint tenant. This will provide security to the surviving spouse but there is no inheritance tax advantage as the tax position will still be as outlined above.

(b) H could transfer the house to C by way of a PET. The obvious disadvantage is that if H and W continue to live in the property then, unless this is for full consideration, this will constitute a gift with a reservation, and thus the inheritance tax advantage will be lost. There is no security for the surviving spouse.

(c) H could create a tenancy in common, enabling each of H and W to dispose of their undivided share by will (utilising some/all of their respective nil rate bands) to C. This will give greater security to the surviving spouse, who will have a right to occupy the entirety pending sale; however, once a share in the property has passed to C, a sale of the property could not be prevented if this was C's wish. Although the risk may appear minimal, all practitioners will know that tensions can arise within what ostensibly appears to be the most united of families.

The conclusion may be that the family home is not well suited to be an instrument of tax planning.

17.3.2.8 Using the reliefs

Prior to changes made by the Finance (No. 2) Act 1992 much energy was devoted to devising schemes enabling the family company or farm to be passed on to the next generation without attracting inheritance tax. Now that agricultural property relief and business property relief have been increased (in many situations) to 100% such schemes have been rendered redundant. Indeed, provided that the rates remain as they are, there is no advantage for inheritance tax in passing on the farm or business *inter vivos*. A lifetime transfer may well have advantages, however, in securing the continuity of management of the farm or business.

For the wealthy client, consideration could be given to investing in property qualifying for these reliefs — remembering that there are minimum periods of ownership. This would reduce the value of the chargeable estate on death.

17.3.2.9 Using settlements

The use of the nil rate band discretionary trust has been explained at **17.3.2.3**. Transfers into interest in possession trusts and to accumulation and maintenance settlements will be PETs. The advantages of using the latter type of settlement where the transferor wishes to benefit minors has been considered at **7.3.4.1**.

17.3.3 LIFE ASSURANCE AND PENSIONS

So far we have looked at the ways in which the impact of inheritance tax on death can be minimised by making the best use of exemptions and reliefs in making lifetime gifts or settlements. In many cases it will not be possible to avoid the charge altogether, as part of the estate may comprise the

TAX AND ESTATE PLANNING

home and funds required to meet future living expenses. Life assurance can have a vital role in these (as in other) cases, enabling the family's standard of living to be maintained after the death of the main income provider and providing additional funds to meet inheritance tax liability.

From an inheritance tax stance it is most advantageous if the policy is written in trust for family members(s), whether under s. 11, Married Women's Property Act 1882 or by making express provision. The policy proceeds will not form part of the deceased's estate, and will be immediately available for the benefit of the beneficiaries. As mentioned (at **17.3.2.1**) the premiums will be exempt as normal gifts out of income.

In addition, we have seen in **8.4.3** that many pension schemes enable lump sums to be paid to the deceased's dependants at the discretion of the pension trustees and a request can be made to the trustees indicating to whom such benefits should be paid. Such benefits will not be subject to inheritance tax as again the lump sum does not form part of the deceased's estate.

The greatest inheritance tax benefit is obtained if such policy proceeds or lump sums pass direct to the children. Whether this is practical will depend on the needs and resources of the surviving spouse.

17.4 Will Planning

In this section we will study how a will can be structured to minimise inheritance tax on death. A will is a very personal document, and tax planning may have to take second place to the testator's personal aims and feelings, and the needs of the surviving spouse. As mentioned in **17.3.1**, before drafting any will you will need to know the client's overall objectives, the needs of the family, the nature and the extent of the estate, etc.

Whether the will contains gifts conferring absolute interests, life interests or other forms of settlement will largely depend on these factors. We saw in **17.3** that the best way to minimise the impact of inheritance tax was to make the best use of available exemptions and reliefs. Where the size of the estate is such that inheritance tax is a relevant factor (i.e. where the deceased's cumulative total exceeds the nil rate band) the same basic strategy should be adopted. The tables of exemptions and reliefs should be consulted.

Generally as to will drafting and inheritance tax the following points should be considered:

(a) In the case of married couples, they should both make wills.
(b) As the spouse exemption does not apply to cohabiting couples there is little scope to avoid the impact of inheritance tax if it is desired to provide for the survivor of them.
(c) Wills should be regularly reviewed to take account of changing needs and alterations to the estate or tax regime. An element of flexibility can be included in the will so that some of these changes can be taken into account (see **17.4.3** below).
(d) Account should be taken of property that passes outside the will (e.g. property passing by survivorship) and any impact this will have on inheritance tax.
(e) The liquidity of the estate, so far as the ability to pay inheritance tax is concerned, needs to be considered, especially if the bulk of the estate is tied up in the family home. The availability of the instalment option (see **6.8.2.2**) and the effect of debts is also relevant.

We saw in **Chapter 15** that it is possible (in effect) to 'rewrite' the will by deed of disclaimer or variation within two years of death. Nevertheless it is always preferable to have the appropriate will in the first place, as such rewriting will need the agreement of the beneficiaries concerned (and sometimes the consent of the court). In addition, government indications have been given that anti-avoidance measures may be introduced limiting the availability of these tax-saving devices.

TAX AND ESTATE PLANNING

In the remaining part of this chapter we will look at a number of specific issues, discussing different ways of structuring a will to take account of inheritance tax exemptions and reliefs. As before it will be assumed that the testator's aim, after making appropriate provision for the surviving spouse, is to transfer wealth to succeeding generations in the most tax efficient way possible.

17.4.1 PROVIDING FOR THE SURVIVING SPOUSE

17.4.1.1 Absolute or life interest?

The amount of provision that should be made for the surviving spouse will depend on the testator's wishes, the spouses' respective wealth and what property passes to the survivor outside the will. Whether such provision should be by way of an absolute or life interest is likely to be determined by factors other than those related to tax planning (see the discussion of 'testator's priorities' at **18.3.2.4**). In either case, no inheritance tax will be payable on the death of the first to die because of the spouse exemption, although the impact of inheritance tax on the death of the second spouse may be considerable because the combined value of the two estates which will then pass on the death of the second spouse may be considerably in excess of the then nil rate band.

If an absolute interest is given, depending on life expectancy, the surviving spouse could make PETs to issue, thus reducing the value of the estate passing on the survivor's death. If the surviving spouse only has a life interest this will not be possible unless provision is made in the will enabling the trustees to advance capital sums to the surviving spouse who can then make PETs of the same property: a somewhat cumbersome device!

17.4.1.2 What type of property should be left to the surviving spouse?

If practicable, this should not include agricultural or relevant business property qualifying for 100% relief, as the benefit of the relief would be wasted. It would be preferable for such property to be left to the children, making provision for the surviving spouse out of other assets.

17.4.1.3 The family home

In many cases the family home will be left to the surviving spouse outright, whether by way of a residuary or specific gift. In some cases, for non-tax reasons, a limited interest only will be given, whether by way of a life interest under a trust for sale or under a settlement under the Settled Land Act 1925. Provided that the surviving spouse has a right of occupation, there is little to choose from a tax point of view, as in both cases the house will form part of the surviving spouse's estate on death for inheritance tax, and for capital gains tax purposes will either be covered by the main residence exemption on sale, or will not be chargeable because the disposal takes place on death.

17.4.2 USING THE NIL RATE BAND

If all the estate is left to the surviving spouse then the nil rate band of the spouse who dies first will have been wasted. Basic estate planning suggests that if possible the nil rate band should be used.

As to the points to be considered in the drafting of such a gift, see **18.3.2.4**(c).

17.4.2.1 Nil rate band gift

To make full use of the nil rate band the will of each spouse should contain a gift or trust of the nil rate band available on death to their children (or other non-exempt beneficiaries), the residue passing to the surviving spouse. The disadvantage of such a clause is that the nil rate band is normally increased annually, and on death its size may be such as to deprive the surviving spouse of adequate provision. Where the combined estates are relatively modest, below say £300,000 it may be safer to leave a fixed amount to the children, taking at least some advantage of the nil rate band.

TAX AND ESTATE PLANNING

17.4.3 'FLEXIBLE' WILLS

Wills can be drafted with an element of flexibility incorporated into them, so that the decision as to the detailed devolution of the estate can be postponed until after the testator's death. Thus account can be taken of the relative wealth of potential beneficiaries at that time, and of the then prevailing tax regime. The 'mini-discretionary trust' enables the nil rate band to be used, whereas the two-year discretionary trust and the precatory trust rely on inheritance tax 'reading back' provisions similar to those which we have already encountered relating to post death variations in **Chapter 15**.

17.4.3.1 Mini-discretionary trusts

Whether there are sufficient assets to enable full advantage to be taken of the nil rate band without prejudicing the position of the surviving spouse cannot be known with certainty until the death of the first spouse. The mini-discretionary trust enables the position to be considered at that stage, and may be useful where a nil rate band gift may put the surviving spouse at risk.

In such a case the available nil rate band would be settled by the will on a discretionary trust for the perpetuity period on the following terms:

(a) The trustees would be given absolute discretion to appoint capital and income to the beneficiaries. In default of appointment the fund to be divided equally between the beneficiaries.
(b) The beneficiaries would be the surviving spouse and issue.
(c) When exercising their discretion the trustees (who could include the surviving spouse) should give priority to the needs of the surviving spouse.

The advantages are that there will be no inheritance tax on creation as the trust is within the nil rate band. Inheritance tax charges during the lifetime of the trust are likely to be nil or small (see **7.3.3.3**). The whole of the nil rate band has been used and yet the position of the surviving spouse has been protected.

17.4.3.2 Two-year discretionary trusts and determinable life interests

These are two further methods of achieving flexibility in a will. In both cases property, usually the residuary estate, is left to trustees on the trusts set out in the will.

The first, the two-year discretionary trust, enables advantage to be taken of s. 144, Inheritance Tax Act 1984, and could be used where the testator is undecided at the time of the will as to the precise devolution of the residuary estate. Briefly, the residue is left to trustees on discretionary trusts for a class of beneficiaries (possibly the testator's children) for up to two years from the date of the testator's death. The trustees are given power to appoint the property between the beneficiaries during the trust period. Provided that the appointment is made within two years of the testator's death, then inheritance tax on the death estate will be calculated as if the will left the residue to the beneficiaries in the shares in which they then receive it. As mentioned above, the effect is similar to that we have seen resulting from a post-death variation in **Chapter 15**, save that the testator has here anticipated that a 'variation' will be made.

The object of the second method is to transfer the estate to children (or granchildren) by way of a 'compulsory' PET. In outline, the testator, having used up the nil rate band in making gifts to the children, leaves a life interest in the residue to the surviving spouse (spouse exempt for inheritance tax purposes), the ultimate beneficiaries being the testator's children. This life interest is, however, expressed to be determinable (after say, six months) by the trustees. If the trustees exercise their discretion to terminate the life interest, the effect for inheritance tax purposes is that there has been a PET of the residue by the surviving spouse to the children. If that spouse survives for a further seven years the residue will pass to the children without becoming liable to inheritance tax.

TAX AND ESTATE PLANNING

The relative merits of these devices are beyond the scope of this book, but details can be found in specialist tax books. They are merely included here to illustrate the wide range of options available, where the testator's wealth is sufficient to warrant their consideration.

17.4.3.3 Precatory 'trusts'

Where the testator is unsure at the time of the will to whom certain chattels (e.g. jewellery, antiques) should be given a precatory 'trust' may be used. Thus, such property may be given by will to the personal representatives or other legatee 'in full confidence but without imposing any trust' that they will distribute amongst (say) family members. Such a provision creates no binding obligation, but if such distribution is made within two years of the testator's death no additional inheritance tax is payable beyond that which was payable on the testator's death (s. 143, Inheritance Tax Act 1984).

There are no special capital gains tax rules so the transfer will be treated as a disposal by the personal representative or legatee.

Similarly there are no special income tax rules.

17.4.4 SURVIVORSHIP CLAUSES

The use of survivorship clauses has been discussed at **7.3.4.3** (and see further **18.4.6.3**(a)). One reason for their inclusion is to prevent the testator losing control of the devolution of the estate if the beneficiary dies shortly after the testator.

From an inheritance tax standpoint, survivorship clauses should be considered in all cases where absolute or life interests are given by will, as:

(a) Where the beneficiary is not the testator's spouse it will prevent a double charge to tax if the beneficiary does not survive for the survivorship period (although quick succession relief would be available in these circumstances).

(b) Where the beneficiary is the spouse, such a clause can prevent the nil rate band being wasted. For example, Hubert leaves his estate of £150,000 to his wife Wilma, who also has an estate of £150,000, subject to her surviving him by 30 days — and if she fails to do so, there is a gift over in favour of their children. Wilma has a will in similar terms, and neither spouse has used up any part of their nil rate band. If Wilma survives Hubert, but dies within the survivorship period, Hubert's estate will pass to the children free of inheritance tax because of his nil rate band. Wilma's estate will also pass to the children free of inheritance tax because of her nil rate band. If there had been no survivorship clause, Hubert's nil rate band would have been wasted. Conversely, there can be cases where a survivorship clause is inappropriate. If in the above example, Hubert had already used up his nil rate band and Wilma had little or no estate, and the deaths were in the same order, a survivorship clause would have ensured that Wilma's nil rate band would be wasted!

17.4.5 GIFTS TO MINORS

Many wills contain residuary or other gifts to be held in trust for persons who may be minors at the date of the testator's death (e.g. the testator's children or grandchildren). Such gifts may be vested or contingent (e.g. on the child attaining a specified age). In such a case the property will be settled property for inheritance tax purposes, and if the gift is contingent (but not yet vested) also for capital gains tax purposes. In drafting such gifts particular attention should be given to the following.

17.4.5.1 Accumulation and maintenance settlements

The beneficial inheritance tax treatment of accumulation and maintenance settlements is only available if the requirements set out in s. 71, Inheritance Tax Act 1984 are fulfilled (see **7.3.4.1**). In drafting such a gift, care must be taken to ensure that the requirements of s. 71 are not infringed.

TAX AND ESTATE PLANNING

For example, the primary requirement is that one or more of the beneficiaries will become entitled to the property or to an interest in possession in it, on or before attaining the age of 25. Even if the right to capital is contingent on the beneficiary attaining an age greater than 18, s. 31(1)(ii), Trustee Act 1925 will normally ensure that the beneficiary will be entitled to the income at 18, and therefore acquire an interest in possession. Once there is an interest in possession a charge to inheritance tax will of course arise on the death of the beneficiary, even if there is still only a contingent interest in the capital. Unless the gift or other estate of the beneficiary is large such inheritance tax liability is likely to be negligible or small.

17.4.5.2 Capital gains tax treatment of vested and contingent interests

If the beneficiary's interest in the trust is contingent, the property will be settled for capital gains tax purposes (contrast the position where property is held for minors who would otherwise be absolutely entitled). In such a case there is a notional disposal and reacquisition by the trustees when the contingent entitlement vests (see further **18.3.2.5**).

17.4.6 TAKING ACCOUNT OF THE BURDEN OF TAX

The rules relating to the burden of tax (**6.7**) should be borne in mind when drafting specific or pecuniary gifts to non-exempt beneficiaries. In particular, it should be made clear in the will whether such gifts are subject to tax, or free of tax — in which case the tax will be paid out of the residue. In the absence of a provision in the will, a gift of UK free estate will generally be free of inheritance tax which will be a testamentary expense payable out of residue — s. 211, Inheritance Tax Act 1984.

The issue of the burden of tax can be particularly relevant where a gift is given to the children, followed by a gift of residue to the spouse (or any other exempt beneficiary). If the gift is within the nil rate band there will be no difficulties: no inheritance tax is payable. If, however, the gift exceeds the nil rate band then consideration must be given to whether this gift should bear its own tax. If it does, then the value of the gift will be taken to be its gross value for working out the liability to inheritance tax. If however the gift is free of tax, then as the residue is given to an exempt beneficiary, it must be grossed up (see **6.7.2.1**) to work out the value transferred for inheritance tax purposes, and this may reduce the value passing to the surviving spouse to an unacceptable level. The rules relating to burden of tax where part of the residue passes to a non-exempt beneficiary and part to an exempt beneficiary should also be considered, although these rules cannot be varied by the will.

17.4.7 TAKING ACCOUNT OF THE PERSONAL REPRESENTATIVES' LIABILITY TO PAY INHERITANCE TAX

The will should ensure that the personal representatives will be in a position to discharge any inheritance tax for which they are liable to account to the Revenue. The liability to pay inheritance tax is dealt with at **6.6** above, and personal representatives are only liable to the extent of assets which they received or would have received but for their own neglect or default. The following points are particularly relevant here.

17.4.7.1 Primary liability

Personal representatives are primarily liable to account for tax on the free estate of the deceased and settled land which devolves on them. The personal representatives may thus be liable to account for tax for which the estate is not liable and in respect of property which does not vest in them (for example, joint property passing by survivorship and nominated property). In such a case they have a right to recover the tax from the person in whom the property is vested (s. 211(3), Inheritance Tax Act 1984). Although the subsection does not specifically so provide, the will could vary this by providing that such tax will be borne by the estate.

TAX AND ESTATE PLANNING

17.4.7.2 Secondary liability

As mentioned at **17.3.2.2** above, the personal representatives have a secondary liability in respect of unpaid tax on lifetime gifts. We will see at **18.4.6.2** that the will could provide that the estate is primarily liable for such tax, if those are the testator's instructions.

EIGHTEEN

WILL DRAFTING

We have left this chapter until the end because of our belief that a discussion of this topic is best embarked upon against the background of an appreciation of the main principles of the law of succession (including the impact of taxation) *and* the practice involved in the administration of an estate. Once you have an idea of some of the problems that may be encountered, it is perhaps easier to appreciate the form of the dispositive provisions and the range of administrative matters the will ought to address. However, a case can certainly be made for discussing this topic at an earlier stage — for example, after material contained in the first three (or the first seven) chapters has been studied — leaving the subject matter considered in the later chapters to reinforce the issues discussed here.

During the course of this book we have encountered a number of sound reasons why a client might be encouraged to make a will. We will begin this chapter with a brief summary of the main advantages that may be gained by doing so (**18.1**). We will then turn our attention to the making of a will, starting with a consideration of a solicitor's duties in this connection (**18.2**). Next, we will examine the task of obtaining instructions (**18.3**). Then we will consider the structure and content of the will (**18.4**) and end the chapter with a few points relating to codicils (**18.5**).

18.1 Why Make a Will?

There are a number of reasons, of which the following are perhaps the most important.

18.1.1 CONTROL OF DISPOSITION

Wills allow testators to determine the disposition of their estates on death. If there is no valid will, we have seen (in **Chapter 2**) that the distribution of a deceased's estate is governed by the intestacy rules.

18.1.2 SELECTION OF EXECUTORS

Testators can select those whom they wish to carry out their wishes by appointing executors — whose authority to act stems from their appointment and is effective from the date of death (see **8.3.1**). If there is no will (or if there are no executors ready, willing and able to act) the court will appoint administrators, who have no authority to act until the issue of the grant (see **8.3.2**). As to the appointment of executors, see further **18.3.2.3(d)** and **18.4.4** below.

18.1.3 ADDITIONAL POWERS

As we saw in **13.2**, a will can (and should) incorporate a range of additional powers — i.e. in addition to those available under the general law — to facilitate the administration of the estate and for the benefit of those entitled to the estate (see further **18.3.2.3(c)** and **18.4.7** below).

WILL DRAFTING

18.1.4 GUARDIANS

For many younger clients, the ability to appoint guardians for their infant children may be a particularly cogent reason for making a will (see further **18.3.2.3**(e) and **18.4.4.4** below).

18.1.5 TAX

In **17.4**, we looked at a range of possible tax advantages which might flow from appropriately drafted wills. Tax mitigation is certainly an issue to be considered with the client when taking instructions for a will — both in the context of the will itself and possibly in conjunction with lifetime measures which might also be undertaken. However, it is always important to temper the client's (and perhaps your own) enthusiasm to save tax with realism; what is tax efficient may not, from other points of view, be in the best interests of clients or their families.

18.2 Duties of Solicitor Instructed to Prepare a Will

The following is a brief summary of the principal duties of solicitors asked to draft a will for a client.

18.2.1 CONDUCT ISSUES

The Solicitors' Practice Rules 1990 and The Law Society's rulings on matters of professional conduct apply, of course, to this as to other activities of solicitors acting in their professional capacity. The following matters are of particular importance in this context.

18.2.1.1 Third party instructions

Instructions received from someone other than the intended testator (e.g. from a relative or a bank manager) raise several conduct issues. They include:

(a) Rule 1. Of particular importance here is the need to have in mind the 'freedom of choice' aspect of this Rule. It will be necessary to make it clear to the proposed testator that, whilst you are happy to act (assuming you are able and willing to do so), they are entirely free to instruct any solicitor of their choice.

(b) Rule 3. The introduction must not be in breach of this Rule, which is concerned with introductions and referrals of business.

(c) An appreciation of who is your client. The intending testator is your client, not the person who makes the initial approach to you. It is therefore essential that you obtain written confirmation not only that the client wishes you to act, but also as to the terms of the instructions. In practice, you should ideally arrange to interview the intending testator.

18.2.1.2 Solicitor as beneficiary

We saw in **1.1.3.2** that if the will substantially benefits the person who drafted it there will be no presumption of knowledge and approval — one of the essential elements of a valid will. In these 'suspicious circumstances' the gift will fail — unless the suspicion can be removed by the person seeking to propound the will. For solicitors, there is an additional conduct issue of potentially much more serious consequence.

The Law Society has ruled that where a client intends to make a gift by will (or *inter vivos*) to their solicitor (or the solicitor's partner, employee or the members of the families of any of them) of a significant amount — either in itself, or having regard to the size of the client's estate and the reasonable expectations of prospective beneficiaries — the solicitor must advise the client to be independently advised as to that gift. If the client declines, the solicitor must refuse to act.

WILL DRAFTING

The Society's ruling applies even where the intended beneficiary (or donee) is a relative of the testator. It does not apply, however, where the gift is to be made to the solicitor to be dealt with in accordance with the testator's wishes (e.g. under a secret trust) so that the solicitor does not take any personal or financial benefit. However, as a precaution the solicitor in such circumstances should carefully preserve the instructions on the basis of which the will is drawn. Further, the testator's wishes should be expressed in writing, signed by the testator.

Whether a gift is 'substantial' or of a 'significant amount' is a matter of judgment. Neither the 'suspicious circumstances' nor the conduct problems just outlined will apply to a 'token' gift, nor to the standard charging clause included where solicitors are appointed executors (see further **18.4.4** below). If you are in doubt as to whether you have a problem, err on the side of caution!

18.2.2 COMPLIANCE WITH CLIENT'S INSTRUCTIONS

It is the solicitor's duty to ensure that the will drafted gives effect to the client's instructions. We have seen (in **1.4.1.4**) that there is a limited power of rectification which may, after the death, allow correction of clerical errors or a failure to understand the client's instructions — but even where this is possible, considerable delay and expense will be involved. We have also seen (in **15.2**) that it may be possible to effect a variation of the will after the death (and thereby 'put matters right') — but this might not always be possible without the assistance of the court, which will again involve delay and expense (let alone the possibility that the court might not 'play ball'!).

Clearly, therefore, the solicitor must obtain full instructions from the client on a number of matters (see further **18.3** below) — and this will in almost all cases necessitate an interview with the client.

18.2.2.1 Advice concerning the will

Although the will drafted at the end of the day must be the client's (rather than the solicitor's) will, this does not mean that the solicitor's role in taking instructions should be merely 'passive'. It is entirely proper for the solicitor to give advice on possible dispositions and their tax implications so that clients can make informed decisions as to what is appropriate to their circumstances. Sometimes you will be forced into this position by the client who says (in effect) 'what do you think I should do?'. However, you should also take an active role in discussing the range of possibilities even with clients who come to you with a detailed list of dispositions and a seemingly clear idea as to what they wish to do. It may well be that they are unaware of other (possibly better) ways of achieving their basic aims.

18.2.2.2 Lifetime arrangements

It may also be appropriate to raise with the client the possibility of making lifetime gifts to mitigate the impact of taxation (see **17.3**). Life insurance policies in favour of others (the proceeds of which would not, as we have seen, be treated as part of the client's succession or taxable estate) might also be considered. If so, and in the case of any other investment advice, bear in mind the requirements of the Financial Services Act 1986.

18.2.2.3 Review

It is important to remind clients of the need to keep their wills under review. What is appropriate for today and the foreseeable future might not be so where family and/or financial circumstances change.

Although you must not 'tout' for business, there is nothing 'unprofessional' in a solicitor informing existing clients of changes in the law (e.g. in tax rules) which make it desirable that they consider making a new will.

WILL DRAFTING

18.2.3 CAPACITY

We examined the need for the testator to have the requisite capacity to make a will in **1.1.2** above. Although this is not a 'live' issue in the majority of cases, if there is any doubt about the testator's capacity or any suspicion that this might be challenged the solicitor drafting the will should take steps at the time of its preparation and execution, in order to be able to deal with the issue should it arise in the future. In the nature of things, it is not otherwise likely to be easy to establish the existence of the requisite capacity when the matter is raised on the testator's death — perhaps some years after execution of the will.

In any such case, therefore, it would be wise to try to arrange for a medical report to show that the testator has the requisite capacity — and (ideally) for the medical practitioner concerned to act as one of the witnesses. The solicitor taking the testator's instructions should also aim to be present at the execution of the will (where possible perhaps acting as one of the witnesses) and should make and preserve a detailed file note of his view of the testator's capacity.

18.2.4 FORMALITIES

The solicitor drafting the will also has the responsibility of ensuring that the will is duly executed in accordance with the provisions of s. 9, Wills Act 1837 (as amended) which were discussed at **1.1.4** above and not forgetting s. 15, Wills Act 1837 (**1.4.3.4**). Ideally, the solicitor or an employee conversant with the formality requirements should attend at the execution of the will. In any event, it is a good idea to make and preserve a note of the details of the execution (time, place and names and addresses of witnesses and anyone else present at the time) in case any doubt as to due execution arises in the future.

18.2.5 DUTY TO WHOM?

Clearly, the solicitor has a duty to the testator both in contract and tort. However, since any breach would not cause any financial loss, the client's estate could only recover nominal damages.

However, it is also clear that the solicitor, in relation to the drafting and execution of a will, also owes a duty of care to the beneficiaries whom the testator intends to benefit.

18.2.5.1 *Ross* v *Caunters* [1980] Ch 297

In this case, the solicitor had omitted to warn the testator (to whom the will was sent for execution) that a spouse of a beneficiary should not be a witness (where this happens, we saw (in **1.4.3.4**) the gift to the beneficiary fails). He had further failed (when the will was returned after execution) to check whether it was properly attested, to notice that the beneficiary's spouse was one of the witnesses and had failed to draw this to the testator's attention. For these reasons, the solicitor had been negligent and the judge went on to hold that the solicitor's duty of care to the client (the testator) extended to third parties whom the client intended to benefit. The beneficiary was therefore entitled to damages to compensate for the loss of the legacy which would have been received had the gift not failed.

Although the case was concerned with a failure to ensure due execution of the will, it is clear from the judgment that there would be a breach of the duty of care to the beneficiary where the will is negligently drafted.

18.2.5.2 *Clarke* v *Bruce Lance & Co.* [1988] 1 All ER 364

The decision in this case places an important limitation upon the impact of the decision in *Ross* v *Caunters*. Here, the defendants made a will for a testator under which the plaintiff was left a service station. Subsequently, the testator granted a lease of this property to X, and later the defendants drew up a variation of that lease granting X an option to purchase after the testator's death at a fixed price. This was, in due course exercised, and the plaintiff sued the defendants for his loss. It was held that he was not entitled to damages: the solicitors owed no duty of care to the beneficiary when acting for the testator in a subsequent transaction which adversely affected the value of the beneficiary's gift.

18.2.5.3 *Kecskemmett* v *Rubens Rabin, The Times,* 31 December 1992

Here the testator sought by his will to give the plaintiff (his son by his first marriage), half of the proceeds of sale of certain properties. These were, in fact, held by the testator and his second wife as beneficial joint tenants, so that on the testator's death they vested beneficially in the testator's second wife by virtue of the *jus accrescendi*.

Macpherson J held that the solicitors were in breach of their duty of care in preparing the will (which duty extended to the plaintiff) in not ascertaining the nature of the tenure of the properties and failing to advise the testator of the need to sever the joint tenancy in order to be able to give effect to the proposed gift.

18.2.5.4 *White* v *Jones, The Times,* 9 March 1993

In this case, the Court of Appeal held that solicitors who, through inexcusable delay, failed to draw up a will before the testator's death were liable in negligence to the disappointed prospective beneficiaries.

18.3 Taking Instructions

A good set of instructions is the only secure foundation upon which the client's will can be constructed.

18.3.1 GENERALLY

As has already been suggested, an interview with the intending testator is likely in almost all cases to be essential in order that the solicitor can obtain the necessary information to form the basis upon which to advise the client and ultimately to draft an appropriate will.

18.3.2 INFORMATION REQUIRED

This is best collected by using a checklist: by doing so, it should be possible to ensure that essential information and issues to be considered are not overlooked. Most firms will have their own version of a suitable checklist: the issues which this needs to address can be grouped under three headings:

(a) Personal details (**18.3.2.1**)
(b) Size and nature of the 'estate' (**18.3.2.2**)
(c) Contents of the will (**18.3.2.3**).

18.3.2.1 Personal details

The full name, address, age and occupation of the testator will be required. You will need similar information regarding any spouse, children or other dependant(s) — since in order to be able to give suitable advice you must have a picture of the client 'in context'. Thus, for example, you may need to form a judgment as to whether a possible problem might arise (and which ought to be addressed now) in relation to the Inheritance (Provision for Family and Dependants) Act 1975 — see **Chapter 3**. You should enquire whether any of them have special needs — e.g. arising from a disability.

WILL DRAFTING

In addition, you should enquire as to the existence and whereabouts of any previous will. (If only minor adjustments to this are required, consider whether they may be satisfactorily achieved by means of a codicil.)

18.3.2.2 Size and nature of the 'estate'

A general picture needs to be formed of what assets the testator has and (in very round figures) their value. This is essential if you are to have any hope of giving sensible advice to the client: the sort of will which might be appropriate for someone with an estate of £1 million is likely to be very different from that which is possible where the estate is valued at £100,000.

It will not generally be necessary to be too specific about details: it will normally be sufficient, for example, to discover that the testator has stocks and shares worth approximately £25,000 without compiling a detailed list of the precise holdings and their exact value.

The term 'estate' is used here in a very wide sense. What you need to know about includes all of the following:

(a) Assets vested in the deceased's name alone.
(b) Assets owned with other(s) as a beneficial tenant in common.
(c) Any foreign property interests.
(d) Life policies and pension scheme benefits which will pass under the terms of the will.
(e) Any property which will pass outside the will — such as assets held with other(s) as a beneficial joint tenant; property the subject of a statutory nomination; trust policies (whether under s. 11, Married Women's Property Act 1882 or otherwise); discretionary pension scheme benefits (and whether there has been any 'nomination' in respect of them).
(f) Any trust interests currently enjoyed — such as a life interest.
(g) Liabilities — in particular any mortgage debt (and whether it is covered by any life insurance).
(h) Any 'expectations' — i.e. known and likely inheritances. Thus it would, for instance, be important to know that the testator is entitled to the remainder interest under the terms of a grandparent's will on the death of the testator's parent who is the life tenant.
(i) Any lifetime gifts already made or contemplated. This information is obviously needed to enable you to make an assessment of the client's inheritance tax position: but any such lifetime provision will also need to be taken into account in planning the will.

Where the testator is married, a similar picture of the spouse's estate needs to be established. You cannot properly advise your client without knowing something about the spouse's position. If, for example, the spouse is already well provided for the opportunities for passing property direct to the children so as not to waste the testator's nil rate band are much increased. Ideally, the spouse should also be encouraged to make a will!

Likewise, check whether any provision has already been made for the children. It may be, for instance, that they are beneficiaries under a trust set up by a deceased grandparent's will.

18.3.2.3 Contents of the will

Once you have a picture of the client's personal details and the size and nature of the estate you are then ready to consider the dispositions etc. which the client wishes to include in the will.

It is, as has already been hinted, likely that you will need to offer advice and make suggestions. What is appropriate for the individual client will obviously very much depend upon that client's particular circumstances and priorities. Generalisations are, therefore, not easy to make: however, some situations which are commonly met in what might be termed 'family wills' are considered in 18.3.2.4 and 18.3.2.5 below.

WILL DRAFTING

What information do you need from the client in order to be able to prepare the will?

(a) *Legacies*. Does the client wish to make any:

(i) specific gifts? If so, explain the doctrine of ademption (**1.4.3.2**) and identify whether they are to be free of tax (**6.7.1** and **17.4.6**), expenses (**16.1.1**) and (if appropriate) mortgage (**14.3.4.1**).

(ii) general or pecuniary legacies? If so, are they to be free of tax (**6.7.1** and **17.4.6**) and from what part of the estate are they to be paid (**16.1.2**).

(b) *Residue*. Who are to be the residuary beneficiaries? Is there to be a survivorship clause (**17.4.4**)? What provision is required for substituted beneficiaries (so as to avoid a partial intestacy (see **Chapter 2**) in the event of a beneficiary predeceasing or failing to survive for the survivorship period)? What provision is required as to the payment of debts (including secured debts)?

(c) *Administrative powers*. Are extensions, modifications or exclusions required of the powers under the general law in respect of:

(i) insurance (**13.2.6**)
(ii) appropriation (**13.2.2**)
(iii) receipt by/on behalf of infant beneficiary (**13.2.3**)
(iv) investment — including power to purchase land for residence (**13.2.10**)
(v) maintenance (**13.2.11**)
(vi) advancement (**13.2.12**)
(vii) loans to beneficiaries (**13.2.12**)
(viii) statutory and equitable apportionment rules (**13.1.2**)
(ix) to run business (if testator sole trader) (**13.2.9**).

Not all of the above will be relevant in every case (much will depend upon whether a trust arises (e.g. because a life interest is conferred by the will, or some of the potential beneficiaries might be minors). It may be that you will not discuss these in detail with the client at this stage, but later when the will has been drafted.

(d) *Executors and trustees*. It is possible for the testator to appoint any number of executors — though as we have seen (in **8.9**) a maximum of four may apply for a grant in relation to any property. A sole executor has full authority to act, but unless a trust corporation (such as a bank) is appointed it is usually sensible to appoint at least two individuals to cover the possibility of one predeceasing or being unable to act.

If under the terms of the will a trust will (or might) arise trustees should also be appointed. They will usually be the same persons as are appointed executors. Indeed, even if the will does not create any trust interests, practitioners will often nonetheless appoint trustees; at least this has the benefit that trustees will be 'in post' should they ever be needed (e.g. if a codicil makes a gift to a beneficiary who happens to be a minor). If trustees are appointed, it will be desirable to appoint at least two individuals (or a trust corporation) so that there are sufficient to be able to give a good receipt for capital money.

It may also be necessary to consider the appointment of executors to deal solely with particular assets — for example, where the testator is a sole trader, appointing someone with experience in the type of business concerned to act in relation to that particular asset may make a lot of sense.

The client may have firm ideas as to whom to appoint, but you may be called upon to advise as to the relative merits of possible appointees. They include:

(i) *Friends or relatives*. Such an appointee has the merit of being known to the testator and (in all probability) to the intended beneficiaries. Indeed, there is no reason in principle why a beneficiary (who will have a clear interest in attending to the administration of the estate) should not be appointed — though the possibility of a potential conflict of interest should not be ignored. Nor should any known antagonism between the proposed appointee and the beneficiaries.

Another 'advantage' of appointing 'lay' executors and trustees is that they will be prepared to act without payment (though you should consider with the testator whether perhaps a legacy might be appropriate as a 'reward' for their services). However, this advantage may prove to be more apparent than real if (as is common) the executors instruct solicitors to act for them!

It will be important for the testator to be confident (especially if the case is 'complicated') that the persons chosen will be capable of coping with the task — and to check their willingness to act.

Ideally, the proposed appointee (or, if there are several, at least one of them) should not be of a generation older than that of the testator. It is also important that, if several persons are to be appointed, they be known to be capable of 'getting on' with each other, otherwise there may be real difficulties in the administration of the estate.

(ii) *Solicitors (or other professional advisers, such as accountants)*. Such appointments have the advantage of entrusting the administration of the estate to 'experts', and this may be particularly important where the estate is complex. However, they will certainly wish to be able to charge for their services, and to enable them to do so a charging clause must be included in the will.

Individual solicitors etc. may be appointed. This has the advantage that the testator will at least know who the proving executors will be, but problems may arise if the appointees die, retire or leave the firm. Consequently, provided the client is happy with the idea, it is increasingly common for the appointment of a firm of solicitors rather than named individual members of the firm (see further **18.4.4** below).

(iii) *Trust corporations*. The main advantage of appointing such a corporation (e.g. a bank) is continuity. Banks will generally insist upon the use of their own standard appointment clause (incorporating a charging clause, permitting the bank concerned to charge in accordance with its charging scales) and will usually wish to see a draft of the will when this has been prepared. This is a standard request, but you should inform the client of it and obtain consent to this being done.

Such an appointment may be suitable if there are likely to be long running trusts or the estate is particularly complex, but is likely to be an expensive solution in a more straightforward case. Very often, when the appointment of a bank is being considered, it will be the case that instructions to prepare the will were received from the bank concerned. As indicated in **18.2.1.2** above, it is then particularly important to remember that the testator is your client who is entitled to be advised about the appointment of executors and trustees in exactly the same manner as any other client.

(iv) *The Public Trustee*. It will probably be a very rare case in which you might advise the appointment of the public trustee (a corporation solely created by statute — the Public Trustee Act 1906) as being appropriate. The only advantages of doing so appear to be continuity and that the state is effectively liable for loss occasioned by a breach of duty! The public trustee is entitled to remuneration and can refuse to act (except on the grounds that the estate is too small): he will usually decline an appointment which would involve the running of a business.

(e) *Guardians*. If the testator has infant children, consideration should be give to the appointment of a guardian until they attain their majority. Under s. 5, Children Act 1989 a guardian may be appointed in writing or by a will.

Under the Act, a parent with 'parental responsibility' may appoint a guardian. In broad terms, a child's mother has parental responsibility irrespective of marital status: the child's father automatically 'qualifies' if he has been married to the mother at any time since the child's conception. In other situations, the father will be able to appoint a guardian only if parental responsibility is conferred on him by court order or by agreement with the mother. When a child is legally adopted, the adopting parents acquire parental responsibility.

By virtue of s. 5(7) and (8), an appointment by one parent will not normally take effect until after the death of the surviving parent if the survivor has parental responsibility (whether automatic or conferred): in other words, in such a case the surviving parent is automatically sole guardian of the infant child concerned and the appointment by the deceased parent is 'deferred'. The only exception to this is where the deceased parent had immediately before death a 'residence order' in their favour: in such a case, the appointment by the deceased parent takes effect immediately (i.e. jointly with the surviving parent, who can apply to the court for the guardianship to be terminated (s. 6(7)) if unhappy with the situation).

In addition, if the child's parents have never been married to each other, an appointment by the mother will take effect upon her death even if the father survives — unless parental responsibility has been conferred upon the father as above. If this is the case, the appointment will be deferred unless the mother had a residence order in her favour immediately prior to her death — in which case the guardian will act jointly with the father.

If guardians are to be appointed, two matters need to be addressed. First, the testator should check that the proposed appointees are willing to act. Second, the guardians may need a larger property in which to house their 'expanded family', and consideration should be given to the inclusion of a power to fund this — e.g. by means of a loan at a preferential rate of interest or by authorising a purchase in the joint names of the guardians and the trustees.

(f) *Directions as to disposal of the body etc.* It is quite common for testators to include in their wills any 'special request' for the disposal of their remains (e.g. for cremation, burial at sea, etc.). Whilst there is nothing 'wrong' with this practice, it is perhaps more sensible to encourage testators to make their wishes known to those who will be likely to be making the funeral arrangements. It is, after all, quite possible that the will might not be looked at until after the funeral has taken place!

The same comments apply to any wishes the testator may have in relation to organ donation or use of his or her body for medical education or research.

18.3.2.4 Testator's priorities

In perhaps the majority of cases you will be concerned with the drafting of 'family wills' where the testator is seeking to make provision for a surviving spouse or partner and any children. What the appropriate provision might be in a particular case will depend upon a number of factors — especially the testator's priorities, the size and nature of the estate and the needs and resources of the potential beneficiaries concerned.

Further, the 'solution' in any case must be arrived at bearing in mind the possibility of 'disappointed' members of the family or other dependants making claims under the Inheritance (Provision for Family and Dependants) Act 1975 (**Chapter 3**) on the grounds that reasonable financial provision has not been made for them.

In the discussion which follows, references are made to the situation where the testator leaves a surviving spouse. Where the testator is not married but wishes to provide for a cohabiting partner as well as children, essentially the same choices will arise, but the following points should be borne in mind.

First, the partner has no 'succession rights' to the testator's property under the intestacy rules: such rights can only be acquired under the terms of the will. It is, of course, possible for the testator to confer property interests upon the partner *inter vivos* — e.g. by outright gift or by ensuring that property is held by them as beneficial joint tenants. Second, the partner will only have a claim under Inheritance (Provision for Family and Dependants) Act 1975 if within the terms of s. 1(1)(e)

— i.e. as someone who immediately before the death of the deceased was being wholly or partly maintained by the deceased (otherwise than for full valuable consideration), and the dispositions on the death do not make reasonable financial provision for the maintenance of the partner concerned. Third, there will be no question of inheritance tax spouse exemption applying, whether on an *inter vivos* gift or on death.

Where the testator has a spouse and children it is likely that they will be the main beneficiaries under the will. A fuller discussion of the range of possibilities will be found in 17.4, but a brief reminder of the main tax points and other issues involved in selecting the appropriate 'option' in a particular case is included here.

(a) *Absolute interest to surviving spouse.* This will clearly confer the maximum possible benefit upon the surviving spouse. However, since the property passes outright to the survivor, the testator loses any further control of it and cannot, therefore, be sure that what is not needed by the surviving spouse will end up with the children. This is so even if the spouse currently has a will in terms similar to that made by the testator, because (as we have seen) the will may be revoked either by a later will, or automatically upon the surviving spouse's remarriage.

There will be no inheritance tax charge on the testator's death (because of the spouse exemption), but any of the testator's nil rate band available at the date of death will be 'wasted'. The property becomes, of course, part of the spouse's estate for tax purposes.

(b) *Life interest to spouse, remainder to children.* As the surviving spouse will here receive an interest in possession, the inheritance tax position is effectively the same as for the absolute gift. The spouse exemption applies, and the property supporting the life interest is deemed to be part of the spouse's estate. However, the surviving spouse is only entitled to the income for life — and the testator retains control over the ultimate destiny of the capital. If ensuring that the children ultimately benefit is the testator's priority, this is certainly how it can be achieved: but will this type of disposition provide adequately for the spouse?

(c) *Legacy to children, residue to spouse.* So far as the property passing to the surviving spouse is concerned, the comments made in (a) above will apply. The gift to the children does allow the testator to ensure some provision for them — and use some/all of any available nil rate band for inheritance tax purposes. A gift of a fixed sum may be made, but the maximum tax benefit from the gift to the children can be secured by the use of a formula gift — along the lines of 'such sum as may at the date of my death be paid without attracting any charge to inheritance tax at a rate above nil'. The danger with using such a formula, however, is that with the passage of time the nil rate band might have risen to such an extent that when the testator dies the amount passed to the children by the gift is a much higher proportion of the estate than the testator contemplated at the time the will was made. To prevent the surviving spouse being prejudiced, a maximum amount could be specified.

(d) *Legacy to spouse, residue to children.* This too will allow use to be made of any available part of the testator's nil rate band, with the estate passing to the spouse being exempt. It is probably only a viable proposition where the spouse is independently wealthy, and even then the risk is that it might not adequately provide for the spouse in the longer term.

18.3.2.5 Gifts to children

Again, the issues have been discussed more fully elsewhere: however, as they are particularly important to have in mind when taking instructions and drafting the will, a reminder of them is given here.

(a) *Vested or contingent gift?* This fundamental question needs to be addressed in all cases where gifts to minor children are included in the will.

Basically, if the gift is vested it is 'unconditional' and although it will have to be held by trustees until the beneficiary attains the age of 18, it will be part of the beneficiary's estate — passing on the beneficiary's intestacy on death whilst still a minor, and liable also to inheritance tax in that event as part of the beneficiary's estate. At 18, the beneficiary can call for payment — and the testator may wish to consider (especially if a substantial sum is involved) whether this is an appropriate age at which to gain control of the gifted property.

A contingent gift requires the fulfilment of some condition before it vests — such as attaining the age of 18: in this case, if the beneficiary dies before attaining 18, the gift fails and there will be no question of an inheritance tax charge as part of the beneficiary's estate. If the contingency is attaining, for example, the age of 21, then if the beneficiary dies at (say) 19 the gifted property will not pass as part of the beneficiary's succession estate — but will be treated as part of the beneficiary's taxable estate because of the effect of s. 31, Trustee Act 1925 (see **13.2.11**). For this reason, if the vesting of the capital is postponed to an age greater than 18 it is wise to consider the postponement of the vesting of the income until the same age by an appropriate variation of s. 31.

For capital gains tax purposes (see **7.2**), a vested gift may have some advantages: the property concerned will be treated as the beneficiary's (even whilst under 18) and any gains on a disposal treated accordingly. Thus, they will be liable to tax at the rate(s) appropriate to an individual and an individual's annual exempt slice will be available (currently £5,800). There will be no disposal for tax purposes when the beneficiary attains 18. On the other hand, if the gift is contingent there will be a deemed disposal when the condition attached to the gift is fulfilled. Any disposals in the meantime will be taxed as gains of the trustees (usually at 35%) and will be subject to the trustee's annual exempt slice only (currently £2,900).

So far as income tax is concerned (see **7.1**), where the beneficiary's interest is vested the trustees will pay at 25% and the income will form part of the beneficiary's income for tax purposes — even if being accumulated. Thus, as the case may be, the beneficiary may have a repayment claim or be liable to higher rate tax (claiming credit for the basic rate already effectively paid). Where the beneficiary's interest in the income is contingent only, the trustees will normally be paying tax at 35%. In such cases, only income not being accumulated will be included as part of the beneficiary's income for tax purposes.

(b) *The possibility of further children.* To avoid the testator having to remember to amend the will if further children are born, a class gift should be considered (see **1.4.1.5**).

(c) *Substitutional gifts.* Routinely, thought should be given to the position if the minor beneficiary should predecease the testator. We have seen (in **1.4.3.3**) that s. 33, Wills Act 1837 may provide a statutory substitutional gift in the case of gifts to the testator's own children or remoter issue. In other cases, an express provision will be necessary and should, in practice, be included even in cases where s. 33 might 'save the day'.

18.4 Structure and Content of the Will

Having obtained the client's instructions and advised as necessary, it is now possible to turn to the drafting of the will itself.

In drafting wills, practitioners rely extensively upon precedents. It is not our intention here to attempt to provide you with a set of precedents: you will have access to collections of these on your course. Consideration of the detailed content of individual clauses and practise in using them will be essential functions of the drafting exercises you will be asked to undertake during the course. Rather, our aim is to consider the basic elements of will drafting and the sorts of issues which the various clauses included in a will need to address.

Successful will drafting needs an understanding of what the client wants, what the options are and (flowing from these considerations) what the will needs to achieve — so that the person drafting the will can select appropriate precedents to produce the 'right' will for the client.

WILL DRAFTING

In a sense, what follows is a distillation of points made previously in this and, indeed, in earlier chapters of this book. We will begin with a look at the basic structure of a will and then turn to an examination of the content of the various clauses of 'standard' wills.

18.4.1 STRUCTURE OF THE WILL

Traditionally, wills are drafted without punctuation, though the will is normally divided into numbered clauses.

The usual pattern is:

(a) Commencement
(b) Revocation clause (may be part of the Commencement)
(c) Appointment of executors etc.
(d) Specific and general legacies (if any)
(e) Residuary gifts
(f) Administrative provisions
(g) Date (may be part of the Commencement)
(h) Attestation clause.

In all but perhaps the simplest cases, it is likely that a precedent will have to be adapted to fit the needs of the particular will. This needs to be done carefully, and special care will be required where more than one source of precedent is being used.

18.4.2 COMMENCEMENT

The purpose of this is to identify that what follows is the 'last will' of the testator, whose full name and postal address should be given. It is usual also to state the testator's occupation.

18.4.3 REVOCATION

We saw (in **1.2.1.5**) that a later will normally revokes an earlier will, but that this is not inevitable. For the avoidance of doubt, and even if the testator has not previously made a will, it is best practice to include a revocation clause which (logically) should be the first in the will. Indeed, it is often incorporated as part of the Commencement. You cannot rely upon the statement in the Commencement that this is the testator's 'last will': something more is needed, such as: I REVOKE all previous wills and testamentary dispositions.

18.4.4 APPOINTMENTS

18.4.4.1 Executors and trustees generally

We discussed the possible appointees in **18.3.2.3** above, and the normal practice of appointing (usually the same people) trustees as well as executors. Having made the appointment, it is usual to continue with something like the following:

(hereinafter called 'my Trustees' *which expression shall include where the context so admits the trustees for the time being of this my will or any codicil hereto*).

The words in italics are included to ensure that it is clear that any powers conferred by later provisions of the will upon 'my Trustees' are not merely personal to the executors and trustees who are originally appointed.

If individuals are appointed, a substitute appointment may be provided for in the event of the original appointee(s) being unable or unwilling to act.

18.4.4.2 Solicitors

Solicitors may be appointed by name like any other executor or trustee. Where it is desired to appoint a firm, rather than named solicitors, the clause used should address the following matters.

First, it should appoint the partners 'at the date of death'. If this is not specified, the appointment will be construed as of the partners at the date of the will. This nullifies one of the advantages which can be obtained by appointing the firm rather than the individual solicitor(s) — namely, dealing with the problem of the partner who has died, retired or left the firm.

Second, the firm may not be known by its present name or may have amalgamated with another firm: the clause should therefore deal with these contingencies.

Third, it is usual (though not essential) to express the wish that only two of the partners should take the grant. This is almost certainly what would, in practice, happen in any event — since it may be administratively inconvenient to have as many as four partners acting.

Whether the appointment of solicitors is as named individuals or as a firm, a charging clause will be necessary. This may be conveniently dealt with as part of the appointment clause, or may be included as a separate clause later in the will — usually as one of the administrative powers at the end of the will. Whichever course is adopted, the clause must be sufficiently widely drawn so as to allow the solicitor(s) to charge for all the work done by them or the firm in and about the administration of the estate. It is important that this is expressed to include acts which a trustee who is not a solicitor could do — otherwise a charge will only be possible in relation to strictly legal work. Sometimes the clause is expressed to allow payment 'without abatement'; the reason for this is to prevent the possibility of the benefit of the charging clause abating along with the other pecuniary legacies (see **16.1.3**).

18.4.4.3 Other professionals

The same comments apply to appointments of, for example, accountants or other professionals.

Banks all have their own (different) preferred appointment clauses incorporating provisions allowing them to charge according to their respective scales.

18.4.4.4 Guardians

If an appointment of guardians for infant children is required, the appropriate clause is usually included after the appointment of the executors and trustees. As we saw in **18.3.2.3** above, the appointment will normally only take effect on the death of the child's surviving parent.

18.4.5 SPECIFIC AND GENERAL LEGACIES

As we discussed in **18.3.2.3**(a) above, it is important that the testator's instructions be taken as to whether such gifts are to be 'free of tax' (the position in most cases if nothing is said) or 'subject to tax' — and the appropriate provision included in the will. With specific gifts, the clause should also deal with the question of 'expenses' — i.e. insurance and costs of transfer which will be borne by the legatee unless otherwise provided. In the case of a gift of land, the question of whether the gift is to be 'free of mortgage' needs also to be addressed.

Particularly with specific gifts, take care to identify the property given as clearly as possible: so, for example, a gift of 'my diamond necklace which was given to me by my grandmother' rather than simply 'my diamond necklace'. Remember also that specific gifts are subject to the doctrine of ademption (**1.4.3.2**), and (subject, of course, to the client's instructions) an 'anti-ademption' provision might be appropriate. For example, a gift of 'Blackacre or other the property which I may own and occupy as my residence at the date of my death' will cover the case where the testator moves house after making the will.

The possibilities are almost limitless! However, there are a few situations which perhaps merit special mention.

18.4.5.1 Personal effects

It will frequently be the case that the testator wishes to pass personal effects to (say) the surviving spouse. This is best done by means of a gift of 'my personal chattels as defined by s. 55(1)(x), Administration of Estates Act 1925'. You will perhaps recall that (as we saw in 2.2.2.3) there can be problems with assets such as a car used partly for business purposes. This is best dealt with by adding a phrase such as '... but including any car whether or not used for business purposes'.

Often, a gift of personal effects is given in the will through the medium of a 'precatory trust' — i.e. an absolute gift in the will coupled with a wish (expressed not to be binding) that the beneficiary distribute the assets concerned in accordance with the terms of (e.g.) a letter from the testator. As we saw in 17.4.3.3, provided this is done within two years of the death there are no adverse inheritance tax consequences: it will be as if the testator had made the gifts directly to the intended beneficiaries (s. 143, Inheritance Tax Act 1984).

Another possibility is that the testator wishes relatives or friends to be able to choose a 'keepsake'. There are a number of issues which need to be addressed in such cases, including:

(a) a time limit within which any such selection must be made (and if several people are to be given the right to select, some thought will also need to be given to possibly setting a 'pecking order' or including a provision for resolving any disputes).
(b) what is to happen in the event of a beneficiary predeceasing or failing to make a choice within the time limit.
(c) whether a limit on the value of items selected is needed.

18.4.5.2 Shares

Whether the gift is general or specific, it is important that the clause to give effect to a gift of shares addresses the following.

First, the shareholding should be precisely described, and the source of the payment of any charge upon those shares at the date of death should be identified (e.g. residue).

Second, the clause needs to cover the possibility that, as a result of amalgamation, takeover or reconstruction, the current holding is represented by a different holding at the date of death.

18.4.5.3 Gifts to institutions

Whenever the testator is making a gift to an institution (e.g. a charity) the following matters must be dealt with by the clause giving effect to the gift.

First, it is essential that the institution be precisely identified. Its full correct name should be given, and its address. In the case of a charity, its registered charity number is often quoted for good measure. If the name is not absolutely 'spot on' the gift may fail.

Second, it is important to provide for the possibility that the institution has, by the date of death, changed its name, ceased to exist or amalgamated with another institution. You may recall that in the case of a charity (but not any other institution) it may sometimes in such situations be possible to be authorised (by the court or the Charity Commissioners) to apply the gift *cy près*. The ideal solution (whether or not the gift is charitable) is for the will to provide what is to happen in such cases, e.g. 'my Trustees shall pay it to the (charitable) organisation which in their opinion most nearly fulfils the objects' of the original donee institution.

Third, the clause should provide a simple means for the trustees to obtain a receipt and thus be discharged in relation to the gift. This will be especially important where the gift is to an unincorporated institution such as a members club — where, in the absence of a sensible receipt clause, it might be necessary to obtain the receipt of all the current members! Something along the lines of 'The receipt of someone who appears to be the secretary, treasurer or other proper officer of the (charity) shall be a sufficient discharge of my Trustees' will deal with the potential problem. The phrase 'appears to be' will remove the necessity for the trustees to make enquiries as to the propriety of the official's appointment!

18.4.5.4 Permission to occupy

Sometimes, the testator wishes to provide a property for the occupation of a beneficiary — such as the surviving spouse. This is usually best done behind a trust for sale: the property concerned is given to the trustees upon trust for sale (with the usual power to postpone) and a direction that the beneficiary be allowed to occupy according to the testator's instructions (e.g. rent free and for so long as they wish). Again, subject to the client's instructions, the clause may go on to provide that the beneficiary should pay all the outgoings (including insurance premiums) and keep the property in good repair. Further, there is usually included a provision that the house should not be sold without the consent of the beneficiary — who may request the sale and reinvestment of the proceeds in an alternative property.

The clause should also determine what is to happen when the beneficiary dies or no longer wishes to occupy (e.g. that the property should then fall into residue).

18.4.6 RESIDUARY GIFTS

The residue will usually be given either directly to the beneficiaries whom the testator wishes to benefit, or to the trustees upon trust for sale (often this is done even where no trust is actually created by the will).

18.4.6.1 Payment of debts and legacies

Whichever form the residuary gift takes, there should (unless property has been specifically 'earmarked' for the payment of these items) be a provision for the payment of debts and pecuniary legacies (see **14.3.4** and **16.1.2.1**). Where the gift is direct to the beneficiaries it will be expressed to be 'after' or 'subject to' their payment; where there is a trust for sale there should be a direction for payment out of the proceeds of sale.

Remember that a general direction for the payment of debts does not cover the payment of any mortgage debt. This will be borne by the beneficiary taking the property, unless the gift is expressed to be 'free of mortgage' or the general direction for the payment of debts is specifically expressed to include the mortgage concerned. (See **14.3.4.5**.)

Funeral and testamentary expenses (in effect, the executorship and administration expenses) are normally also included in the direction.

18.4.6.2 Payment of inheritance tax

In the majority of cases, the tax attributable to the transfer deemed to take place on death will be a testamentary expense (**6.7.1**). This will include the tax on any tax-free gifts in the will.

The clause can be drafted to embrace more than just the tax in respect of the 'death' estate. If the provision included in the will is for payment of (e.g.) 'all tax payable by reason of my death' then tax on property which would normally bear its own tax would also be included — such as joint property, foreign property, nominated property, settled property, former PETs, LCTs and even gifts with a reservation! Clearly, it is important that both you and the client are clear as to what tax is to be covered by the clause and that this is in turn clear from the will.

18.4.6.3 Beneficial interests

The terms of the gifts required in any particular case will obviously depend upon the instructions of the testator. We have considered the sorts of provisions which enable the testator to leave a 'flexible will' in **17.3.3**. In other circumstances, it is likely that the residuary gift will take the form of an outright gift with substitutional gifts in the event of the primary gifts failing; or successive interests (such as to the testator's spouse for life with remainder to the children).

In these cases, there are some general observations which may usefully be made.

(a) *Survivorship clauses*. These have already been discussed (in **7.3.4.3** and **17.3.4**). They are usually for 28/30 days and should not for tax purposes be longer than six months. From a succession viewpoint, the inclusion of such clauses prevents the *commorientes* rule in s. 184, Law of Property Act 1925 applying; allows the testator control over the destiny of the gifted property where the beneficiary survives but dies within the prescribed period; and saves the inconvenience and cost of a 'double administration' where the testator's and beneficiary's deaths occur in rapid succession. From a tax viewpoint, the inclusion of such a clause may prevent a double charge to tax where the testator and beneficiary are not spouses; where they are, it can prevent the potential wasting of the testator's nil rate band due to the 'bunching' of the spouses' estates.

In the case of spouses, it is important that the clause provides for the substitutional gift to take effect not only if the beneficiary spouse predeceases or fails to survive for the specified period, but also 'if the gift should for any other reason fail'. This is to overcome the problem of s. 18A, Wills Act 1837 and the decision in *Re Sinclair* (see **1.2.1.4**).

Whilst survivorship clauses are routinely included in cases where the gift is outright, the precedents rarely seem to suggest this where a life interest is being conferred. However, since for tax purposes the consequences are essentially the same for either type of gift, perhaps survivorship clauses should always be included. The '*Re Sinclair* extension' of the clause is not, however, needed because the effect of divorce is automatically to accelerate the remainder interest (s. 18A, Wills Act 1837 — see **1.2.1.4**) even if this is expressed in the will to be dependent upon being alive at the date of the life tenant's death.

(b) *Named beneficiaries or class gifts?* If the gift is to be to named beneficiaries, the drafting problems are simply to ensure that the will makes it clear what shares are to be taken by the various beneficiaries, and what is to happen if any of them should predecease the testator.

Where the testator wishes to benefit, say, grandchildren, we have seen that it may be wiser to frame the gift as a class gift (see **1.4.1.5**). In such cases, it will be necessary to have in mind the class closing rules and their implications will need to be considered with the client. It is also necessary that there should be no ambiguity as to the composition of the class. Thus, for example, if the gift is to be to 'nephews and nieces' this will be prima facie a gift to the testator's blood relatives fitting the description — and not those related by marriage. Further, it is again important that the clause giving effect to the gift should identify what is to happen in the event of any member of the class predeceasing.

(c) *Substitutional gifts*. Such gifts are essential for the proper working of survivorship clauses. It is good practice in any event routinely to suggest the inclusion of substitutional gifts — e.g. to grandchildren in place of any children who have predeceased — so as to minimise the risk of a partial intestacy — even where such a substitution might in any event be made under s. 33, Wills Act 1837 (see **1.4.3.3**). Indeed, it is a good idea to consider the inclusion of a 'long stop' beneficiary (such as a charity) in the event of all the 'family trusts' failing.

Where the provision to be included is to be of a substitutional gift in favour of children to follow a gift in favour of the surviving spouse, a decision will have to be made as to whether the children's entitlement to take should be determined at the date of the testator's death or at the death of the survivor of the testator and the spouse. The answer may differ depending upon whether the spouse's interest was absolute or a life interest only.

Where the spouse is given an absolute interest, it seems that most precedents suggest that the children living at the testator's death should take. However, a case can certainly be made for the alternative view — that it should be those alive at the death of the survivor of the two. In the sort of case we are considering, the children can only become entitled if the spouse does not survive for the survivorship period prescribed in the will. A child could die between the deaths of the testator and of the spouse: if that child had already a vested interest in the testator's estate that interest would now pass under the child's will or intestacy. If the child, in order to take, had to be alive at the death of the survivor, the child's interest would still be contingent on its death — so that any further substitutional gift in favour of the grandchildren could take effect under the terms of the testator's will.

If the child has to be alive at the death of the survivor of the testator and the spouse there is, however, a problem with s. 18A, Wills Act 1837, in that if there has been a divorce there is no acceleration of the substitutional gift in the same way as of the remainder interest where the spouse was given a life interest only.

When the interest of the children follows a life interest, the class of children eligible to take is usually defined as those alive at the death of the life tenant. However, in this event there could be difficulty if the life tenant and remaindermen wished to bring an end to the trust and distribute the capital immediately. Their agreement to do this could not be put into effect without the assistance of the court since grandchildren (who might not yet have been born) could have an interest in the property.

18.4.7 ADMINISTRATIVE PROVISIONS

As we saw in **18.3.2.3** above, a variety of administrative provisions may be considered for inclusion in the will, depending upon the circumstances of the particular case. The clauses discussed here are those which you might most frequently need to consider. The list of clauses (and the comments made about them) should not be considered as exhaustive!

If your will contains only absolute gifts in favour of adult beneficiaries, then it will only be necessary to consider including clauses relating to insurance (**18.4.7.4**), appropriation (**18.4.7.5**) and possibly the exclusion of the statutory apportionment rules in the Apportionment Act 1870 (**18.4.7.7**).

If the testator is making gifts (whether original or substituted) which are contingent, or are vested but any of the potential beneficiaries may be minors, or there are successive interests, then *in addition* you will need to consider clauses relating to powers of maintenance (**18.4.7.1**), advancement (**18.4.7.2**), investment (**18.4.7.3**), infants' receipts (**18.4.7.6**) and (if there are successive interests) equitable apportionments (**18.4.7.7**).

In any situation where the testator is a sole trader, an appropriate provision to allow for the continued running of the business should be included (**18.4.7.8**).

18.4.7.1 Maintenance

The power of maintenance under the general law has been considered in **13.2.11**. It is usual in practice to extend this by giving the trustees an absolute discretion, rather than having to comply with the objective standards set out in s. 31(1), Trustee Act 1925. You can achieve this by drafting your own maintenance provision, or more simply by providing that the statutory provision should be modified by substituting the words 'as my Trustees shall in their absolute discretion think fit' for the words 'as in all the circumstances be reasonable' in s. 31(1).

If it is the testator's wish to postpone the vesting of capital until an age greater than 18 (say 21) then, as has previously been suggested, it is likely to be appropriate that the vesting of the income should be similarly postponed (**18.3.2.5**). In such an event, s. 31 needs to be further varied by providing for the substitution throughout the section of the age of 21, so that the duty to accumulate with the power of maintenance in s. 31 will continue until that age is attained.

18.4.7.2 Advancement

Again, the statutory power has been considered previously (at **13.2.12**). It is usual in practice to remove the 50% ceiling upon advancements contained in s. 32, Trustee Act 1925. Under the section, any such advancements must be brought into account: it is common to provide in the will that the trustees shall have a discretion as to whether to require this. Further, where there is a prior life interest, the statutory power can only be exercised with the life tenant's consent: this requirement may be specifically excluded (it is apparently not so excluded merely because the trustees are given an 'absolute and uncontrolled discretion' as to the making of advancements — *Henley* v *Wardell, The Times*, 29 January 1989).

If there is a life interest, there is no statutory power to advance capital to the life tenant. It is usual in such cases, therefore, to provide for this in the will.

Allied to the power of advancement, it is common practice to provide a power for the trustees to make loans to any beneficiary as the trustees think fit.

18.4.7.3 Investment

The statutory powers relating to investment (considered in detail in **13.2.10**) are generally accepted as being far too restrictive. The will should, therefore, contain a widely drawn power. That most commonly conferred is a power to act in relation to investments as if the 'absolute beneficial owner' of the trust funds for investment.

We have seen, also, that authorisation under the general law for investment of trust monies in the purchase of land is limited: a general power to do this should therefore be included. It is also important to provide for the possibility of purchasing a residence for a beneficiary, which is not permissible under the general law.

18.4.7.4 Insurance

The very limited power of insurance in s. 19, Trustee Act 1925 has been discussed in **13.2.6**. A clause authorising comprehensive insurance to the full value must be included — even though someone under the will is absolutely entitled to the property (under the general law, even the limited power in s. 19 is not available in such a case). It is common to provide also for payment of the premiums from either income or capital: and for the insurance monies in the event of a claim to be treated as proceeds of sale of the insured property — this allows the trustees the freedom not to have to replace the property, but rather to invest in something else if they think fit.

18.4.7.5 Appropriation

We have discussed the statutory power (which is found in s. 41, Administration of Estates Act 1925) in **13.2.2**. In practice, it is usual to provide in the will that this power may be exercised without the need for the consents (of the beneficiaries) required by s. 41. Under the general law, the value for appropriation purposes is the value at appropriation; sometimes, in order to avoid the trustees having to incur the expense of a revaluation of property being appropriated they are given the power to appropriate at the value at the date of death — or perhaps a discretion to use either value.

WILL DRAFTING

18.4.7.6 Infants' receipts

The problems faced by personal representatives having to hold assets for minor beneficiaries have been considered in **13.2.3** and **16.1.5**. It is useful, in practice, for the will to provide a simple means of discharging the personal representatives in such a situation — by empowering them to accept the receipt of the infant's parent or guardian, or of the infant himself if aged at least 16.

18.4.7.7 Apportionments

There are two sets of apportionment rules — statutory and equitable — and these have both been considered previously (in **13.1.2** and their tax implications in **Chapter 4**). In practice, these rules are usually excluded by a simple clause in the will. The statutory rules in the Apportionment Act 1870 may usefully be excluded from operation in any will: it is only 'essential' to exclude the equitable rules where the will contains gifts of successive interests in property — though many practitioners routinely exclude the operation of both sets of rules in all cases.

18.4.7.8 Business

It will only be necessary to consider the inclusion of any powers in the will relating to the testator's business where the testator is a sole trader. The basic problem has already been discussed (in **13.2.9**): under the general law, personal representatives have only a limited authority to carry on the business, access to limited resources to do so, and are fully liable for debts etc. incurred in the process (though subject to a right of indemnity from the estate).

Hopefully, steps will have been considered and taken in the testator's lifetime as to the succession to the business. If not, a power should be included in the will to enable the personal representatives to carry it on as a going concern; to utilise other resources in the estate (and not just the capital employed at the date of death) for this purpose; to appoint manager(s); and for a full indemnity from the estate for any liabilities and losses incurred.

18.4.8 DATE

A will should show the date of execution (though it is not necessarily 'fatal' to its admissibility if this is omitted, so long as the court can be convinced that it is indeed the testator's last will). The date is sometimes incorporated into the Commencement, but many practitioners prefer to include a date clause at the end of the will, immediately above the space for the testator's signature and the attestation clause. Something along these lines is usual: 'IN WITNESS whereof I have hereunto set my hand this . . . . . day of . . . . . 199 '.

18.4.9 ATTESTATION CLAUSE

As we saw in **1.1.4.7**, the inclusion of such a clause is specifically not a requirement of s. 9, Wills Act 1837. However, a suitable attestation clause should be routinely included since this will raise a presumption of due execution. If there is no such clause (or only an inadequate one) compliance with the requirements of s. 9 will have to be proved (see further **11.2**).

An attestation clause should show (as a minimum) compliance with the statutory requirements. It need not be lengthy: the following simple clause is sufficient:

> SIGNED by [the Testator] as her
> last will in our joint presence
> and then by us in hers

Where the testator is blind or illiterate, or someone else signs on behalf of the testator, we saw (in **1.1.3.2**) that there is no presumption of knowledge and approval and that this will have to be established if the will is to be admitted to probate. The best way of dealing with this is to have the

WILL DRAFTING

will read over to the testator in the presence of the witnesses and to include an attestation clause showing that this was done and explaining the circumstances of the execution of the will. For example:

> THIS WILL having been read over to [the Testator] in our joint presence when [the Testator] appeared thoroughly to understand it and approve its contents was SIGNED by [the Signatory] in his presence and at his direction as his last will in our joint presence and we then in the presence of [the Testator] and at his request subscribed our names as witnesses

18.4.10 ARRANGEMENTS FOR EXECUTION

It should be the aim whenever possible to have the execution of the will supervised by a solicitor or responsible member of staff who is conversant with the formality requirements. As we have already seen (in **18.2.5**) a solicitor who negligently fails to ensure proper execution of the will is liable in damages to a disappointed beneficiary, the measure of damages being essentially the loss of the intended gift.

Ideally, the testator (having first read it through to check that all is as required) should sign the will in the presence of two witnesses who should then sign the will as witnesses (adding their addresses and occupations) in the presence of the testator and of each other. This goes beyond the strict requirement of s. 9, Wills Act 1837, but there is no harm in that! Hopefully, there will not be any alterations — but if there are, remember to have them initialled by the testator and the witnesses (**12.3.5**).

The witnesses should not be beneficiaries or married to beneficiaries — otherwise the gifts to those beneficiaries will fail under s. 15, Wills Act 1837. In this context, remember that a charging clause is a 'benefit' for the purposes of s. 15! (**1.4.3.4**).

Once the formalities have been completed, a photocopy of the original should be made, or the draft copy made up to show details of the execution. This should then be carefully preserved in case the original is lost or accidentally destroyed — in which event, as we have seen in **11.6.1**, it may be possible to prove the will by means of the copy. The client's instructions as to the safe keeping of the original should be obtained.

If for any reason the will has to be sent to the client for execution, very carefully and clearly drafted instructions should be included to guide the client through the correct procedure. What do these instructions need to address?

First, the client should be instructed to read the will to check that all is in order. If there are any mistakes, or the client wishes any alterations to be made, no attempt should be made to make these but you should be contacted immediately.

Second, if satisfied, the testator should be told to date the will and sign it in the presence of the witnesses as outlined above.

Third, the client needs to be warned of the effect of s. 15, Wills Act 1837.

Fourth, the testator should be asked to return the executed will to you so that you can check that all appears to be well and make a copy.

18.5 Codicils

A codicil is an 'addendum' or 'appendix' to a will and used where only minor adjustments to the will (such as the appointment of a replacement executor, or a change to the amount of a legacy) are required. It is not a good idea in practice to have too many codicils: if the testator has more than two or three it is better to advise a fresh start!

The codicil begins (like a will) by introducing the testator and identifying the nature of the document as a [first] [second] codicil to the will [dated ...], and should recite the dates of any previous codicil(s).

The required adjustment(s) are then set out and the codicil ends with a clause stating: 'IN all other respects I confirm my said will [and codicil(s)]'.

The codicil must be executed in the same manner as the will itself, a typical attestation clause being:

SIGNED by [the Testator] as a Codicil to
her last will in our joint presence and
then by us in hers

INDEX

Ademption, gift, of 18–19
Administration of estate *see* estate
Adopted children, gifts to 16, 166
Affidavit evidence
  alterations 127
  attempted revocation
    burning, tearing or obliteration 130
    generally 130
    something attached 130–1
  codicils 131
  due execution
    deponent 128
    generally 128
    no satisfactory evidence 128
    rule 12(3), NCPR 128
    rule 16, NCPR 128
  form 127
  generally 127
  identity 132
  knowledge and approval 129
  missing wills 131
  rectification 131
  swearing 128
  terms, condition and date of will
    alterations 129
    date 129–30
    incorporation 129

Benjamin order 165
Body, disposal of, directions as to 217

Capital gains tax
  beneficiaries and 51
  contingent interests 206
  disclaimers and 173
  estate, distribution of, and 184–5
  generally 49
  personal representatives
    deceased, gains of, and
      assessments 49
      gains 49
      losses 49

Capital gains tax – *continued*
  estate, gains of, and
  disposals by
    chargeable event 50
    gains 50
    losses 51
  position on death 50
  transfers to legatees
    definition 51
    not a disposal 51
  tax planning *see* tax and estate planning
  trusts and settlements *see* trusts and settlements
  variations and 175–6
  vested interests 206
Caveats *see* court proceedings
Citations *see* court proceedings
Class gifts 14–15, 224
Codicils
  affidavit evidence and
    missing codicil 131
    revoked codicil 131
  drafting 229
  republication 10–11
  revival 11
  revocation and 7–8, 131
  validity 6
Court proceedings
  caveats
    date and duration of 134
    definition and purpose 134
    entry of 134
    meaning 134
    warning of 134–5
      effect of 135
  citations
    definition and purpose 135–6
    procedure on issue 136–7
    subsequent procedure 137
    types of 136
  generally 133
  solemn form procedure

INDEX

Court proceedings – *continued*
    appearance, default of 138
    compromise 138
    costs 138
    issue of writ or summons 138
    pleadings 138
      default of 138
    when required 137
  standing searches
    definition and purpose 133
    procedure 134

Death, registration of 155–6
Devises
  see also gifts; legacies
  income tax and 46
  meaning 17
  residuary 18
  specific 17
    payment of 181–2
Disclaimers
  legal effect of 172
  meaning 171
  restrictions on right to disclaim 171–2
  successions effects of 171–2
  taxation consequences of
    capital gains tax 173
    inheritance tax 172–3
      income tax 173
    stamp duty 173
  variations distinguished 174
Divorce, revocation of will by 7

Estate
  administration of
    financial needs of deceased's family 155
    financial services
      personal representatives 168
      solicitors 168–9
    generally 153
    grant, on receipt of
      advertisements 158–9
      payment of debts
        insolvent estate
          generally 163
          protection of personal representatives 164
          secured creditors 163
          unsecured creditors 163–4
        solvent estate
          contrary provision 162–3
          generally 160
          marshalling 162
          secured creditors 161
          statutory order 161–2
          property not included in 162

Estate – *continued*
  personal representatives
    protection for 164
      application to court for specific relief 168
      claims under inheritance 167
      future and contingent liabilities 165–6
      inheritance tax 166
      leaseholds 167
      missing beneficiaries or creditors
        Benjamin order 165
        indemnity 165
        insurance 165
        payment into court 165
      rectification 167
      section 48, Administration of Justice Act 168
  registering the grant 159
  sales of assets
    generally 160
    tax implications 160
    the will 160
  searches 159
  inheritance tax
    payment of
      direct payment to Revenue 157
      generally 156
      loan
        bank, from 156–7
        beneficiary, from 157
      sale of assets 157
  instructions 154
  papers to lead to grant
    lodging 157–8
    preparing 156
  registration of death 155–6
  swearing or affirming the oath 157
  distributing
    assents
      land
        beneficiaries, protection of 190
        effect 190
        form 190
        personal representatives, protection of 190
        power to assent 189–90
        purchasers, protection of 190
      pure personality 189
    estate accounts
      capital account 188
      discharge 188–9
      distribution account 188
      form 187–8
      income account 188
      transfer of assets 189

INDEX

Estate – *continued*
  financial services 191
  generally 181
  legacies, payment of
    pecuniary legacies
      abatement 183
      appropriation 183
      generally 182
      no provision in the will and no partial intestacy 182
      partial intestacy but express trust for sale of the residue in the will 183
      partial intestacy and no express trust for sale of the residue in the will 183
      provision in the will 182
    receipts 183
    specific legacies and devises 181–2
  personal representatives
    trustees, as
      generally 191
      intestacy, where 191–2
      will, not under 191
      will, under 191
  residue, ascertainment of 183
    administration expenses
      funeral expenses 185
      legal costs 185–6
      professionals, fees of 186
    capital gains tax 184–5
    income tax 184–5
    remuneration 186–7
Executors, appointment of 209, 215–16, 220

Family and dependants
  provision for
    anti-avoidance provisions, necessity for 40–1
    application
      categories of applicant
        child
          deceased, of 33, 37
          family, of 33, 38
        dependant 34
          being maintained 34, 38
            immediately before death 34
            proof of 34
        spouse
          deceased, of 33, 37
          former, deceased, of, not remarried 33, 37
      county court, to 32
      High Court, to 32
      time limit for 31
        late applications 32
        practical consequences of 32
    basis of claim 31
    generally 31

Family and dependants – *continued*
  reasonable financial provision
    failure to make, testator's reasons 36
    family provision order
      periodical payments, variation of 38
      property available for 40
        deceased's severable share of joint property 40
      types of 38–9
        consequential directions 39
        inheritance tax 39
        interim payments 39
        lumps sum payment 38–9
        marriage settlements, variation of 39
        periodical payments 38
          termination on remarriage 38
        property
          order for acquisition of 39
          settlement of 39
          transfer of 39
    generally 35
    guidelines 36–8
      relevant to all applicants 36–7
      relevant to particular categories of applicant 37–8
    maintenance standard
      generally 35
      level of maintenance 35
    surviving spouse standard 35
      court's discretion to apply 35
      judicial separation, where 35

Gifts
see also devises; legacies
  children, to 15–16, 218–19
    adopted children 16, 166
    illegitimate children 16, 166
  class 14–15, 224
  failure of
    ademption 18–19
    beneficiary, or spouse of, witness will, where 20
    gift contrary to public policy 20
    lapse 19–20
    uncertainty 18
    Wills Act, section 15 20
  inheritance tax and
    gifts in consideration of marriage 56
    gifts with a reservation 54–5, 200
    gifts to charities 57
    small gifts 56
  institutions, to 222–3
  minors, to 205–6
  personal effects 222
  reservation, with 54–5, 200

INDEX

Gifts – *continued*
    residuary 149
    shares 222
    specific 149
    substitutional 219, 224
Grants of representation
    amendment of
        appointment of additional personal representative 92
        Inheritance (Provision for Family and Dependants) Act, section 2, order under 92
        minor errors 91
        redemption of spouse's life interest 91
    grant not necessary
        generally 84
        property not part of deceased's estate 85–6
        property not passing to personal representatives 85
        property in deceased's estate 85
        small sums due to estate 84
    issue of, effect of
        administrators 83
        executors 83
        foreign grants 83
            Northern Ireland, issued in 84
            resealing 84
            Scottish confirmations 84
        generally 83
    non-contentious business 81–2
    oaths *see* oaths
    personal representative
        capacity
            corporations 93
            generally 93
            mental or physical incapacity 93
            minors 93
            rule 24, NCPR 94
            section 116, Supreme Court Act, discretion under 93–4
            section 50, Administration of Justice Act 94
        number
            additional
                rule 25, NCPR 95
                rule 26, NCPR 95
            administrators 95
            executors 95
        renunciation
            administrators 96
            executors 96
        several claimants
            administration 94
            probate 94
    probate jurisdiction 81

Grants of representation – *continued*
    revocation
        consequences of 92
        grant wrongly made 92
    revocation of, physical or mental incapacity of grantee 92
    solicitors instructed by personal representatives
        responsibilities of, generally 82
        responsiblities of
            initial duties 82
            later duties 83
    types of
        letters of administration
            beneficial interest 88
            generally 87
            personal representatives 88
            rule 22, NCPR 88
            with will annexed 86–7
                deceased having foreign domicile 87
                rule 20, NCPR 87
                rule 21, NCPR 87
        limited as to property 89–90
        limited as to purpose
            administration *ad colligenda bona* 89
            administration pending suit 89
            grant *ad litem* 89
        limited as to time
            administration for the use and benefit of a minor 88–9
            grants in case of mental incapacity 89
        probate 86
        special grants
            administration *de bonis non* 90
            attorney grants 91
            cessate grants 91
            double probate 91
            settled land grants 90
Guardians, appointment of 210, 216–17, 221

Hotchpot *see* intestacy

Illegitimate children, gifts to 16, 166
Income tax
    beneficiaries
        general/pecuniary legatees 46
        generally 45–6
        residuary 46
            absolute interest 47
            Income and Corporation Taxes Act, section 699 47–8
            limited interest 46–7
        specific legatees or devisees 46
    disclaimers and 173
    estate, distribution of, and 184–5
    generally 43

INDEX

Income tax – *continued*
  personal representatives
    deceased's income, and
      assessments 43
      'continuing' income 44
      delay 44–5
      income arising before death,
        generally 43–4
      trust income 44
    estate's income, and
      equitable apportionments 45
      liability 45
      loan to pay inheritance tax 45
      tax deduction certificates 45
  trusts and settlements *see* trusts and settlements
Inheritance tax
  account, duty to 67
  burden
    general position on death
      no provision in the will 66
      provision in the will 65–6
      recovery of tax paid 66
    generally 65
    partially exempt transfers (PETs)
      generally 66
      part of residue exempt, part chargeable 67
      tax-free legacy to non-exempt beneficiary, residue to exempt beneficiary 66–7
  calculation of tax on death
    death estate
      commorientes 60
      generally 60
    disclaimers and variations 61
    lifetime transfers (LCTs) 60–1
    potentially exempt transfers (PETs)
      generally 61
      taper relief 61
      value charged 61
  certificate of discharge 185
  disclaimers and 172–3
  estate, distribution of, certificates of discharge 185
  excluded property 195–6
  exemptions and reliefs 195
    applying on death only
      death on active service 60
      quick succession relief 59–60
      woodlands 58–9
    applying to lifetime transfers and on death
      agricultural property relief 58
      business property relief 57–8
      gifts to charities etc 57
      heritage property 57
      transfers between spouses 56–7

Inheritance tax – *continued*
    applying to lifetime transfers only
      annual exclusion 55–6
      gifts in consideration of marriage 56
      normal expenditure 56
      small gifts 56
      generally 55
    generally 53
  liability
    lifetime chargeable transfers (LCTs) 64
      supplementary charge on 64
    purchasers 65
    tax on former PETs 64
    transfer on death 65
  lifetime dispositions 53
    lifetime chargeable transfer (LCTs), chargeable immediately 53–4
    potentially exempt transfer (PET) 53
  minimising effects of *see* tax and estate planning
  nil rate band, use of 196
  payment of
    by instalments 68
    direct payment to Revenue 157
    funding 124
    general rule 67
    loan
      bank, from 156–7
      beneficiary, from 157
    residuary gifts 223–4
    sale of assets 157
  survivorship clauses 79, 205
  tax planning *see* tax and estate planning
  transfers on death
    estate 54
      excluded property 54
      gift with a reservation 54–5
    generally 54
  trusts and settlements *see* trusts and settlements
  valuation
    general rule 61–2
    special rules
      changes in value 63–4
      land 62–3
      liabilities 63
      life assurance policies 63
      quoted securities 62
      related property 62
      unquoted securities 62
  variations and 174–5
Inland Revenue accounts
  corrective accounts 124–5
  excepted estates 112
  Form CAP A–5C 125
  Form IHT 200 115–24

INDEX

Inland Revenue accounts – *continued*
  Form IHT 202   113–14
  generally   111–12
  inheritance tax, funding payment of   124
Intestacy
  basic position   21–3
  capitalisation of a life interest on   179
  Crown and   26
  entitlement   22
    hotchpot
      children and issue   27–9
      rules   27
      surviving spouse   27
    issue   23, 26
      hotchpot rules   27–9
    order of   26
    other relatives   26
    spouse
      no issue but parents or siblings of whole
          blood (or issue of), where   24
      special rules applying to   24–5
        matrimonial home, appropriation
            of   25
        redemption of life interest   24–5
      surviving, where
        generally   23
        hotchpot rules   27
        personal chattels   24
        spouse alone   23
        spouse and issue   23–4
  generally   21
  lifetime dispositions   53
  statutory trusts   22–3
    for sale   21–2

Legacies
  see also devises; gifts
  contingent pecuniary   149
  demonstrative   17
  drafting   215, 218
  general   17, 221–3
  income tax and   46
  meaning   17
  payment of   181–3
  pecuniary   17, 149
    payment of   182–3
  residuary   18, 215
  specific   17, 221–3
    payment of   181–2
Lifetime chargeable transfers (LCTs)
  chargeable immediately   53–4
  liability   64
  recalculation of tax after death   60–1
Lifetime dispositions *see* inheritance tax

Minors
  gifts to   205–6
  grants of representation
    capacity   93
    limited as to time, administration for the use
        and benefit of   88–9
  maintenance of, personal representative, ad
      ministrative powers of   147–8
  property of, trustee, appointment of   143

Oaths
  administrators   157
    applicants   105
    capacity in which grant sought   107–8
    clearing off   105–6
    de bonis non
      capacity   109
      minority and life interests   108–9
      prior grant   108
      reason for present application   108
      value of estate   109
    gross and net estate   108
    minority and life interests   106–7
    with will annexed
      applicants   103
      capacity   104
      clearing   104
      minority and life interests   103–4
      personal representatives, duties of   105
  executors, for   98–103
    applicants   99
    deceased, details of   100
    executor's title
      all appointed
        all applying, where   101
        not all applying, where   101–2
      partners in a firm   102
      relationship to deceased   101
    jurat   103
    other matters   103
    personal representatives, duties of   102
    settled land   101
    value of estate passing under grant   102–3
  generally   97–8

Partially exempt transfers   66–7
Personal representatives
  application for provision for family and
      dependants, time limit for, consequence
      of   32
  beneficiaries
    remedies available to
      general administration actions
        appointing judicial trustee   151
        costs   151
        jurisdiction   150

Personal representatives – *continued*
    order for administration 151
    parties to proceedings 151
    reasons for commencing proceedings 150
    removal of personal representative 151
  generally 150
  personal action
    personal representatives, against 151
    recipients of estate assets, against 152
  tracing, right of 152
 rights of during administration
  date for payment of entitlement under will or intestacy 149–50
  generally 148
  right to compel due administration 149
capital gains tax and *see* capital gains tax
duties of
 fundamental
  duty to administer 140
  duty to collect deceased's assets 139
  need to establish title to assets by production of grant 139–40
  property of deceased not vested in personal representative 140
 legal and equitable apportionments 140
estate
 administration of *see* estate
 distributing *see* estate
grants of representation and *see* grants of representation
income tax and *see* income tax
liability of 141
powers of
 administrative
  advance capital, to 148
  appointment of trustee of minor's property 143
  appropriate, to 142
  delegate, to 144
  exercise of 148
  generally 142
  implied indemnity 144
  insure, to 143
  invest, to 145–7
  maintain a minor, to 147–8
  postponing distribution 143
  run deceased's business, to 144–5
  sell, mortgage or lease, to 142
property not passing to, grant not necessary 85
removal of 151
trustees, as 191–2

Post mortem changes
 capitalisation of a life interest on intestacy 179
 disclaimers *see* disclaimers
 'flexible wills' 179
 generally 171
 Inheritance (Provision for Family and Dependants) Act 1975, orders under
 procedure
  costs 178
  county court, in 176, 177–8
  High Court, in 176–7
 tax effect of 178
 variations *see* variations
Potentially exempt transfers (PETs)
 former, tax on 64
 lifetime gifts 53, 198–9
 recalculation of tax after death 60–1
 taper relief 61
 value charged 61

Settlements *see* trusts and settlements
Solemn form procedure *see* court proceedings
Solicitors
 appointment of 221
 beneficiaries, as 210
 financial services
  generally 168–9
  investment business
   discrete 169
   non-discrete 169
 wills, drafting of *see* wills
Standing searches *see* court proceedings

Taxation *see* capital gains tax; income tax; inheritance tax; Inland Revenue accounts; tax and estate planning; trusts and settlements
Tax and estate planning
 capital gains tax planning
  inheritance tax planning and, conflict between 196
  lifetime tax planning and 196–7
 generally 193
 inheritance tax planning
  capital gains tax planning and, conflict between 196
  excluded property 195–6
  exemptions 195
  nil rate band, use of 196
  reliefs 195
 lifetime tax planning
  capital gains tax provisions and 196–7
  client's objectives, considering 198
  life assurance and pensions 201–2

INDEX

Tax and estate planning – *continued*
  lifetime gifts
    exemptions, using 198
    family home 201
    making PETs 198–9
    nil rate band, using 199–200
    order in which made 200
    reliefs, using 201
    reservation, with 200
    settlements, using 201
    transfers between spouses 200
  will planning
    burden of tax, taking account of 206
    'flexible' wills 204–5
    generally 202–3
    gifts to minors 205–6
    inheritance tax, personal representatives'
      liability to pay, taking account
      of 206–7
    nil rate band, using 203
    surviving spouse, provision for 203
    survivorship clauses 205

Trusts and settlements
  capital gains tax
    beneficiaries
      bare trust 73
      settled property 73
    generally 71
    liability
      settlor, of
        settlement created on death 72
        settlement created *inter vivos* 71–2
      trustees, of
        actual disposals 72
        generally 72
        notional disposals 72–3
  income tax
    beneficiaries
      with no right to trust income 70–1
      with right to trust income 70
    generally 69
    liability
      trustees, of
        generally 69–70
        trustees special rate 70
  inheritance tax
    accumulation and maintenance settlements 78
    charitable and similar trusts 78
    generally 73–4
    settlement
      creation of 74
      interest in possession
        beneficial, with
          chargeable events 75
          charging basis 74–5
          exemptions and reliefs 76

Trusts and settlements – *continued*
        generally 74
        reversionary interests 76
      without
        creation of the settlement 77
        generally 77
        rates of tax and cumulation 77–8
        subsequent chargeable events 77
  survivorship clauses 79

Variations
  disclaimers distinguished 174
  meaning 173–4
  succession effects of 173–4
  taxation consequences of
    capital gains tax 175–6
    income tax 176
    inheritance tax 174–5
    stamp duty 176

Wills
  affidavit evidence and *see* affidavit evidence
  alterations 9–10
    effective 9–10
    ineffective 10
    invalid, consequences of 10
    precautions 10
    Wills Act, section 21 9
  ambulatory 1
  codicils *see* codicils
  construction 11–20
    date from which will speaks 13–14
    devises
      see also devises
      meaning 17
      residuary 18
      specific 17
    extrinsic evidence 12–13
    general principles 11–12
    gifts
      see also gifts
      absolute 16–17
      children, to 15–16
      class 14–15
      failure of
        ademption 18–19
        beneficiary, or spouse of, witness will, where 20
        gift contrary to public policy 20
        lapse 19
        uncertainty 18
        Wills Act, section 15 20
    legacies
      see also legacies
      demonstrative 17
      general 17

INDEX

Wills – *continued*
    meaning 17
    pecuniary 17
    residuary 18
    specific 17
  life interest 16–17
  omitting, changing and supplying words 14
  presumptions 12
    words and expressions
      dictionary principle 12
      non-technical 12
      secondary meaning 12
      technical 12
destruction of 8
disposal of body, directions as to 217
divorce, revocation by 7
drafting
  administrative provisions
    advancement 226
    apportionments 227
    appropriation 226
    business 227
    generally 225
    infant's receipts 227
    insurance 226
    investment 226
    maintenance 225–6
  appointments
    executors 209, 215–16, 220
    guardians 210, 216–17, 221
    other professionals 221
    solicitors 221
    trustees 215–16
  attestation clause 227–8
  codicils 229
    see also codicils
  commencement 220
  execution, arrangements for 228
  generally 209, 220
  inheritance tax, minimising effect of
    burden of tax, taking account of 206
    family home 203
    'flexible wills' 204–5
    generally 202–3
    gifts to minors 205–6
    nil rate band, using 203
    personal representatives liability to pay inheritance tax, taking account of 206–7
    providing for surviving spouse 203
    survivorship clauses 205
  residuary gifts
    beneficial interest 224–5
    debts and legacies, payment of 223
    inheritance tax, payment of 223–4

Wills – *continued*
  revocation clause 220
  solicitor, duties of
    capacity 212
    client's instructions, compliance with
      advice concerning will 211
      lifetime arrangements 211
      review of will 211
    conduct issues
      generally 210
      solicitor as beneficiary 210–11
      third party instructions 210
    formalities 212
    persons duty owed to 212–13
    taking instructions
      generally 213
      information required
        estate, size and nature of 214
        gifts to children 218–19
        personal details 213–14
        testator's priorities 217–18
        will, contents of 214–17
  specific and general legacies
    generally 221–2
    gifts to institutions 222–3
    permission to occupy 223
    personal effects 222
    shares 222
  structure of will 220–8
executors, appointment of 209, 215–16
'flexible' 179, 204–5
guardians, appointment of 210, 216–17, 221
incorporation by reference 11–12
inheritance tax and *see under* drafting *above*
intestacy *see* intestacy
marriage, revocation on 6–7
missing, affidavit evidence and 131
mutual, revocation of 6
nullity of marriage, revocation by 7
reference, incorporation by 11–12
republication 10–11
revival 11
revocation
  attempted, affidavit evidence 130–1
  clause 220
  codicil 7–8
  conditional 9
  destruction 8
  divorce/nullity 7
  general position 6
  later will 7–8
  marriage 6–7
  mutual wills 6
survivorship clauses 79, 205, 224
trustees, appointment of 215–16
validity 1–6

INDEX

Wills – *continued*
    capacity
        basic test 2
        generally 2
        lack of 2
        proof of 2
    codicils 6
        see also codicils
    formalities
        signature 4
            attestation clause 5
            with intent to give effect to will 3, 4

Wills – *continued*
        witnesses to 5
            attestation 5
    Wills Act, section 9 3–4
    wills in writing 3, 4
generally 1–2
intention 3
    omitting, changing and supplying
        words 14
    professional conduct 3
    proof of 3
        extrinsic evidence 12–13
    requirement 3